MORAL FORMATIONS

DISCIPLINE AND RELIGION IN THE IRISH ARMY, 1922–32

MORAL FORMATIONS

DISCIPLINE AND RELIGION IN THE IRISH ARMY 1922-32

DANIEL AYIOTIS

EASTWOOD BOOKS

First published 2024 by Eastwood Books

Dublin, Ireland
www.eastwoodbooks.com
www.wordwellbooks.com

First edition

Eastwood Books is an imprint of the Wordwell Group

Eastwood Books
The Wordwell Group
Unit 9, 78 Furze Road
Sandyford
Dublin, Ireland

ISBN: 978-1-913934-59-0(Paperback)
ISBN: 978-1-916742-61-1 (Ebook)

British Library Cataloguing in Publication Data.
A catalogue record for this book is available from the National Library of Ireland
and the British Library.

Copyediting by Heidi Houlihan
Layout and design by Wordwell
Printed in Ireland by Sprint Books

CONTENTS

ACKNOWLEDGEMENTS

I had the idea to write this book very shortly after I submitted the final manuscript of my previous one to the publisher. In going through a century's worth of records to research *The Military Archives: A History*, I was particularly fascinated by the records of the first ten years of the Army's – and the state's – existence, for reasons that I hope become evident as you read. So the idea for the theme of this book developed organically and without too much difficulty. However, in getting it from a concept to a finished product I benefited from the knowledge, kindness and generosity of many people whom I would like to acknowledge.

First and foremost, all my team at the Military Archives and the Military Service Pensions Collection project team. Special thanks to Rosemary Dunne and Hannah Kavanagh for their guidance with the Department of Defence '2/' file series and to Noelle Grothier for guiding me to some of the gems among the Archives' privately donated collections. Thanks are due to Military Archives' volunteers Tony Kinsella, Gerry McCann and Richard Cummins, who were a great asset to me in conducting my research, keeping their eyes peeled for material relevant to this book as they came across it in the course of their own projects.

Thanks to Noelle Dowling of the Dublin Diocesan Archives for a warm reception and assistance while looking at the Archbishop Edward Byrne papers.

Thanks to Prof. Eunan O'Halpin, Dr Michael Kennedy, Dr Eoin Kinsella and Dr Pat McCarthy for general words of encouragement and answering my questions when I got stuck here and there.

Thanks to Ronan Colgan at Eastwood and his team for their support in bringing this book to the shelves.

Finally, very special thanks to my wife Victoria, for her constant encouragement and support.

A NOTE ON TERMINOLOGY

In this book, *the Army* refers to the military forces of the Provisional Government/government of the Irish Free State, known as the *National Army* from 1922–24 and after that as the *Irish Army* or simply the *Army*.

The National Army was formed in early 1922, as the Irish Republican Army (IRA) split over the Anglo-Irish Treaty. By the time it became redesignated as the Defence Forces in October 1924, as provided for by the Defence Forces (Temporary Provisions) Act, 1923, the National Army Air Service (formed in June 1922) had become the Air Corps. There was a short-lived Coastal and Marine Service formed during the Civil War which was disbanded in 1924, and a Marine and Coastwatching Service formed in 1939, but the Army and Air Corps would not be joined by a proper Naval Service until 1948. Perhaps it is for this reason (as well as misplaced public perceptions relating to the exact nature of Ireland's espoused policy of military neutrality) that there is a common misconception in Ireland that we do not have an 'army' but a 'defence force' or that the two titles are synonymous. The Defence Forces consists of three services – the Army (land component), the Naval Service (maritime component) and the Air Corps (aerial component). In this book, the general focus is on the Army as the vast majority of incidents described occur within that service rather than the much smaller Air Service/Air Corps. While the force was given the title of the 'Defence Forces' in 1924, it was predominantly constituted of army personnel and formations. Where I do refer to the Defence Forces as opposed to just the Army, it is generally in reference to matters of regulations or directions from General Headquarters that applied, by their statutory or regulatory nature, to the organisation as a whole. For all practical purposes, however, the terms are interchangeable.

INTRODUCTION

'Philosophy is its own time apprehended in thoughts.'

Georg Wilhelm Friedrich Hegel

It is apt to introduce this book with a quote from Hegel, given the importance of the themes of both history and freedom in his philosophy. Writing this introduction last, it is clearer to me now that the numerous intertwining threads which revealed themselves during my research – religion, morality, discipline, regulation, law, values, health, bodily autonomy, identity, conformity, and ethos – converge to form what is most accurately described as the *philosophy* of the Irish Army's first decade. This book examines how these various forces were employed in the 'moral formation' of the Irish soldier in order to instill in him, to quote the Head Chaplain, 'a standard in discipline and behaviour, such as would be a credit to the young Army of a Christian state'.[1]

While the Army's task and purpose became increasingly ambiguous and neglected by the government after the Civil War, and very noticeably so during the decade under examination in this book, its overarching philosophy remained constant and contiguous with the ideals of the Irish state. Hegel's words are fitting in that this book presents the young Army situated within the context of its own time and place. It does not set out to either pummel or pedestalise. The primary sources speak for themselves as the book discusses the various social forces, both internal and external, exerted upon and within the Irish military immediately post-independence: 'its own time apprehended in thoughts'.

The Army is a fascinating vehicle for the exploration of social themes during the early years of the Irish state. As a volunteer, professional, democratically mandated force, its members were drawn freely from among Irish society: *a part of it*, not *apart from it*. Combined with the rigours of military administration and record-keeping, it is an accurate weathervane for wider contemporaneous trends in Irish society. At the same time, the Army, like all professional armies, had (and has) its own unique culture. During the period under discussion, it was made up exclusively of men.[2] They were generally young, physically active, robust and, by virtue of their profession, generally inclined towards a certain level of patriotism, conservatism and loyalty to the state. In this regard, an examination of the Army represents a canary in the mineshaft. Within the Roman Catholic and male-dominated society of the time, the Army, as the domain of archetypal masculinity and the closest thing Ireland had to a 'warrior caste', represents a kind of litmus test indicating wider social values, aspirations and neuroses.

As well as the most conspicuous influences that feature in this book – those of the moral, political, legislative and judicial authorities – the influence of the medical establishment must be included within its remit. For example, Damien Brennan has notably written in this field with particular reference to the state's mental asylum system and its application as a tool of intervention in ensuring social conformity.[3] Brennan's research has revealed a system 'driven by factors such as law, economics and vested interests, including the creation of a medical treatment hierarchy that "continues today"'.[4]

The other influential force in the formation of the Army's identity and character was Irish culture. This is perhaps the most ambiguous and aspirational as, unlike those referenced above, it was not represented by a single institution, encompassing everything from Gaelic games to the Irish language and from modern history to ancient mythology. It was, nonetheless, just as significant. As John Gibney has described the tension between identity and culture during the 1922–32 period:

> The Cosgrave government always had issues with questions of identity. An official commitment to the Irish language had been enshrined in law by the 1920s, which pointed to a degree of fidelity with the ideals of the Gaelic Revival that had preceded the revolution, though this was perhaps more symbolic than real, given the continued decline in Irish speaking communities – the Gaeltacht – throughout the twentieth century.[5]

Of course, the level of influence of all the above-mentioned themes is at the national level and not exclusive to the Army. Returning to the metaphors of the Army as weathervane and canary, however, the old Hermetic maxim of 'as it is above, so it is below' applies. Each of these national institutions are seen reproduced in miniature within the Army, in the forms of the Chaplaincy, General Headquarters/Department of Defence, Legal and Medical Services.

When it was formed in 1922, the National Army was pregnant with national aspirations and laden with the weight of both symbolism and expectation. Taking its official title from the Gaelic name of its antecedent organisation, the Irish Volunteers, Óglaigh na hÉireann traced its lineage from that military organisation established in 1913 to defend Home Rule, through the 1916 Easter Rising, its reorganisation as the Irish Republican Army (IRA) which fought the War of Independence and finally, following in line with the democratic will of the Irish people, forming the military arm of the Irish Free State and successfully prosecuting the Civil War. I acknowledge that this is a foreshortened version of events, that the legislative basis of the Army was initially questionable, and that the title Óglaigh na hÉireann was also claimed as rightfully their own by those who rejected the Treaty and took up arms against the National Army. For transparency, while I believe I have been balanced in my analysis where this is relevant, I am upfront about my opinion that the modern Irish Defence Forces is the sole and rightful heir to the title Óglaigh na hÉireann. My having served as one of its officers for over two decades, this should be no surprise. Having been a professional archivist since 2015 and, more recently, having developed a taste for historical research and writing, I am also friends with several historians who would claim the natural right of succession, or at least equal contention for that right, for the anti-Treaty IRA with reasoned argument. While I disagree, I am glad that we can enjoy that level of civility and plurality in our public and historical discourse on the subject.

The story of Óglaigh na hÉireann and the story of the birth of modern Ireland are inextricably linked. The split into co-claimants of the title is often described as a matter of head versus heart, the head accepting the limited independence of the Free State as a steppingstone to further freedom, with the heart considering it a betrayal of the republic declared in 1916. To tease this out, looking back at the beginning of the twentieth century with hindsight from its end, it is useful to consider Francis Fukuyama's analysis of the tensions that exist within liberal democracy – liberal democracy being the ultimate, albeit unknown at the time, destination of the Irish independence movement. This tension arising from:

> the incomplete correspondence between peoples and states. States are purposeful, political creations, while peoples are pre-existing moral communities ... The realm of States is the realm of the political, the sphere of self-conscious choice about the proper mode of governance. The realm of Peoples is sub-political. It is the domain of culture and of society, whose rules are seldom explicit or self-consciously recognized even by those who participate in them.[6]

Those analysts who are critical of the Treaty and the Free State often point to this same difference between achieving an independent Irish state and an independent Irish nation. Indeed, the concept of nationalism was one intrinsic to the formation of the Free State and one which was very much in vogue at the time, as it was once again at the end of the twentieth century following the collapse of the Soviet Union. Writing in the 1980s, Ernest Gellner's description of nationalism clearly aligns with the Ireland of 1922–32, particularly in consideration of partition and Roman Catholicism and the ensuing tensions when one nation was split between two states:

> Nationalism is a theory of political legitimacy, which requires that ethnic boundaries do not cut across political ones, and, in particular, that ethnic boundary within a given state ... should not be separate from the power holders.[7]

The Army then, in its early years, was seen by many of those most influential within it as the vehicle through which these elements could be reconciled – perhaps this was making the best of what

the Treaty offered, or perhaps it was an *ex post facto* justification
of an incomplete revolution that failed to secure an all-island
republic. Ireland's army was to be Gaelic, Godly, loyal and manly,
and the Irish soldier 'an example to be always looked up to by all
classes of the community in Irish life'.[8] Christianity, most conspicuously in the form of Roman Catholicism, was a common
fountainhead for all of its various streams of thought and influence. This is not surprising. From the pastoral Christianity of
St Patrick, through the resistance of Gaelic Catholicism to the
Protestant reformation of Henry VIII and its ensuing sectarianism towards Irish Catholics, to its significant role in the Gaelic
Revival and the national movement, the Roman Catholic Church
was an enduring mainstay of Irish identity. Following independence, it provided a firm platform on which to establish national,
and martial, identity.

A key juncture along this path, the one responsible for the tone
of Roman Catholicism in Ireland at the establishment of the Free
State, was the appointment of Paul Cullen as Archbishop of Dublin
in 1852. Colin Barr has described his later elevation to cardinal as
partly in recognition of his 'taming the Irish church and moulding
it along Roman lines'.[9] Diarmaid Ferriter has attributed to Cullen,
as one of the 'chief architects of modern Irish Catholicism', the
attendant 'authoritarianism, distrust, pessimism and class prej-
udices that became intrinsic to institutional Irish Catholicism'
and a transition to an 'emphasis on communal outward devotion
and obedience rather than interior and personal spirituality'[10] of
Ss Patrick or Colmcille. Niall O'Dowd has traced the course of
Roman Catholicism in Ireland specifically identifying the critical
ill-effect of Cullen and his observance of Jansenism, a strict, ascetic,
morally rigorous theology with an emphasis on original sin, human
depravity, divine grace and predeterminism.[11]

It is understandable, given our contemporary knowledge of the diabolical legacy of the institution of the Roman Catholic Church in Ireland (see, for example, the Ryan or Murphy Reports if you think *diabolical* is an excessive description), that Christianity could be considered a redundant or reductive framework for the following social-historical case study. Another writer might prefer an intersectionalist, or feminist, or post-colonialist framework, all of which would elucidate different perspectives. Christianity however, as Tom Holland has described it, remains 'the most influential framework for making sense of human existence that has ever existed'.[12] The breadth and depth of Christian thought is such that it contains both thesis and antithesis (which itself hearkens back to Hegel, specifically his dialectics), one which has synthesised liberal values and concepts such as human rights, secularism and marriage equality, as much as it has conservative values and even some of humanity's worst contrivances like anti-Semitism, sectarianism and slavery. As Holland describes it, to evaluate 'both the achievements and the crimes of Christian civilization is not to stand outside its moral frameworks but rather … to stand within them'. The standards by which some (admittedly not many) of the figures in this book were critical of Catholic conservative influences draw as much from two millennia of Christian thought as those against whom they railed. Nor should my earlier comment about the ultimate destination of Ireland's fight for freedom being liberal democracy be misconstrued as itself inconsistent with a focus on Christian influence. Similarly to Holland, Larry Siedentop has described how the sweep of Christian thought over two millennia has shaped concepts of moral agency and equality, and placed the individual as the 'organizing social role in the West' which has resulted in modern Western liberalism.[13] In this book, Christian thought, specifically Irish institutional Roman Catholicism, informs the religious, disciplinary, regulatory, medical and legal systems that were put in place for the young Army. At the same time, in a broader Christian sense – perhaps it could be described as a pre-Cullen Catholic sense – it informs the standards by which we now judge the extent of their successes and failures in this endeavour.

SETTING THE SCENE

It should be no surprise then, that the Roman Catholic attitudes and beliefs that influenced and characterised the Free State influenced and characterised its army. Diarmaid Ferriter has described how Richard Mulcahy's vociferous rejection of accusations that young IRA men executed during the Civil War were being denied access to a priest 'underlined a consistent theme throughout this dark period and beyond: whatever divided a people ravaged by Civil War, they had their faith in common and, with that, a special regard for men of the cloth and their role'.[14]

An examination of early Irish legislation demonstrates the influence of Roman Catholicism. The 1925 statement of the Catholic hierarchy condemning divorce, which resulted in the suspension of a private members' bill coming before the Dáil, is an illustrative example.[15] Three such bills had been introduced in the Oireachtas (the national parliament of Ireland, consisting of an upper (Seanad) and lower (Dáil) house) the year before but had no chance of being passed for two reasons. Firstly, from a procedural perspective, the constitution made no allowance for divorce; there existed no provision within Dáil Standing Orders for divorce bills and the Joint Committee on Standing Orders had no power to deal with such bills without authorisation from both houses. Secondly, the overwhelming majorities in both houses of the Oireachtas were Roman Catholic, with the *Irish Times* ruefully reflecting that 'this is a Roman Catholic country; there is a preponderating majority of Roman Catholics in both Houses of Parliament, and their Church's teaching on the subject of divorce known to all the world'.[16] Thomas Mohr has described how this was decried by many, including the Senators W.B. Yeats (Protestant) and Ellen Cuffe, Countess of Desart (Jewish), as Catholic morals being forced on non-Catholics.[17] Similar Catholic moral influences informed legislation such as the Censorship of Publications Act (1929) and reports such as the Interdepartmental Inquiry into Venereal Disease (1926) and the Report of the Committee on Evil Literature (1927). This is not surprising, however, within the context of the time or place. Most of the population of the Irish Free State, about 93 per cent, was Roman Catholic in 1922. Many prominent members of the government – including President W.T. Cosgrave and Richard Mulcahy, to name just two relevant to the events in this book – were devoutly so. It would have been anathema to them not to accept Church advice on state affairs.

It was not a Catholic theocracy either though. Religious discrimination in the Irish Free State was nowhere near comparable to that of the majority Protestant Northern Ireland. Mohr has described how, in general, the Cumann na nGaedheal government of 1922–32 was more representative of Protestants, both directly and indirectly, than their successors, Fianna Fáil. The 1922 Constitution was secular, with provisions specifically aimed at assuaging the anxieties of non-Catholics. Fianna Fáil's 1937 constitution enshrined the 'special position' of the Catholic Church within the state. It was certainly not a secular constitution, setting the tone with its opening words: 'In the Name of the Most Holy Trinity, from Whom is all authority and to Whom, as our final end, all actions both of men and States must be referred.'[18]

There were various provisions in the early 1920s (admittedly, sometimes merely overtures) towards representing religious minorities in the Free State, not least for the sake of public harmony and to reassure religious and social minorities such as non-Catholics and southern unionists who found themselves within a new and overwhelmingly Catholic state. Cosgrave, for example, had vehemently opposed Church suggestions of discriminating based on religion in making appointments to the civil and public service, a position not shared by his successor, Éamon de Valera.[19] One of the primary reasons for the establishment of the Seanad (Senate), in which non-Catholics were represented in disproportionately high numbers when it was established in 1922,[20] was to provide some political representation for religious minorities in the legislature of the Irish Free State, although this reality was never reflected in the text of the constitutional provisions that created and regulated it.[21] The guarantee of three 'university' seats for Trinity College Dublin, a stronghold of Protestantism, was initiated for this reason. The state's use of a proportional representation (PR) voting system for electing representatives to the Dáil, which is still used, was also introduced as a means of facilitating minority representation.[22] These concessions towards religious minorities, it must be noted, were only intended as a temporary measure and not a permanent one at the expense of egalitarian principals.

This outline of the legislative and religious tone of the new state is not intended to be comprehensive, nor does it need to be as there is already a decent body of work published on the subject, some of which provided a rich source of secondary research for this book. It does, however, give an insight into the ethos of the time, and some context as to why many important figures aspired to mould the young men joining the Army's ranks into the pioneers of a Christian state.

CHAPTER 1

PIONEERS

On 6 December 1921, the Anglo-Irish Treaty was signed between Ireland and Great Britain, bringing a formal end to the War of Independence, a ceasefire having been in place since 11 July. Just over a month later, on 14 January 1922, the Provisional Government was established to administer the twenty-six counties that would constitute Saorstát Éireann (the Irish Free State) in the interregnum before its official establishment on 6 December 1922. The withdrawal of the embedded machinery of British governance after centuries of occupation resulted in administrative chaos. Compounding this, the terms of the Treaty divided the country, as well as the IRA that had fought for its independence. The Provisional Government had to carry on regardless, proceeding with implementing the Treaty and the Herculean task of establishing a functioning state, aware that the split in the IRA could very well precipitate conflict of some sort. This necessitated the immediate formation of a professional, regular army.

The first appearance of uniformed members of this new National Army[1] was at the ceremony to mark the handover of Beggars Bush Barracks in Dublin, the first military post to be taken over by the Provisional Government, on 1 February 1922. The company-strength unit involved, known as the Dublin Guard, was formed from members of Michael Collins' 'Squad' and the Active

Service Unit (ASU) of the Dublin Brigade IRA, all of whom were experienced veterans of the War of Independence. They paraded that day under the command of Captain Paddy O'Daly, who would later gain infamy for his involvement in the Ballyseedy Massacre as well as several other ignoble incidents. Following the appearance of its first uniformed troops the expansion of the National Army began immediately, with 3,500 men enlisted by April. By May, the Dublin Guard was at brigade strength with O'Daly now promoted to the rank of general.

With the formal outbreak of the Civil War on 28 June 1922, and the need to expand the National Army to a war footing, its size eventually peaked at approximately 55,000 members. Even acknowledging the various nuances and arguments of what remains a contentious part of Irish history, the Treaty had the support of both the Dáil and a war-weary public. A disciplined and organised army was essential to fight the undemocratic and illegal anti-Treaty IRA insurgency, implement and maintain law and order, vouchsafe the establishment and endurance of democracy, and ensure the survival of the nascent state.

Throughout the Civil War, the National Army operated within an ambiguous legal framework, having not been formally constituted by the Dáil. Its nucleus had been drawn from a revolutionary organisation – the IRA – which, having emerged from a successful guerrilla campaign against the British, was torn apart by the Treaty. Those who supported the Treaty found themselves committed to fighting the faction that was seeking to disrupt the emergence of the new state. As it was described in the late 1920s by the General Staff, the National Army's 'outlines were no mere projections of military theory and organisation but were the outcome of the dire necessity of a situation in which the very existence of itself and the State for which it struggled were at stake'.[2]

DISCIPLINE

However, building a professional and disciplined army from scratch, and the need for immediate and rapid recruitment, are incompatible goals. The Irish experience was no exception and the results were predictable. In September 1922, Commandant Dermot MacManus expressed his concern in relation to the Army's discipline and professionalism to its Commander-in-Chief and Minister for Defence, General Richard Mulcahy, in no uncertain terms.[3] MacManus described the junior officers and senior non-commissioned officers (NCOs) as 'hopelessly inefficient'. The fact that the junior officers were appointed from the rank and file meant that they possessed no greater education, military or otherwise, than the men they commanded and led. MacManus described to Mulcahy how 'often the men are of a better type than their officers' and their 'average military knowledge' he assessed as 'nil'.

He presented to Mulcahy a military command structure that was undermined by informality and over-familiarity; one in which it was common practice at the smaller barracks and posts for officers and men to mix socially, drink together, and call each other by their Christian names. The result of this was that when the officers had to assume authority or admonish the men under their command, they received no respect or obedience from them. Third-party comments confirmed this dire situation for MacManus, who regularly heard reports from priests, civil servants and other civilians of how soldiers had expressed to them the sentiment that 'if only we had officers we could trust, who would not lead us blindly into death traps'. The 'monotonous spadework which means success in modern war', the adherence to attention to detail and routine tasks that are an essential part of the training of professional military leaders, were lacking in most officers; where they possessed it, they lacked the authority to enforce it. MacManus directly attributed operational failures by the Army to this neglect of proper military operating procedures such as patrolling, building adequate defensive positions and fortifications, and weapons handling and control skills – all of which require self- and collective discipline as much as mechanical knowledge of their performance. The Army paid dearly for this. Recent research conducted by Lisa Dolan and Tony Kinsella of the Irish Military Archives demonstrates that the number of Army deaths during the Civil War was higher than believed in the past, being in excess of 810 men.[4]

While it was difficult to effect major changes in the middle of prosecuting the Civil War, it was clear to MacManus that if discipline was not addressed immediately then the only possible outcome was 'national disaster'. MacManus advocated a ruthless combing out of officers, only retaining those demonstrating the sufficient degree of competency and demoting to the ranks any officer who did not meet the required professional standards. 'It is better to have NCOs in command temporarily,' he said, 'than bad officers.' Only when this was accomplished could discipline be tightened up and, in tandem with regular and properly constituted courts martial, could real justice be given to all ranks.

The London-born, Sandhurst and Trinity College-educated MacManus was as well placed as any to make these observations. Joining the British Army in 1911, as an officer in the Royal Inniskilling Fusiliers he had fought in the First World War and been wounded at Gallipoli. Leaving the British Army in 1918 he joined the IRA in 1920, serving under Cathal Brugha. He had been appointed as Inspector of Training in 1921 and as Deputy Director of Training in January 1922. In July, he was attached to General Eoin O'Duffy's staff as they were deployed to take Limerick, a turning point in the Civil War. What he had identified and was advocating was the critical need for the professionalisation of the Army in order to bring it in line with other modern European forces. He advised Mulcahy that the science of war had been consistent and unalterable for as long as there had been human beings, and that its principals were universal. Disciplined leadership was non-negotiable. As highly trained and disciplined officers could not be produced at a moment's notice, he saw no alternative to the appointment of ex-British Army officers as unit adjutants and staff officers on the command and divisional staffs. The standard of military competency attained in foreign armies, he lamented, was not understood or appreciated by the broad number of National Army officers, which was a hindrance to professionalisation in itself. A similar lack of appreciation of the utility of 'foreign' service was evident in the Civic Guard mutiny of May 1922, when resentment festered over the seemingly preferential treatment given to men with Royal Irish Constabulary (RIC) service over IRA men, even though this new police force had to be established from a standing start within a period of mere weeks.

All was not lost, however. While even the best junior officers, as MacManus described them, were hopelessly behind the standard of other European armies, they were 'second to none in pluck and grit'. The raw material was there at least. The most intuitive methods of instilling discipline in the Army were the establishment of formal legislation to underpin it (which came the following year in the form of the Defence Forces (Temporary Provisions) Act) upon which regulations and instructions could be based, and an army legal system to enforce military law. Just how crucial this was is confirmed by the statement of the Judge Advocate General, Cahir Davitt, to the Army Inquiry Committee in 1924:

Recruiting for the National Forces during the period from June '22 till the end of the year was free and unchecked, and ... a large

proportion of the criminal element found its way into the Army
... nearly every criminally disposed person had a gun either from
the Government or from Mr de Valera, and needless to say the
Government service, on account of the pay involved, was the
more attractive. Old soldiers, experienced in every kind of military
wrong-doing, were placed under the command of officers necessarily inexperienced and the resulting state of discipline is not to be
wondered at.[5]

There were, for example, the General Regulations as to Discipline
issued by Mulcahy on 1 November 1922, but this was not derived
from any Act in the same way that current Irish Defence Forces
Regulations (DFRs) derive their statutory authority from the
Defence Act. Such instruments, however, are generally of use to
dissuade and punish. The patriarchs of the National Army wanted
to ensure that not just the disciplinary standards but also the moral
character of its men reflected those expected, as it was described in
the official army journal *An tÓglách*, of 'pioneers in a new State'.[6]

The Army did not just grow contiguously with the new state,
the two were intimately linked. The capacity of a government to
exercise its democratic mandate and defend its territorial boundaries through organised and lawful force of arms is a fundamental
element of any state establishing and securing its legitimacy. More
than this, the history of the Defence Forces and the modern Irish
state are inextricably linked – from the founding of the Irish
Volunteers (Óglaigh na hÉireann) in 1913, through its evolution
into the IRA and the struggle for independence, its subsequent
split birthing the National Army, to the modern Irish Defence
Forces over a century later. Óglaigh na hÉireann remains the official
title of the Irish Defence Forces, deliberately maintaining a direct
link to its antecedent organisation founded in 1913. This synergy

between army and state was even more prominent in 1922 when, for example, simultaneously holding senior military appointments and political office was normal practice.

'THE MOST CONSERVATIVE-MINDED REVOLUTIONARIES'

Kevin O'Higgins' well-known quip about being 'the most con-servative-minded revolutionaries that ever put through a successful revolution'[7] has become a hackneyed trope epitomising Cumann na nGaedheal variously as counter-revolutionaries or failed revo-lutionaries, conservatives responsible for a decade characterised by stagnation and the suffocation of revolutionary aspirations. Jason Knirck has refuted such claims without acting as an apologist for Cumann na nGaedheal's failings, making the case that they remained committed to the ideals of the independence struggle. He nuances this by acknowledging that revolutions have to be con-solidated, and this requires all parties involved to choose 'which parts of revolutionary ideology to emphasize, which to deempha-size and which to ignore', a process which 'often never resolves into a unified narrative'.[8] Cumann na nGaedheal, within the context and confines of the hand they had been dealt, successfully built the foundation of the modern Irish state, arguably a revolutionary act in itself.

Representative of the more radical claims of counter-revolution is Gerry Adams' description of the British execution of the key leaders of the 1916 Easter Rising as a very deliberate removal of the independence movement's greatest thinkers and writers, 'removing the revolutionary leadership that had come through against all the odds to organize the rising and to make the Proclamation'.[9] While this claim may have some validity, it is arguably a tenuous position on the whole. Michael Laffan, for example, has stated in relation to the executions that 'far more men were killed than was necessary to remove dangerous revolutionary leaders'.[10] But this is not the same as evidencing that the independence struggle was bereft of extremely passionate, creative, idealistic or intellectual leadership after 1916. More revealing is Laffan's observation that not long after the executions the 'leaders were already passing into legend as sober and pious martyrs ... and the rebellion's legacy had taken on a semi-religious tone'.[11] With the seven proclamation signatories in particular idealised, immortalised and ensconced within the pantheon of republican heroes in the collective Irish consciousness, how could any mere mortal, or mortal endeavour, that followed live up to their legacy?

However valid the accusation of counter-revolution may or may not be, for Cumann na nGaedheal the Civil War represented the social and moral disintegration of the nation. Almost a year to the day from the shelling of the Four Courts, Kevin O'Higgins declared to the Dáil that:

> Throughout this country within the last year, the moral standard has been lowered and there has been such a wave of degradation that many people have lost all rudder and compass to guide them in matters of right and wrong; they have thrown the moral law to the winds, the law of God as well as the law of man.[12]

Knirck points out that Mulcahy viewed the National Army not as the 'selfless band of idealists' that the Volunteers had been portrayed as, but 'no better or worse than the general population from which it was drawn'. At its worst interpretation, for men like Minister for Finance, Ernest Blythe, and Attorney General, Hugh

Kennedy, the social degeneracy was due to 'the inherent weakness of the Irish people' which had been 'liberated by independence and self-government'.[13]

Since the Gaelic Revival, the concept of 'Gaelicness' had been an inextricable but intangible signifier of the aspirational independent Ireland. Now that it was no longer aspirational, defining a 'Gaelic Ireland' was proving evasive. The Irish language was the most tangible touchstone, but after that its measure was ambiguous.[14] It was from within this milieu that the hopes and aspirations placed in the Army, particularly by Mulcahy, arose. Not all of his contemporaries shared this outlook: Ferriter has described how Justice James Creed-Meredith had been 'perplexed at Mulcahy's contention that the post civil-war army could unite the country by leading a cultural resurgence'.[15] To Mulcahy, however, as 'the inheritors of that strength and of that bravery' typical of the great Michael Collins,[16] the Army presented a self-contained, discreet, loyal branch of the state that traced its origins back to the foundational organisation of the independence struggle, the Irish Volunteers, itself tracing its symbolism to the ancient Fianna. The Army, more than any other state institution, had the potential to embody the ideal of 'Gaelic' manhood, becoming both a scion of the old Gaelic traditions and the vanguard of the new state.

CHAPTER 2

RELIGIOUS FERVOUR

By virtue of both his rank and disposition, the story of the moral formation of the Army begins with the Minister for Defence, later also its Commander-in-Chief, General Richard Mulcahy. While he joined the Irish Republican Brotherhood (IRB) in 1908 and the Irish Volunteers in 1913, Pádraig Ó Caoimh notes that, even in light of his pre-standing revolutionary and nationalist zeal, it was at a retreat with the Jesuits at Milltown Park during Holy Week of 1916 that he answered the call to arms and joined the Rising, in what Ó Caoimh describes as a 'watershed moment'.[1] Like many of his contemporaries, Mulcahy had received a Christian Brothers' education, one that aimed to instil boys with a combination of employability and spirituality. Together with his scholarly acumen, Mulcahy's 'spiritual training' imbued him with 'qualities which happened to meld harmoniously into emancipative patriotism'.[2]

FR RICHARD DEVANE, SJ

On 1 May 1922, a letter landed on Mulcahy's desk from the Jesuit priest, political activist and social reformer, Fr Richard Devane. Devane was a Limerick-born priest of entrenched Catholic and nationalist views. Educated by both the Christian Brothers and the Jesuits, he was ordained as a diocesan priest in 1901 and initially posted to a parish in Middlesborough, England. The impoverished working-class environment of the industrialised north of England, which stood in contrast to his native Limerick, solidified his belief in the importance of both campaigning for the social and spiritual welfare of the working classes and the importance of middle-class leadership in matters both spiritual and national.

Devane returned to his native Limerick in 1904, where one of his diocesan responsibilities was as chaplain to New Barracks on Lord Edward Street (present day Sarsfield Barracks, still occupied by the Irish Army). His nationalist, reformist and spiritual zeal saw this chaplaincy end after he was involved with the boycotting of a delivery of English newspapers destined for the barracks, which he deemed to be culturally and morally degenerate influences. His experiences during this time, particularly regarding what was termed 'Khaki Fever' (local women consorting with British sol-diers), coloured his views of young women and their need for social support and reform.[3]

Upon seeing that the transition to self-government, in the form of Home Rule, was on the cards for Ireland in the second decade of the 1900s, Devane wanted to ensure that 'the transition was man-aged in an orderly manner and believed that it was something in which he could and should play a role'. Devane believed that it was necessary for change in Irish society to be properly managed in order 'to ensure that Home Rule was the end product; and the Catholic Church was the only organisation that could manage this change'.[4] This idea grew from his assessment of the 'Catholic influence that had ensured the relatively smooth transition of land ownership in Ireland' following the Land War of the late 1800s[5]

11

and his opinion of the Church as the 'natural moulders of public opinion'.[6]

In 1918 Devane joined the Society of Jesus (Jesuits), an order to which he was well suited as one renowned for its influence on Catholic thought and education. This would give him the opportunity to 'speak and write about some of the most important social issues affecting the country during the early years of the new Free State'.[7] Throughout the first decade of Irish independence, Devane contributed to several significant moral and social movements including: the clearing of the Monto 'red light' area of Dublin along with Frank Duff, the founder of the Legion of Mary; the Interdepartmental Committee on Venereal Disease; the Committee on Evil Literature; the Carrigan Report; and Catholic Action (a movement of lay Catholics advocating for increased Catholic societal influence).

RETREATS AND SODALITIES: BULWARKS AGAINST MORAL PERILS

In mid-July 1920, Devane was appointed as the spiritual director of the Jesuits' Milltown Retreat Centre in Dublin. His position on the matter of religious retreats gives an insight into his later interest in the National Army and its implications, believing that retreats would 'help to ameliorate the lawlessness and societal damage caused by the Anglo-Irish War of Independence and, later, the Civil War. More importantly, it would strengthen the role of the Catholic Hierarchy in an independent Ireland.'[8]

Less than a year later, the Archbishop of Dublin, Edward Byrne, transferred Devane to the Jesuit's new retreat centre for working men at Rathfarnham Castle, a position he would hold until 1932.

This centre represented a new departure for the Jesuits in Ireland, away from their established practice of catering for the spiritual needs of the middle-class and into providing for the spiritual guidance of working-class men, something which they had already established in mainland Europe and which fell very much within Devane's bailiwick.

It was in this capacity that Devane contacted Mulcahy, on a subject entitled 'The New Army: Some problems and suggested solutions'.[9] In his letter, Devane expressed his concerns that:

The herding of men, incidental to life in any Army, always entails moral dangers, and the lowering of the general moral standard. It is unnecessary to prove this assertion: experience shows that the soldier in every country is an easy victim and too often a willing prey.

Tradition in a regiment is a tyrant that brooks no opposition. If the tradition be loose and low, the recruit soon becomes corrupted. Indifference to, or half-veiled contempt for religion and its practices grows rapidly where a few strong-willed bullies or blackguards assert themselves; the quiet type of man remains passive and allows things to drift. Thus evil tradition is formed. Prayers are said, if at all, in bed; the frequentation of the Sacraments is a matter of jest; 'foul language' is the normal topic of conversation; women are discussed as mere play-things – or worse; drink spreads rapidly, and drunkness [sic] becomes a matter of no wonder – but a boast of a jest.

To pre-empt this inevitable drift into wickedness, Devane decided it prudent to write to Mulcahy in order that he might assist the newly established Army in getting off to a good start in such matters. A good start, he believed, would make Irish soldiers an exception to the general rule of their counterparts abroad – religious, sober and moral. Devane cautioned Mulcahy that its first year would decide the moral fate of the Army, but that:

> If a healthy tradition is laid down from the beginning by making serious efforts to maintain a high moral standard in the barrack room, as well as outside, we may confidently hope, considering the fine human material we have to work on, that the happiest results shall ensue.

Devane impressed upon Mulcahy that those responsible for the training and formation of the Army should have deeply impressed upon them their responsibility for 'making the name of the Irish Soldier a synonym for true manliness, clean living, chivalrous spirit and religious fervour'. It would not be sufficient, he said, for commissioned officers and senior NCOs to do this casually, but that they should 'have the opportunity of preparing themselves adequately for the work of moulding the tradition of the New Army by making a specific Retreat for that purpose'. If senior officers would set the example in this, Devane said, 'it would give great impetus to a Retreat Movement' within the new force. Once established, this series of religious retreats would prepare the way for the establishment of a series of 'Missions' which 'could be arranged for the men in the various barracks having as special features the formation of a Regimental Sodality' and the establishment of an Army temperance association.

Devane also provided practical suggestions for introducing religious life into the structure of barrack life:

> If possible, each Barracks should have its own Chapel with the Blessed Sacrament reserved and made as devotional as possible so as to attract the men. Confessions should be heard there so as

to facilitate the men approaching the Sacraments regularly. If the Chapel be sufficiently large the men's Sodality should meet there. Arrangements could be made for night prayers or evening devotions – e.g., Rosary recited by the men, and occasionally Benediction of the Blessed Sacrament be given.

As a general suggestion, to promote esprit de corps and foster good spirit in the troops, it might be worthwhile considering the desirability of establishing or subsidising a 'Soldiers' Journal' where the moral and spiritual sides of the soldier's life should get due prominence. A pretty good circulation should be guaranteed through NCO promotors in various Units and advertisements of Army purveyors could easily be secured.

As the director of the centre at Rathfarnham Castle, Devane was happy to facilitate the organisation of any such retreats for the men of the Army and offered his services to discuss these matters with Mulcahy or his deputies.

ATTITUDES OF THE ARMY LEADERSHIP

The National Army had only been in existence for a few months at the time of Devane's approach, and in the first half of 1922 it was in the process of taking over barracks and posts from the British throughout the country and generally getting its act together. It was still covertly supporting the IRA in the north of the country, supplying them with weapons in cooperation with anti-Treaty IRA in the south, and planning for the (albeit unsuccessful) Northern Offensive. From the end of March 1922 and the IRA Convention, the split between the pro- and anti-Treaty camps was beginning to solidify. The spectre of civil war loomed. Despite the genuine and intense efforts of senior figures on both sides to reconcile and reconstitute the unity of the erstwhile comrades-in-arms with their respective positions, Mulcahy and Collins were forced to strengthen the National Army in anticipation. Meanwhile, on 13 April 1922, Dublin anti-Treaty IRA occupied the Four Courts in the centre of Dublin City and established a headquarters for themselves, seizing several more positions shortly afterwards. Among the opponents of the Treaty, divisions were also becoming discernible between moderates and hardliners.

One of those most firmly camped within the moderates was Liam Lynch, who subsequently fought and died as the IRA Chief of Staff during the Civil War. Lynch had desperately wanted to avoid the tragedy of former brothers- and sisters-in-arms of the Irish independence struggle turning their guns against one another. On 28 May 1922, the 'Collins-De Valera Pact' was ratified, an agreement that pro- and anti-Treaty politicians would jointly contest the election scheduled for the following month with a view to forming a coalition government.

As both a soldier and a statesman, it might reasonably be assumed that Mulcahy had enough on his plate in May of 1922 without having to initiate a series of religious retreats and sodalities within a force that still did not even know exactly how many members it had (this was the reason for the National Army Census, which was conducted on the night of 12/13 November 1922). Such an assumption, however, is incorrect. Mulcahy was a devout man with an 'innate Catholic conservatism'[10] and as such he acted swiftly upon Devane's suggestions, expressing his gratitude for the memorandum and committing to taking his earliest opportunity to get in touch with Devane to discuss his proposals.

On 25 May 1922, just over a month before the Civil War formally began, Mulcahy circulated Devane's memorandum, along

with his own ideas around retreats and chaplaincy, to senior figures. In his letter, Mulcahy proposed to them that:

> I would like to take early action in this matter along the lines as,
> perhaps, the following:
> 1. To arrange a weekend Retreat for Officers at the Rathfarnham
>   Castle on two succeeding weekends, so as to give two relays of
>   Officers a chance of attending.
> 2. Then, a week or so later a week's Retreat for the men of
>   Wellington Barracks, to be held either in Wellington Barracks
>   or possibly in St Kevin's Church – preferably in the Barracks. It
>   would consist of Mass and lecture in the morning and evening
>   devotions and sermon in the evening. The 4th Battalion
>   Companies, both GHQ and Executive, might possibly be asso-
>   ciated with the Wellington Barracks men for this retreat.
> 3. On the following week a similar Retreat for the Portobello men,
>   to be held in either Portobello Barracks or in Rathmines Church,
>   and if possible the 3rd Battalion Volunteers, both GHQ and
>   Executive, to be associated in the matter.[11]

Five days later, one particular reply arrived back to Mulcahy, on
paper headed 'Óglaigh na hÉireann, General Headquarters, Four
Courts, Dublin' and bearing the title 'Chief of Staff' under the
sender's signature block. It was from an unconditionally support-
ive Liam Lynch, who expressed his hope that 'the regular soldier
would be an example to be always looked up to by all classes of
the community in Irish life' and that 'special, wholetime, army
Chaplains should be appointed that they may stay in continual and
close touch with the men'.[12] Lynch advocated practical measures as
well as spiritual, suggesting that an army act be passed through the
Dáil as soon as possible, defining sentences for various offences, in

order to build the Army up on suitably disciplined and moral lines. Drunkenness, for example, he suggested should be punished by dismissal, and he urged Mulcahy to address the establishment of an Army legal department and court-martial regulations as a matter of urgency. Even though the Civil War was looming large it should be no surprise that Lynch and Mulcahy were still in close communication. As soldiers, Mulcahy and Lynch (as well as Collins) left no stone unturned to try to resolve the Army split right up until the last possible minute. They had, unlike more intransigent figures like Kevin O'Higgins or Arthur Griffith, been 'immersed in Óglaigh na hÉireann's esprit de corps'.[13]

The reply from the National Army's Adjutant General, Gearóid O'Sullivan, expressed his opinion that the need for 'some definite organisation or religious services' for the troops was growing increasingly acute, as senior ranking officers were having to give all their attention to the ongoing split:

> The higher commands have their minds occupied by vexed questions of army union and disunion, political unity and political chaos. I fear that officers not worried with such little things are not getting anything done in the way of non-military work.[14]

O'Sullivan strongly advocated Mulcahy contacting Archbishop Byrne about having a 'Chaplain General' appointed, under whose jurisdiction 'all Regulars in barracks and training camps' would fall once appointed, and that the government should immediately make contact with the Holy See in relation to the same.

The National Army's own Chief of Staff, Eoin O'Duffy, was also enthusiastic, deeming the appointment of a Chaplain General 'a necessity'.[15] O'Duffy's concerns leant towards the mystical, encouraging Mulcahy that arrangements should be made for chapels to be established and for the Blessed Sacrament to be kept in barracks. In relation to the chapel in Beggars Bush Barracks, where he himself was based, he informed Mulcahy that 'it is possible the building has been desecrated by the Auxiliaries, and certain ceremonies are necessary'. Despite the ongoing 'vexed questions' over the Treaty split, the matter of the moral and spiritual formation of Irish soldiers was something that leaders on both sides could agree upon, regardless of their position on the Anglo-Irish Treaty – positions over which they would be at war the following month.

SPIRITUAL LIFE AT THE CURRAGH

It was not only in Dublin that the spiritual life of soldiers was being cultivated. Two weeks before the scheduled handover of the Curragh Camp by the British (16 May 1922) O'Sullivan wrote to the Bishop of Kildare and Leighlin, Patrick Foley. As Adjutant General he was responsible for the recruitment of chaplains. He explained the anticipated significance that the Curragh would play in the life and formation of the Army – as the location of several special services (engineering, signals etc.) it would be a training and transit hub for troops from all around the country. O'Sullivan deemed it of the utmost importance that not only a chaplain, but the right chaplain, was appointed at the bishop's earliest convenience. O'Sullivan requested Fr P.J. Doyle of Naas, a man known to him personally and recommended by Michael Collins himself, but Foley opted to appoint Fr Patrick Donnelly. The Catholic ethos desired for the Curragh Camp was described by O'Sullivan to Foley in the following terms:

We hope that the changed position of our country and our people will be fully appreciated, even in the Army; and that there the fullest advantage will be derived from the fact that the Army Command is now in the hands of Catholic Irishmen. This will mean that religious ceremonies would be more than a formality.

It is therefore considered advisable to have a special Chaplain attached to the Curragh. This is the only command in Ireland where this will be the case, and as Officer cadets for all Ireland will be trained there, the standard set up in the Curragh will be that to be imitated afterwards throughout the country.

The General Staff therefore is anxious that any Priest appointed should be as much as possible in sympathy with the social and political outlook of the Officers and men likely to be under his spiritual direction.[16]

From Sunday 11 to Sunday 18 June of 1922, Donnelly arranged a week-long religious retreat for troops stationed at the Curragh. This came about following a meeting in late May, arranged by O'Sullivan, between Donnelly and Devane. Devane conducted the retreat along with two other Jesuit colleagues, Fr Michael Garahy and Fr Daniel J. Flinn. Donnelly had proposed to Mulcahy that the retreat would be an opportunity to establish a Temperance Society at the Curragh Camp. Mulcahy had a special and personal interest in this work however, writing to Donnelly informing him that he 'had some particular ideas in connection with the Missions for each of the Barracks' and had 'wanted to work in the whole question of Consecration, Sodalities, etc., and make the scheme a uniform one'[17] specifically utilising Devane and certain members of the Jesuit order. There was clearly a miscommunication at some stage as it was through Devane that Donnelly had organised the retreat, Donnelly having first become aware of Devane's intention through Mulcahy himself. Nonetheless, it demonstrates the direct and personal interest that Mulcahy was taking in the establishment of religious devotion in the Army and the fact that this was not something being imposed solely by the clergy. Donnelly deferred to Mulcahy in the matter of the organisation of the Sacred Heart and Total Abstinence Sodality, accepting that these matters must be 'left over for the present', but informing him that he was:

> Convinced, and so are the Jesuit Fathers here, that it would have been a great mistake to postpone the Retreat any further. The important thing was to give the troops a good start and to establish a sound tradition before any looseness or laxity crept in. I believe the Retreat has done an immense amount of good and has laid down a foundation for future spiritual development.

It was not only the spiritual formation of soldiers with which the Catholic Church was concerned; as soon as the children's schools at the Curragh reopened in 1923, the bishops were keen to exert their influence. With their re-opening, Mulcahy, as Minister for Defence, insisted that he would act as schools' manager, the General Officer Commanding (GOC) would act as correspondent, and the senior chaplain in the Curragh would have free access to superintend religious instruction. The bishop (Foley) objected, on the basis that this differed very little from the operation of the earlier *model schools*.[18] Instead, he proposed that the Minister for Defence should act as patron to the schools, with the local chaplain and GOC as joint managers. Mulcahy objected and remained as manager until his retirement as minister the following year, and he and Foley remained on bad terms as a result of the dispute.[19] The bishop raised the matter with the new Minster for Defence with the support of the new GOC of the Curragh, Seán Mac Eoin.[20]

The revised school management structure was to the bishop's satisfaction, with the head chaplain at the Curragh, Fr Donnelly, becoming sole manager and Mac Eoin serving as patron.

DEVOTIONAL APPEALS

What emerges from examining the Civil War period is a sense of urgency with regard to ensuring the moral formation and spiritual welfare of the National Army. This impetus was not only on the part of the Catholic Church, but was a mutual position shared with those in authority within the Army. On 21 June, precisely one week before the outbreak of the Civil War, Mulcahy wrote to the Defence Council – the Chief of Staff, Adjutant General and Quartermaster General – identifying: the consecration of barracks; sodalities; and the wearing of religious emblems by members of the Army, as matters presently requiring their consideration. These were clearly matters of priority. The Army has always reflected wider Irish society and Ireland was a devoutly Catholic country at that time. Having the support of the Catholic Church, as well as the press, had ensured that Mulcahy and Collins dominated the political debate during the Civil War.[21] Nonetheless, it may stretch credulity that the following anonymous note, originating from County Clare and dated 12 October 1922, was sent to the highest political office in the country, that of the President of the Executive Council (W.T. Cosgrave) for the attention of the Commander-in-Chief of the National Army (Mulcahy having assumed the appointment following Collins' death in August 1922). Not least that it was then forwarded by the President's office 'for favour of observations' to Mulcahy five days later, with the Civil War in progress. If nothing else, it is a fascinating insight into the religious climate of the time, as well as something of a novel curiosity:

Dear Sir,

As an Irish Catholic and a lover of our poor country I confidently appeal to you, the Commander in Chief of our Army, for a great national favour. It is this – consecrate at once – in any words that come from your heart – the Army and its dead and all whom it is bound to protect – to the Sacred Heart of Jesus and His Virgin Mother under the title of 'Our Mother of the Sacred Heart – the first Tabernacle on earth of the God-Man,' and I promise you a bloodless victory over all enemies.

Though I do not know you personally, I know your family history and I feel you will grant my request. It was the Consecration of France to the Sacred Heart by her brave Catholic military leaders that kept the Germans out of Paris in the late war.

We are at a crisis now and there is no time to wait for an imposing Church ceremony. The Sacred Heart will accept your Consecration and please God in the happy future His image will be borne aloft in Erin's flag.

Later on I will give you my name and address. This is being written in Clare and sent on to Dublin to be posted, fearing a raid I am doing this on the advice of the most saintly person I know in this locality – a woman who gets all she asks for in prayer.

I am, dear Sir,
Yours faithfully
'A Lover of Ireland.'[22]

In this particular matter, Mulcahy's sensible reply to Cosgrave was that the proposal was 'not feasible'. It was not, however, the only devotional appeal to arrive on the desk of the Commander-in-

Chief during the early months of the Civil War. One individual sent a handwritten prayer 'found in the grave of Our Lord Jesus in the year 1003'.[23] The Sisters of Mercy based at Ballyraggat, County Kilkenny, sent 'a sample of a Religious "Comfort" – suitable for soldiers' which contained a badge of the Sacred Heart, a Miraculous Medal and a crucifix, all of which 'could be easily carried in the pocket book'.[24] The Sisters requested that Mulcahy be 'good enough to hand it to one of the men and ask him to procure orders' at a cost of 1/8 each, with 'proceeds for charity'. Mollie Hand, of Warrington Place, County Dublin, on more than one occasion, sent Mulcahy religious leaflets hoping he would be kind enough to distribute them among his troops.[25] And Ms A.M. Hearne, of Smarmore Castle, Ardee, County Louth, sent Mulcahy a 'Shield of St Patrick to be carried in your pocketbook' and which 'had been devised for our soldier boys to carry with them, as a reminder of the faith that is within them, and a shield against dangers'.[26]

FORMALISING RELIGIOUS RETREATS

It is understandable that Mulcahy spearheaded spiritual initiatives in Dublin. This was very much aimed at instilling unity of purpose and consolidating loyal men to the Army and the state, since 'the tradition of local initiative and personal bailiwicks was weaker in the capital compared to the circumstances prevailing everywhere'.[27] Mulcahy's interest in ensuring the spiritual welfare of the force continued into 1923. In January, he contacted Fr John J. Hannon, a Jesuit based at their institute of philosophy and theology at Milltown Park, Dublin. Mulcahy expressed his interest in National Army officers, who would be at the Curragh for training from early February, having the opportunity to partake in a Jesuit-led weekend retreat. There would be four groups of approximately sixty officers, one for each weekend, with his preferred location being Clongowes Wood College (County Kildare) or Dublin (either Milltown or Rathfarnham).

Fr Hannon in turn contacted Fr John Fahy, a Jesuit based at St Francis Xavier's Church at Upper Gardiner Street, Dublin. Unfortunately for Mulcahy, retreats were in high demand at the time. Clongowes was fully subscribed with not a bed to spare. Milltown and Rathfarnham were also fully booked for the period of February to April. With earlier notice, Fahy said he would 'gladly have given preference to the Officers for the sake of the greater spiritual good of the national service'.[28] All that he could offer, however, was a weekend at Rathfarnham for thirty-five officers from 23–25 February or a limited number of mid-week retreats.

Despite Milltown and Rathfarnham being unavailable, a solution was found and the retreats took place at the Hibernian Military School[29] in the Phoenix Park, Dublin. Mulcahy sent a courtesy letter to the local parish priest, Fr John P. McSwiggan, to let him know that these National Army retreats would be taking place within his clerical district. Fr Fahy made arrangements that, once the archbishop had granted his consent, Fr Henry B. Fegan would lead the retreats with the assistance of Fr Daniel J. Flinn.

In a letter from Fahy to Hannon, dated 7 February 1923, he recommended that 'for several reasons – not least being the reason of a military nature – we must do all we can to avoid all publicity or advertisement'.[30] When this letter was viewed by Mulcahy, he expressed his curiosity to Hannon, wondering 'what is his objection in this matter. From the point of view of the success of these Retreats … example is all-powerful.'[31] Most likely it was not meant in a disparaging sense as Hannon saw fit to forward the letter to Mulcahy as a matter of course, but it was a peculiar request none-theless. Perhaps it was intended to mitigate potential ill-feeling or even repercussions from anti-Treatyites, given the Church's official stance of condemnation against those who took up arms against the Free State.

The archbishop's consent came on 12 February, in which he congratulated Mulcahy on his efforts. 'Retreats by the Jesuit Fathers,' he told him, 'were bound to do the officers who go through the religious exercises a great deal of good' and make them 'a good example to the men'.[32] The retreats were duly organised for February through April. The judicious choice of location meant that they were able to accommodate over eighty officers at a time when necessary.

The officers who attended the first retreat proved exemplars of Roman Catholic virtue, something which reflected highly on Mulcahy in the eyes of the Jesuits. In February, Fr Fahy informed Mulcahy that:

> From reports that have come in, it is clear that from our point of view the Retreat at the Hibernian School was an unqualified success. There were hardly any hitches or irregularities, which is very surprising considering that it was the first attempt. Your men were splendid, and they will, please God, realise all your high hopes for them.
>
> You hear many criticisms: I have thought that you would be pleased to hear that men – not perhaps incompetent to judge – give unstinted praise to this good work of yours.[33]

A subsequent letter, sent by Mulcahy to Major General Peadar MacMahon, the GOC of the Curragh Command, on 25 February

1923, gives an insight into Mulcahy's motivations and the connection he saw between the spiritual development of his officers and the development of the new Irish state:

> You know the idea I have with regard to these Retreats, namely, that apart altogether from the fact that we are surrounded by difficulties and dangers at the present time, we are starting out on our great work of National re-building and we are formally commissioning our Officers. And most of them, I feel, will wish for an opportunity at the time of their being commissioned of, as it were, 'dedicating their swords' during a day or so of vigil like the soldiers of more romantic times in other Catholic countries.[34]

The retreat was reported upon in *An tÓglách* and Mulcahy took the time to send a copy to the Archbishop of Dublin. An unnamed officer, who had attended the retreat, described it in terms both mystical and bombastic in equal measure:

> February 17th to 19th saw the start of a great work – one destined with God's help to accomplish great things for Ireland and for God. On February 17th eighty-two officers assembled at the old Hibernian Military School, Phoenix Park, Dublin, for the first week-end Retreat for Officers, under the guidance of the Rev H Fegan, SJ. They devoted the week-end to God and the things of God. With the Father's help they examined their lives in the light of the Eternal Truths, and strengthened by the Grace of God they resolved every one of them to leave that Retreat better Irishmen and better Catholics. From the opening sermon on Saturday night the fervour of the retreatants was manifest. The majority had clearly come for business. They saw there was a big work to be done; they meant to do it, and they did it. In the church they were earnest listeners to Father Fegan's straight, homely

talk, and as afterwards they silently paced the grounds, they were clearly pondering the truths set before them. During the Retreat strict silence was of obligation, and magnificently was it observed by the overwhelming number of the retreatants.

To many the idea of Retreats for soldiers is novel; not to say revolutionary. People have heard of priests and nuns making Retreats, but very few have heard of men leaving their business, or their workshops, and still less of soldiers laying down their arms, in order to give a continuous time to the great business of their Eternal welfare.

Yet the idea is not a new one. The experiment, if such it may now be called, has been tried again and again, and its wonderful success has more than justified the efforts made in the work. Please God success will reward this effort, too! Five other Retreats for Officers have already been arranged, and it is hoped that these five will be the first of a long series, and that soon, too, opportunity may be found to give the men the same glorious chance.

But the beginning has been at the right end. All depends on the officers. The Army will be what the officers make it. And that making, as far as conduct in clean, sober living and true Catholic spirit is concerned, will depend not on the lesson the officers teach, but on the lives the men see them lead. Hence the value of those Retreats. God bless those responsible for them.[35]

TENSIONS

Why then, did Mulcahy devote so much time and energy to religious matters, when he was in the process of fighting the Civil War? The most straightforward answer is that it reflected his own religious devotion and that of wider Irish society, but it is worth exploring within the wider context of the revolutionary period to gain a deeper appreciation. Gavin M. Foster has described the dominant narratives and analyses of the Irish Civil War as being generally devoted to the more obviously defined political and military aspects, as the cost of the 'additional lines of fracture and deeper clashes of material interest in Irish society'.[36] These he characterises as being equally integral to the Irish experience of the Civil War as the political and military aspects. While the republican cause and having a common external enemy maintained unity during the War of Independence, the Civil War allowed these lines to fracture along their respective social stress points. The Catholic Church was firmly ensconced within this milieu.

In an incident in Carlow, for example, anti-Treaty IRA were reported to have 'allegedly threw rosery beads and badges of the Sacred Heart' on the floor of a Civic Guard barracks in the course of a raid. Eoin O'Duffy, at the time the Garda (police) Commissioner, reportedly noted that it was a declining situation of 'first the gun, then the torch, then down with religion and its symbols'.[37] Indeed, the clergy were considered natural allies of the Free State, both by the government and republicans. To those of an anti-Treaty persuasion, the Catholic Church could be considered a cornerstone of the 'bourgeois' Free State; a state that, in their opinion, had capitulated to the British Empire in exchange for 'respectability' – a term that Foster observes was used frequently in a pejorative sense by republicans to describe the class and status aspirations of Treaty supporters. The natural extension of this was how, during the Civil War, the government had organised vigilance committees, to ensure that the appropriate civic attitude was fostered in towns around the country and generally disrupt the IRA and various forms of agitation. It also encouraged the Army to target recruitment at men with 'a stake in the country' who, it was assumed, would consider it in their interests to see order maintained.[38] Considering all of this, it becomes clear that spiritual development within the Catholic faith was not an addendum to the training of National Army soldiers and especially that of its officers, but was an intrinsic part of their overall military ethos and indoctrination.

Mulcahy's retreats were not without their own internal friction either. On 22 March 1923, the Adjutant General (O'Sullivan) informed Mulcahy of a complaint he had received the previous day from Fr Flinn. This was in relation to the second retreat, which had taken place from 3–5 March. Unlike the enthusiastic author of the *An tÓglach* article and his comrades, many of these men certainly did not 'come for business' – at least not of the religious sort. Some arrived by train at Kingsbridge (now Heuston) train station and travelled no further. Some did not attend all the lectures. And some decided to leave before the end of the retreat. The reason, as Flinn informed Mulcahy, was that, just as they were departing the Curragh, they had been given the subject of a very detailed report by their instructors, which they were obliged to write as part of the training course that they were undertaking. It seems, in this example at least, that the more corporeal pressures of military instruction could still sometimes trump matters spiritual.

In April 1923, as the end of the Civil War approached, Fr Francis A. Gleeson, the Dublin Command Chaplain, former British Army chaplain and the subject of the painting *The Last General Absolution of the Munsters at Rue du Bois* by Fortunino Matania, wrote to Mulcahy proposing spiritual retreats for the enlisted men at the Hibernian Military School. Theretofore, the retreats had been exclusively aimed at officers. Gleeson went ahead with one, for both officers and enlisted ranks, but his faux pas was not to be repeated. Both Mulcahy and O'Sullivan admonished Gleeson, deeming it 'undesirable that officers and other ranks would be mixed at those retreats'.[39] It may be argued that such strict social delineation of officers and enlisted ranks was characteristic of the military culture of the time. As Commandant Dermot MacManus had pointed out previously, overfamiliarity between superior and subordinate ranks was endemic and adverse to discipline. It may conversely be argued that Gleeson's lived experience of tending to the pastoral care of soldiers in wartime made him best placed to judge. All may have been equal before God, but perhaps not before the generals.

CHAPTER 3

MANLY LOYALTY TO GOD

Chaplains had been a part of the National Army since early 1922, having been attached to large units and formations with the consent of the Catholic Church hierarchy.[1] Following the initial handover of barracks from the British during 1922, the spiritual welfare of troops had been tended to by local parish clergy on a more *ad hoc* basis, with the seeds of the formation of the Chaplaincy Service being sown when Fr John Pigott was attached to the Army in Dublin.[2] This increased with the outbreak of the Civil War, when chaplains were attached to units and garrisons at the request of local commanders. On 12 July 1922, GHQ issued instructions dividing the country into five military commands: Western, South-Western, Eastern, South-Eastern and the Curragh. In late July 1922, Mulcahy and Collins were engaged in the matter of deciding at which of the Army's current garrisons there should be appointed a 'temporarily full-time' chaplain, including tabulating the sliding scale of allowances for officiating clergymen in conjunction with the Army Finance Officer (Thomas Gorman).[3] In seeking advice, Robert Browne, the Bishop of Cloyne, had recommended that while an army bishop was not necessary, a suitable ecclesiastic (either a diocesan bishop or a nominated 'civilian' priest) should be appointed instead to act as the mouthpiece of the Army's chaplains and through whom the bishop would nominate chaplains. Commissions for chaplains were considered highly desirable as they would lend legitimacy and authority, particularly when dealing with officers.[4]

In late 1922, Mulcahy set about regulating their situation. The matter of pay was formalised by Defence Order No.3, published on 9 November. Following negotiations between the Army Council[5] and the Catholic Church hierarchy, twenty-seven full-time 'Chaplains-in-Charge' and 'Under-Chaplains' were appointed. Smaller posts and soldiers of minority denominations were served by 'officiating clergymen', who were entitled to a sliding scale of pay rates based on the number of soldiers under their care on the Sunday at the commencement of each week. There were 500 of these 'officiating clergymen' in total, including twelve from the Church of Ireland.

January 1923 saw the first large-scale, centrally co-ordinated reorganisation of the National Army. The country was divided into nine regional commands: Dublin, Waterford, Cork, Kerry, Limerick, Claremorris, Donegal, Athlone and the Curragh. Deriving from this, Command Chaplains were appointed to supervise in each command, and in November that same year the first Head Chaplain was appointed. Until the appointment of the latter, the work of the chaplains came under the direction of the staff of the Adjutant General's Branch, within which they were situated.

On the same day that Defence Order No.3 was published, Mulcahy wrote to the Church of Ireland Archbishop of Dublin, The Most Reverend John A. Gregg, informing him that he was 'anxious to put in proper train the matter of formally appointing chaplains and "officiating clergymen" to the Army'.[6] The Church of Ireland clergymen were keen to minster to their flocks, and several made enthusiastic application to Mulcahy to be appointed as 'officiating clergymen'. Among these was the Reverend Canon E.H. Lewis Crosby, later the Dean of Christ Church Cathedral, who became officiating clergyman to sixteen members of the Church of Ireland serving at Portobello Barracks.

In advance of the meeting of the Standing Committee of the Bishops, scheduled for 13 April 1923, Mulcahy requested that a representative of the Department of Defence be received by them in order to discuss 'a more satisfactory and permanent basis for the Chaplaincy'.[7] A sub-committee of chaplains had already made representations on the matter including establishing 'honorary commissions' with 'limited military authority' but the Judge Advocate General (Cahir Davitt) later deemed it unfeasible, both because of the difficulty in defining 'limited authority' and the fact that it would require an amendment to the Defence Forces (Temporary Provisions) Act 1923. Despite being proposed on several further occasions, the system of commissioning chaplains was never introduced to the Irish Defence Forces.

As of 1 February 1923, there were four chaplains attached to the Army in Dublin: Fr John Pigott at Royal (Collins) Barracks; Fr Robert Concannon at Portobello Barracks; Fr William O'Riordan at Beggars Bush Barracks; and Fr John McLoughlin at Wellington (Griffith) Barracks on a temporary basis. However, this was deemed insufficient by O'Sullivan, who informed Archbishop Byrne that a Command Chaplain was required for Dublin, as well as full-time chaplains appointed to the above-mentioned barracks and to Keogh Barracks and St Bricin's Military Hospital.

On 13 February Byrne duly obliged. Fr Francis Gleeson became Dublin Command Chaplain, Fr Eugene Traynor was appointed to Portobello (replacing Fr Concannon), Fr Pigott to Collins, Fr Richard Casey to Keogh, Fr Dominik Ryan to Wellington, Fr

Dermot O'Callaghan to Beggars Bush (replacing Fr O'Riordan), and Fr William Byrne to St Bricin's. The Chaplaincy Service soon expanded outside Dublin with: Fr Patrick Donnelly in the Curragh and his assistant chaplain Fr James Mahon; Fr Joseph Scannell as Cork Command chaplain and Fr John Feely as Athlone Command chaplain; Fr Chrysostom (John Dore) in Ennis, County Clare; Fr Edward Harte in Monaghan; Fr M.J. Clavin at Gormanston Camp in County Meath; Fr William McNeely at Finner Camp in County Donegal; and Fr James O'Connor covering the Diocese of Kerry. The average age of the chaplains was thirty-six, older than many National Army senior officers, and several had previous distinguished service with the British Army during the Great War.[8] The Archbishop clearly regarded the spiritual needs of the National Army as a priority, describing his appointees as 'most zealous and energetic for army work' who would 'do great work for the spiritual good of the army – officers and men'.[9]

The Roman Catholic chaplains in particular were regarded with the same reverence within the National Army as the Catholic Church was generally within the Irish Free State. 'The Bishops,' *An tÓglách* recorded in 1923, 'have paid no small tribute of their esteem for our soldiers in the selection of their first chaplains.' The chaplain's role, according to the article, further demonstrates the inseparable link between the state, Church and Army:

> Commissioned to nurture in our young army that spirit of manly loyalty to God, without which there can never be genuine loyalty to country, they have set themselves to work in no half-hearted way in every branch of the spiritual and cultural side of the Army. Truly Irish of the Irish you will meet them with the troops not only in the barrack church, but in every sphere of activity, whether it be on the sports field to engender in them that grit and persistency, that dis-

cipline of temper which clean and vigorous recreation in a healthy spirit of rivalry begets; or in the reading-room to enthuse them to pick up quietly little grains of knowledge that will help them to become more useful pioneers in a new State.[10]

This formal investiture of the Catholic Church into the culture of the National Army was something for which both parties were eager. Fr Francis Gleeson in particular, perhaps unsurprisingly given his previous service as a chaplain in the British Army, was 'thoroughly convinced of the necessity of having the whole status of army chaplains put on a sound, proper and practical basis from the very beginning'.[11] In March he wrote in detail to Monsignor Hickey on the matter, advocating the adoption of rank and insignia for chaplains given that they were part of an 'organised and graded army which runs its whole system according to rank'. His vision for a properly, militarily-integrated chaplaincy was expansive. He made recommendations on the provision of transport, the clarification of chaplains' duties, the establishment of a Chaplain General with associated staff, a promotion system for chaplains whereby the archbishop filled vacancies based on a system of 'selection on merit', formalisation of pay, allowances, retirement and pension provisions, the design and provision of uniforms, and the provision of accommodation. Despite his experience and frankness, or perhaps because of it, Gleeson did not appear on Mulcahy's list of recommendations for the appointment of the first Head Chaplain.

APPOINTING A HEAD CHAPLAIN

The selection of the first Head Chaplain was not a unilateral decision. The Standing Committee of the Bishops appointed the Archbishop of Dublin and the Bishop of Kildare as the committee to decide upon an Army Head Chaplain. The committee was tasked with selecting about a dozen names of suitable candidates, from which the Army authorities would shortlist three and the Episcopal Committee would make the final selection.[12] 'The chief function of this officer', as it was described in a memo on the subject, would 'be to systematise, coordinate and make fully effective the moral and spiritual agencies of the Catholic Church in respect to the Army as a whole'.

The scheme adopted by the Standing Committee of the Bishops for the requirements of the Army Chaplaincy Service laid down criteria to ensure that a new chaplain's disposition would be congruent with military life. Suitable priests would be at least thirty years old, interested in athletics and possessing organisational ability. The Head Chaplain in turn would ensure that 'uniformity of method' was maintained and represent the view of the chaplains to Army Headquarters. His role would be to coordinate both religious (temperance movements, sodalities etc.) and social work (soldiers' canteens, recreational facilities etc.). The office of the Head Chaplain was designed as a key go-between, reporting to military authorities on matters of military discipline affecting the chaplains, and to the bishop of the diocese on ecclesiastical matters affecting them.[13]

On 30 July 1923, Mulcahy presented his shortlist of candidates, recommending for the position Fr Dominik Ryan, Fr Joseph Scannell and Fr Chrysostom to Archbishop Byrne. On 12 October, Byrne confirmed the appointment of Ryan, a role he would formally assume on 1 November 1923. In response to the news, O'Sullivan wrote to Byrne to:

> Convey the gratitude of the Army to the appointment of this, its first Head Chaplain. The [Army] Council hopes with your Grace that the appointment will do much towards securing that Ireland's Defence Forces will be a standard in discipline and behaviour, such as would be a credit to the young Army of a Christian state.[14]

RELIGIOSITY AND GAELICNESS IN THE 'YOUNG ARMY OF A CHRISTIAN STATE'

An overview of some of the ceremonial events from 1923 demonstrates a strong element of religious devotion within the military and the interconnectedness of the Army's cultural and religious life. On 16 February 1923, St Patrick's Garrison Church in Portobello Barracks, having been beautifully renovated as a Catholic chapel, was solemnly blessed by Fr Eugene Traynor, accompanied by a military brass band and candle bearers.[15] It had, up until then, been used by the Transport Corps as a workshop and stores.[16] It should be noted that, while he was happy for the Army Corps of Engineers to be responsible for the upkeep of chapels, Mulcahy was pragmatic in this regard and prohibited the renovation of those in barracks that would likely soon be closed.[17] The following month, chaplains, blessings and Masses featured significantly in the pageantry and national symbolism of the Army's St Patrick's Day programme.[18] On Spy Wednesday (27 March) at Keogh Barracks, over 400 troops and civilians were treated to a lecture on the Passion Play at Oberammergau, accompanied by lantern slides, by Fr Gleeson. They also enjoyed a programme of sacred music, at the end of which 'the rendering of the "Soldier's Song" brought to a close a most enjoyable evening's entertainment'.[19] Easter Sunday (1 April) saw High Mass at Portobello celebrated by Fr Traynor, attended by Mulcahy and many GHQ staff officers. Those in attendance – the church was described as 'overflowing with the troops' – were treated to an impressive programme of sacred music from an ensemble of military and civilian musicians and vocalists.[20]

The GHQ Irish Language Convention of August 1923 saw the formation of Fáinne na tÓglach – a decoration which would consist of a 'fáinne' (Irish for *ring*) worked in gold thread on the sleeve of the uniform. Nowadays it is worn as a pin badge on the soldier's tunic. Again, the aspirations and inferences of the Army as the moral and cultural vanguard of a new Gaelic, Catholic Ireland are evident. Attended by many Irish-speaking officers, the event was presided over and opened by Fr Pigott. Mulcahy was elected as Ceann (head) Fáinne na tÓglach with Seán Ó Murthuile (Quartermaster-General) and Gearóid O'Sullivan as its Tánaistí (deputy heads). Arising from the convention, O'Sullivan was directed to have a census conducted of all Irish speakers and possible Irish teachers in the Army.[21] The following contribution to *An tÓglach*, summarising the nationalist fervour behind this Irish-language movement in the Army, put it in the following terms that resonate with Mulcahy's previously mentioned and those of Eoin O'Duffy to come later:

> Ireland free, not alone free but Gaelic, was the spirit of Patrick Pearse R.I.P. Part of the work was done when we saw the last of the British soldiers, but a great deal remains to be done. Ireland cannot be said to be free while her children's language, amusements and customs are those of the British. 'Who are better fitted to revive the language, etc., than her own sons, "The Army of Ireland?"' The

men who released her from bondage are the men for the work, and if they arc determined the enemy's language, etc., will go under like her soldiers.[22]

August 1923 also marked the first anniversary of the deaths of Arthur Griffith and Michael Collins. At the Great Parade in the Phoenix Park, the Head Chaplain played a prominent role in the first ceremony marking the Bóthar Buadha (Road to Victory), commemorating Collins and Griffith and attended by the President of the Executive Council of Dáil Éireann and the General Staff. This ceremony was a significant statement by and about the National Army having emerged victorious from the Civil War. 'The time of mourning is past and the Army has mustered from the four corners of the country for the first Bóther Buadha parade – in proud memory of those twain [Collins and Griffith] who first set their feet upon the Road to Victory.'[23] Other remembrance events throughout the country centred around the offering of Mass, as well as services by members of other denominations, including Church of Ireland and Judaism.

It was very much with the end of the Civil War and the 'looseness of morals inevitably connected with war conditions' that the chaplains noted tentative progress in tackling prevailing issues of discipline and morality:

From October 1923 marked progress was noticeable. Concentration of troops and stability of barrack conditions tended to a general improvement. The efforts of the Chaplains then became more organised. Suitable places of worship were properly equipped, and the full influence of religion was exercised. Permanent churches were established at all the principal centres, church parades were better arranged, Missions and Retreats were organised, the results of which were consolidated in the form of the Sacred Heart Sodality.[24]

CHAPTER 4

BOYS LED ASTRAY

Religion was not only a fundamental component of Free State identity during the Civil War. The anti-Treaty side also had a strong spiritual ethos. This is particularly evident in the vivid language around hunger strikes, but also more generally in their self-perception as 'guardians of the soul' or 'keepers of the flame' of the Irish nation.[1] Not all priests supported this 'young Army of a Christian state'. Some were of a more subversive disposition. The Adjutant General and the Archbishop of Dublin had been resolute, in establishing the Chaplaincy Service, that the nominated priests be politically and socially sympathetic to the Free State, Byrne being well aware that some of his priests were of a decidedly anti-Treaty disposition.[2]

One such subversive priest was Fr Joseph Smith of Mount Argus, Dublin. On 15 December 1922, the Director of Intelligence, Commandant General Diarmuid O'Hegarty, wrote to Mulcahy recommending that 'it would be extremely desirable that Fr Joseph's case should be brought to the notice of the Archbishop of Dublin'.[3] It is a small detail but one illustrative of the social hierarchy of the time that O'Hegarty recommended that the best channel through which this could be done was through the President of the Executive Council of Dáil Éireann, the most senior politician in the country.

O'Hegarty had received the information on Fr Smith from a Seamus O'Dwyer, who informed him that:

The Reverend Father Joseph of Mount Argus announced from the altar at eight Mass on Sunday last the 10th [of December] that Seán Hales had been murdered by CID [Criminal Investigation Department] men and that the 'slave state' had murdered four republican prisoners. This man makes use of the altar weekly to incite a very impressionable congregation. I think quiet representation to His Grace of Dublin would be better than any public attentions to this mad man and would be a much severer strain on him as well.[4]

The CID were a plain-clothes, counter-insurgency police force, operating between 1921 and 1923 with a notorious reputation for brutality and abuse up to and including torture and murder. Hales, a pro-Treaty member of Dáil Éireann, was in reality killed by anti-Treaty IRA gunmen. Liam Lynch, the anti-Treaty Chief of Staff who, in May of that year had advocated that Mulcahy have an army act passed through the Dáil and urged the establishment of an army legal department and court-martial regulations as a matter of urgency, had called for the killing of any TDs who had voted for the Public Safety Bill 1922. Faced with the prospect of a protracted and expensive war against experienced guerrilla fighters, the Free State implicitly condoned the use of intimidation and terror in its efforts to force the surrender of the IRA. The Army Emergency Resolution, more commonly known as the Public Safety Bill, came before the Dáil on 27 September 1922.

Referred to by Lynch as the 'Murder Bill', it saw the introduction of emergency legislation giving the Army extensive powers to supress the IRA, introducing military tribunals and state-sanctioned executions of those found guilty of bearing arms against the Free State. Fr Smith believed that Hales' murder was a state-sanctioned false flag operation, conducted in order to 'give the Government an excuse to murder the men who are fighting for the Republic'.[5] While Hales was one of the TDs who had voted in favour of the legislation, he apparently was not the intended target. Frank Henderson, the Officer Commanding of the Dublin Brigade IRA, had ordered only the killing of Pádraic Ó Máille, the Leas Ceann Comhairle (deputy speaker) who was shot alongside Hales but survived.

The publication of the Public Safety Bill was coordinated with the issuing of a pastoral letter from Cardinal Logue and the archbishops and bishops of Ireland. This letter, which priests were directed to read at all Masses on Sunday 22 October 1922, condemned those who expressed their opposition to the Treaty by taking up arms against the government and the soldiers of the National Army. 'They carry on what they call a war, but which, in the absence of any legitimate authority to justify it, is morally only a system of murder and assassination of the National Forces.'[6] The 14 October edition of *An tÓglách* included an arresting extract from the letter on its front page. The spiritual penalty was severe. Excommunication awaited those who 'participate in such crimes, [who] are guilty of the gravest sins, and may not be absolved in Confession, nor admitted to the Holy Communion, if they purpose to persevere in such evil courses'.[7]

Further sources on the 'irregular' activity going on at Mount Argus suggested that Fr Smith was not alone in his views. A letter sent to Mulcahy from a Kevin O'Mahony, who had been assisting at the Mass in question, asked 'how is it that Mount Argus is allowed to be the central depot for all who are up against the Bishops and all those who stand for the Free State?'[8] O'Mahony warned that 'as long at this lunatic priest and his auxiliaries are allowed carry on' there would be no end to the 'boys led astray by these same priests and Sunday after Sunday incited to murder, hate, rob and bomb'.

Mulcahy brought the matter to Cosgrave on 16 December, recommending that he contact the Archbishop of Dublin. Instead, Kevin O'Higgins, the Minster for Home Affairs, contacted the Archbishop on 20 December and on 21 December Cosgrave contacted The Very Reverend Malachy Gavin, the Provincial at Mount Argus. Both letters, while forthright in describing Smith's wrongdoing, are somewhat obsequious in tone. O'Higgins said that 'I make no request for intervention. My colleagues and I are absolutely content to leave the matter to your entire discretion.'[9] Even the formal valediction used by the Minister for Home Affairs is insightful – 'With great respect, I remain, Your Grace's obedient servant, Kevin O'Higgins.' Cosgrave's letter begins with an apology – 'It is with very much regret and reluctance that I have to write to you about the following matter which I am sure is as painful to you as it is to me' – and ends without requesting any specific action on the part of Fr Gavin – 'I refrain from making any comment, but the allegation is false and unworthy of a clergyman and I am deeply grieved that such a thing should occur at all.'[10]

Gavin's reply to Cosgrave demonstrates a very cautious and tenuous attitude to dealing with the situation. It was his opinion that only Smith and one more priest based at Mount Argus were of a militantly anti-Free State disposition, and that the vast majority of priests there were 'in accord with the vast majority of our countrymen'. Nonetheless, his position was a difficult one. He explained to Cosgrave that he had:

Hesitated to have recourse to extreme measures in the hope that peace would be restored … You will know yourself that it is not easy to know how to act in such a case, for these men have a certain number of sympathisers in Dublin, and if action is taken against them, they are at once made martyrs of. It is principally on this account that I have refrained.[11]

The trepidation of the Provincial of Mount Argus to act decisively may seem incongruous, given the power and authority of the Catholic Church in the new state. Ireland had been Catholic and Gaelic before 1922, and with the foundation of the Free State it was becoming more Catholic and Gaelic. One explanation for this, as Susannah Riordan has described it, was that it had come as a shock to the Church hierarchy that a significant number of anti-Treaty Catholics had ignored their pastoral letter and refused to lay down arms against the National Army.[12]

Cosgrave's response arrived on Mulcahy's desk two days later, recommending that Army Intelligence Branch be utilised and that he send someone to report verbatim on the priest's pronounce-ments. On 5 January, word arrived to the Director of Intelligence from one of Mulcahy's staff, Captain Hegarty, to start watching Fr Smith and reporting on the content of his sermons. The reports, he requested, should be addressed for his attention personally, for the sake of discretion.

All of this intrigue was a bit too impractical for the Director of Intelligence. He replied to Mulcahy that he regretted to inform him that he had no one attached to his department who would be qualified to take verbatim notes of a sermon. He also urged caution, not unlike Fr Gavin, that:

Even if such a person were available it is rather doubtful whether the resulting information would be sufficiently valuable to justify us in giving such a handle to enemy propagandists, as the discovery that we were taking notes in a church would give.[13]

Mulcahy's office did not argue the toss, and three days later requested the return of the correspondence and material that they had previously forwarded to the Director of Intelligence in relation to the matter.

While the Public Safety Bill drew battle lines in a more conventional sense, the pastoral letter was symptomatic of a wider religious front in the Civil War. One illustrative example of this was the issue raised by Archbishop Byrne with the Dublin Command Chaplain in relation to Tallaght Camp, which in 1923 was the headquarters of the Army Corps of Engineers. In this case, the National Army authorities at the camp were accused of egregiously denying access to Mass and the Catholic Sacraments to civilians imprisoned there.

Fr Gleeson investigated personally, but found the accusations to be unfounded, making his formal report to the Archbishop that 'it was lying REPUBLICAN PROPAGANDA that prompted these allegations against the Tallaght Camp Authorities'.[14] Upon being interviewed, the seven prisoners held there informed Gleeson that they had never been refused as they had never asked, were indifferent, or did not bother with Mass in the first place. It was not a wasted effort however, as Gleeson was glad to inform Byrne that he had 'induced 5 of the 7 prisoners to make new a formal demand for Mass'. He could find no reluctance on the part of the authorities to facilitate the prisoners' spiritual needs, noting that they would have had them met at any stage of their captivity, 'had they sufficient Catholic Principle to demand them'.

IRREGULAR PRIESTS

Mount Argus was far from an isolated incident of a clergyman opposing the National Army and advocating the use of force against it. On 6 March 1923 Commandant Michael J. Costello, from the Office of the Director of Intelligence (later serving as Director of Intelligence himself) wrote to Mulcahy to acquaint him with the activities of Fr John Costello of St Michael and John's Church, Dublin. Army Intelligence had come into possession of a letter that Fr Costello had sent to Brian Fagan, an anti-Treaty IRA man interned at the Tintown camp in the Curragh. The language constituted incitement in Costello's assessment, but even still, it was considered a matter for the Archbishop's attention rather than the Army. Some of the intercepted letter read as follows:

I was sorry to hear how poorly you were. First I heard you lost a leg altogether, but this rumour was contradicted and I am not clear as to what the truth is in the story. I am told they made you tramp for many miles on an empty stomach and with crutches. I won't say God forgive them for I would not mean it. I say instead 'God don't send them to Hell, but give them a bit of what they deserve.' The honour of Ireland will not be washed clean till a few of these F.S. [Free State] Government Members are set dancing on air. May the Lord have mercy on their souls then? The hour is coming. I meet very few, but everyone is full of confidence that we shall soon have our hearts' desire. The Gilbertian situation is that if the F.S. soldiers wiped the Irish [anti-Treaty] forces out of existence they would themselves be dismissed and left to starve. As it is in the beginning it is now. England failing to conquer Ireland by her own soldiers finds Irishmen to conquer for her.[15]

Mulcahy wrote to Byrne on this matter on 13 March 1923. In this letter, his language is noticeably terser than the earlier correspondence regarding Fr Smith, perhaps a symptom of a hardening attitude as the Civil War progressed. 'It will be understood that the reception of a letter like this from a priest by any of our present day prisoners and the dissemination among them that such views were entertained by a priest, would have very serious results'.[16] He also reminded the Archbishop that Michael Collins had previously brought Fr Costello to his attention.

Indeed, priests were not beyond the reach of the Army as the Civil War progressed. In February, for example, Fr Byrne of Clonaslee in County Laois, who was an active IRA supporter and Treaty opponent, had his house raided. In March, the Army's Chief Legal Officer advised Mulcahy that, in the matter of Fr Byrne, who had been found in possession of 'irregular literature' and 'a letter of protest against the action of the troops', he could certainly be tried by military court. In the same letter, with reference to the case of a Fr Burbage of Geashill in County Offaly, he advised that, 'if his usual discourse from the pulpit is in keeping with his remark made after the ambush of 7th January, he could be tried by Military Court ... for encouraging murder'.[17]

In light of the advice of the Chief Legal Officer, it is insightful to consider how these two cases were addressed. On 22 March 1923, Mulcahy wrote to Bishop Patrick Foley at his residence at Braganza House, County Carlow, in order to make a complaint about the actions and attitudes of Fr Byrne and Fr Burbage. For the sake of forthrightness, Mulcahy enclosed copies of the relevant charge sheets. However, whereas the Chief Legal Officer had said that these were charges with which they *could* be tried, Mulcahy informed the Bishop that these were the charges which, 'if these two priests were ordinary lay-men, would be brought against them before a military court'.[18] In framing the formal charges, Mulcahy explained, the Army authorities had confined themselves to matters of which there was direct and sufficient proof to establish those charges. Mulcahy also alluded to his suspicion that they were guilty of more and worse that could not be formally proven and suggested that the Bishop himself should intervene directly:

> You Lordship will, I am sure, understand that it is possible that the more private actions and attitude of these two priests may be much more serious in themselves and in their results than any offences which it might be possible for us to formally establish against them, and I sincerely trust that your Lordship will be able to influence them against their present line of conduct.

Bishop Foley's reply of 26 March 1923 informed Mulcahy that he had already dealt with the case of Fr Byrne, and that following his own consideration of the evidence, he 'had no alternative to finding that the charge had not been substantiated'.[19] The Bishop's following action was a cynical one with which Irish society has become all too familiar, informing Mulcahy that Fr Byrne 'has recently been removed to another parish, for reasons which, I feel bound to add, had no connection to the charge'. In the case of Fr Burbage, Bishop Foley said that he would be happy to give it his careful consideration, if evidence of a satisfactory character could be produced. The best he felt in a position to do, given the circumstances, was give Fr Burbage 'advice and even warning … as clearly and as effectively as I can consistently with the needs of the case'.

Not all subversive priests were as lucky. In April, Mulcahy had to deal with the case of Fr Edward Ryans of County Leitrim. The charges against Ryans were exceedingly serious. The first: attempting to purchase from National Army troops in Ballinamore a machine gun and ammunition; the second: holding up at gunpoint a man named Rowley in the street in Mohill and threatening to take his life; the third: being an accessory before and after the fact of the murder of a local GP named Dr Paddy Muldoon. In relation to the third charge, recent research has suggested that this was connected to an incident whereby a child fathered by Fr Ryans with his housekeeper had been abandoned on a doorstep in Dublin a few months earlier.[20] Significantly in this case, Major General Seán Mac Eoin, the GOC of the Athlone Command and therefore the officer responsible for the military detention of Fr Ryans, had been a friend of his since the War of Independence.

In April of 1923, while Ryans was in the custody of the Army in Athlone, it was decided that he would be transferred into the custody of the civil authorities instead. He was moved by military escort to the Bridewell station in Dublin and handed over to the Dublin Metropolitan Police to stand trial in connection with abandonment of the baby and the murder of Muldoon.

There was local speculation that Dr Muldoon had informed Bishop Joseph Hoare of Fr Ryans' responsibility for the pregnancy, that he intended giving evidence against Ryans and his housekeeper in the case against them for attempting to abandon the baby, and that for this reason he was killed. Despite the charges against Ryans, and his well-known form for being militantly anti-Treaty and anti-Free State, his correspondence with Mac Eoin reveals that he was still in friendly communication with him and willing to assist him if he could. Evidence has also led to suggestions that there was intervention by the Bishop to hinder the investigation, getting the IRA to claim responsibility for Muldoon's death as an accident, so as not to disgrace the Church. In 1925, the Free State, with the alleged agreement of the Church and the IRA, facilitated Ryans' transfer to the USA; as part of this transfer, Mac Eoin secured compensation of £250 for Ryans in relation to his Ford Model T car, which had been confiscated previously by the Army.

***

51

The Civil War period established that the Catholic Church, as an institution, was firmly on the side of the Free State. By extension, the National Army considered God as being firmly on their side. While the National Army was not homogenously Catholic, with the employment and payment of other denominations of officiating clergy being formalised by Defence Order No. 3 in November 1922, it was overwhelmingly Roman Catholic – a reflection of the broader demographic of the Free State. The Catholic Church was keen, from the earliest days of the National Army, to inculcate its ethos into it intimately. This was not a one-way relationship either – for Mulcahy and his generals, the correct religious attitude of the Army, and its officers especially, was crucial to the success of the 'great work of National re-building' that they were undertaking. Central to developing these men into 'pioneers in a new state' were the chaplains, who would cultivate the necessary 'spirit of manly loyalty to God, without which there can never be genuine loyalty to country'.

To the modern ear, these values and aspirations convey a strongly conservative outlook. Arguably, they also did a century ago to those who took the anti-Treaty side. For many of them, the Catholic Church represented the 'bourgeois' Free State and its supporters' pompous aspirations to 'respectability'. It is important for the modern observer to appreciate the severity of the threat of excommunication for taking up arms against the National Army and the government that the pastoral letter of 1922 implied. While it did not shock the anti-Treaty forces into stopping fighting, it had a profoundly demoralising effect on many and arguably deepened the social rift between those on both sides. There were, of course, those members of the clergy who remained loyal to republicanism over the widely and democratically popular Free State, up to and including supporting the use of force against the National

Army. Even during these embryonic years of the modern Irish state, the correspondence between the National Army hierarchy and the Catholic Church hierarchy in addressing subversive clerics demonstrates the reluctance by the Army to encroach upon the jurisdiction of the Church (in the discipline of clergy, for example) or for the Church to encroach upon the jurisdiction of the Army (in the maintenance of military discipline, for example). They were, like with all strong and successful relationships, establishing their boundaries.

CHAPTER 5

STRICT REGULATIONS

From July 1922, as the call to arms saw the ranks of the National Army swell, Mulcahy formalised its command-and-control structure through the designation of divisional commands, with eight stood-up by the end of August. Within these commands, the Army formed into the conventional structures of brigades, battalions and companies. The recognisable shape of GHQ began to form at this time too, consisting of the Departments of the Commander-in-Chief, Chief of Staff, Adjutant General, Quartermaster General, and the Directors of Operations and Intelligence. As J.P. Duggan observed, formalising the command structure along the conventional lines of a professional military was essential to maintaining an organised and disciplined force. Not only was this fledgling army inexperienced in conventional warfare and needing to be rapidly whipped into shape, but it was the only tool available to the Provisional Government to maintain law and order within the state.[1] It could not impose discipline externally if it could not enforce it internally.

On 27 September 1922, the Provisional Government passed the Public Safety Resolution, a severe piece of emergency legislation providing for the execution of anyone bearing arms against the state. To the Army specifically, it granted powers to bring before a court martial any civilian charged with: 'taking part in, or aiding or abetting, any attack upon, or using force against, the National Forces'; 'looting, arson, destruction, seizure, unlawful possession or removal of, or damage to any public or private property'; 'possession without proper authority' of bombs, explosives or weapons etc.; or 'the breach of any general order or regulation made by the Army Council'.[2] The punishments available to the Army ranged from the imposition of fines to execution. While some propagandists may have painted a picture of the executions as hasty, cold-blooded and hot-tempered, General Seán Mac Mahon's statement to the Army Inquiry Committee in 1924, in reference to military courts and executions during his time as Chief of Staff, demonstrates that these were not entered into in a spirit of recklessness but with discipline to the forefront of the minds of those tasked with this unenviable duty:

> During the month of September, the Dáil met and approved of proposals for setting up of Military Courts to deal with the Irregulars. In connection with this I may mention that the carrying out of executions was perhaps the most severe test on our troops. In an Army such as ours, which had been built in a hurry without the necessary training, and which had no time or means for fostering discipline it made us think carefully as to how the first executions should be carried out. It was proposed that the first execution should be carried out by a squad of officers as so much depended on it at the time and we could not afford to run any risk of our men refusing to carry out the work. It was, however, decided that a firing squad would be picked from the men of the best unit we had in Dublin and that proved successful.[3]

While this gave the National Army a role in enforcing wartime discipline and authority on behalf of the state, there remained a requirement to formalise the system of internal military discipline. Regulatory systems were introduced towards the end of 1922. On 19 October, Mulcahy issued the first Defence Order. These consisted of 'all instructions, regulations, rules and notifications of whatever nature and of a lasting or permanent character which should be communicated for information or guidance of the Forces generally or which apply to a branch of the administrative services'.[4]

Instructions and notifications from GHQ dealing with administration and discipline generally, and which were not deemed suitable for inclusion in Defence Orders, were issued as General Routine Orders (GROs). These were issued by Mulcahy in his capacity as Commander-in-Chief, in contrast to Defence Orders, which were issued in his capacity as Minister for Defence. The first GROs were published on 1 November 1922, the same day as the *General Regulations as to Discipline*.

GENERAL REGULATIONS AS TO DISCIPLINE

Under the *General Regulations as to Discipline*, drafted by the Judge Advocate General Cahir Davitt, and drawing from the existing British model, the conduct of all persons subject to military law was governed by a comprehensive range of offences essential to the maintenance of military discipline. These included mutiny and insubordination, desertion and illegal absence, sleeping or drunkenness while on post, being drunk either on or off duty, making false statements, commandeering vehicles or billets without authority, and, in case anything had been overlooked, 'any criminal offence against ordinary law'.

The schedule of maximum punishments was severe but necessitated by wartime exigencies. The death sentence could be imposed for acts of treachery and cowardice, looting, violence, leaving or sleeping on-post or mutiny. Being drunk while off duty could see a commissioned officer dismissed and an enlisted soldier facing six-months' detention. Illegally occupying a billet could result in imprisonment, and anyone guilty of withholding pay faced dismissal. For offences against ordinary law, the Army could impose the maximum punishment open to a civil court for the same offence.

The *General Regulations as to Discipline* was also the first 'tac aide' (tactical aid memoir) issued to Irish soldiers. Taking the form of a hard-back, notebook-size publication that could fit in the pocket, published by the well-known Dublin publishers Eason and Son, it contained forms of oath to be taken by members of courts martial, sample court martial applications, charge sheets, forms of commitment for military and civilian prisoners and to summons witnesses. Demonstrating a renewed focus on the strict military discipline expected from all ranks that was crucial to inculcating the ethos of the profession of arms in the young force, its closing memorandum implored the owner: 'don't lose this book, and therefore don't lend it; keep it so that you can easily refer to it at any time; make yourself as familiar as possible with its contents'; and 'strictly observe the regulations as they apply to yourself and see that those under your command observe them likewise'. Discipline needed to be ubiquitous and second nature to the Irish soldier.

One interesting digression on this path to establishing a professional, disciplined conventional army, if for nothing else than for another perspective on some politicians' potential vision for the force, was the brief existence of the Special Infantry Corps. The corps was a sort of gendarmerie established within the National Army in January 1923, operating until that December. Rather than being tasked with combatting the IRA, its task was to put down the wave of illegal land occupations, cattle driving and strikes that had flourished during the Civil War in conjunction with the IRA's campaign against the state. The Minister for Home Affairs, Kevin O'Higgins, who was justifiably concerned at the social disintegration, anarchy and outright criminality taking root in certain parts of the country, was instrumental in the corps' establishment. Ironically though, for a man with such ostensibly trenchant views on discipline and law and order, O'Higgins' communication with Mulcahy about the Special Infantry Corps demonstrates that he was not beyond bending the law to enforce order:

> We want a force like this in every County – a force that will be neither exclusively military nor police, but flexible to take on at any moment the functions of either. A great deal of wholesome work could be got in at the moment by men in green uniform under the cover of 'military necessity', and I think we should aim at making the most of this fact before peace comes and pins us down to statutory law ...[5]

If nothing else, it is interesting to speculate hypothetically upon the possible trajectory of both the military and policing in the state had this gendarmerie model endured, not least given the fact that by 1924 General Eoin O'Duffy, a man of known fascistic and dictatorial leanings, would hold the top appointments in both the National Army and An Garda Síochána.

ESTABLISHING THE MILITARY LEGAL SYSTEM

The Office of the Judge Advocate General (JAG – the principal judicial officer in a military force) came into existence on 15 August 1922, as a sub-department of the Adjutant General's Department. It was initially staffed by Cahir Davitt (JAG) with

Colonel G.P. Hodnett as the Chief Legal Officer (CLO). Davitt had serious pedigree. The son of patriot and Land League leader Michael Davitt, Cahir joined the Irish Volunteers in 1915. In 1920 he was appointed as one of two circuit judges of the Dáil Courts, the parallel court system of the separatist Dáil Éireann during the War of Independence. Initially, Davitt served as a civilian, but accepted a commission and appointment to the rank of major general in 1923, recognising that command authority was necessary for his orders to hold any weight.

To carry out the necessary work of courts martial and military courts, Davitt requested and obtained sanction for an established strength of one Chief Legal Officer (colonel), eight Command Legal Staff Officers (lieutenant commandants) and nine Assistant Legal Staff Officers (captains) for the JAG Office.[6] Suitable barristers and solicitors were identified and commissioned during November[7] and December of 1922.[8]

A problem presented itself, however, in the difficulty of the JAG in obtaining the necessary officers to sit on the courts martial. In the case of the Curragh Camp in September 1922, for example, each barracks, which could hold approximately 1,000 men, was controlled by just three officers.[9] Colonel Hodnett requested a list of all available officers from the Director of Organisation (Commandant General Diarmuid O'Hegarty). Concerned that commanding officers would use this list to rid themselves of unsatisfactory officers, O'Hegarty instead gave the shrewd instruction to commanding officers to withhold a sufficient reserve of officers for the purposes of sitting on courts martial when identifying officers for training courses.[10]

By the middle of December, Davitt was of the opinion, based on court martial proceedings that had been forwarded from the commands to the Adjutant General, that 'either the Legal Officers concerned have not even cursorily read the General Regulations as to Discipline, or else they have completely failed to understand the same'.[11] While it was acknowledged that the *Regulations* were nether perfect, nor exhaustive, nor entirely explicit in every detail, and were being applied under the considerably difficult conditions of an active civil war, it had been specifically for this reason that Davitt had sought legal professionals in the first place.

By February 1923, Davitt had evaluated the strength of the Legal Service as insufficient to meet the necessary demands. This was compounded by the fact that, by then, two of his Command Legal Officers and four of his Assistant Legal Staff Officers had resigned, and one Assistant Legal Officer had been shot.[12] Considering this, particularly in light of the reorganisation of the Army's territorial commands in January 1923,[13] Davitt petitioned the Adjutant General for the attachment of additional suitably qualified officers to assist each Command Legal Staff Officer. While subject to the scrutiny and exigencies of the Army Finance Office, particularly in relation to rates of pay and allowances, this increase was duly pursued and secured.

There was plenty of work for legal officers during this time. Analysing the figures for the six months from 1 December 1922 to 1 June 1923, 486 courts investigated 914 offences against 546 members of the National Army. By rank, these broke down to 65 officers, 163 NCOs and 318 privates. Represented as percentages, this meant that 4.32 per cent of the total strength of officers, 3.2 per cent of NCOs and 1.96 per cent of privates accounted for all serious offences in the Army.[14]

Taking a broader view, between the formation of a functioning army court system and the introduction of the *Regulations as to Discipline* there had been 166 trials by court martial. Between December 1922 and August 1923, under the *Regulations* there had been 796, and under the Defence Forces (Temporary Provisions) Act 1923, between August 1923 and April 1924, there had been 274.

Of this total of 1,236 members of the National Army who faced court martial up until April 1924, 335 had been acquitted and 901 convicted. While the majority (664) were punished with detention or other sentences, 188 were imprisoned, 45 were sentenced to penal servitude and 6 were executed.

At face value, these figures may simply suggest an undisciplined force. However, as MacManus had described to Mulcahy, trying to establish a large, disciplined military while in the middle of a war, and doing so rapidly, are incompatible goals. Similarly, Liam Lynch, in May of 1922, had extolled the benefits of proper legislation and regulation to build the Army up 'on suitably disciplined and moral lines'. So as the large numbers that were needed came through the barrack gates, the court system had to ruthlessly weed out as many of those who subsequently proved unsuitable as possible.

THE MOUNTED SERVICES MUTINY OF 1922

Perhaps no word in the military lexicon resonates as forebodingly as 'mutiny'. Mutiny, in professional armed forces, is the ultimate failure of discipline; an unforgivable offence that threatens to undermine the very foundations that make a military force greater than the sum of its parts. In his statement to the Army Inquiry Committee, the Chief of Staff, Seán Mac Mahon, reflected on mutinies during the Civil War period as follows:

We had mutinies in the Army before the Regular force was established. We had a minor mutiny during the first week of the regular Army's existence. We had a major mutiny again before the Army was two months old and I may say we had mutinies and numerous happenings bordering on mutiny from the time the fight started in 1922. We dealt with all such incidents.[15]

Of these several episodes, perhaps none demonstrated how crucial a formalised system of military law was to establishing discipline more than the Mounted Services Mutiny.

The first cavalry unit of the National Army, known as the Mounted Services, was established under Commandant Dominick J. McGreal from the Octagon, Westport, County Mayo. He joined the National Army before the outbreak of the Civil War, on 16 March 1922, signing up on a contract of indefinite period. Very little on him survives at the Military Archives but he must have cut quite the figure – five foot ten with black hair and grey eyes, he bore colourful tattoos of horseshoes, snakes, eagles and scrolls on both arms.[16] McGreal was lauded in the *Freeman's Journal* of 20 July 1922 as 'an expert horseman' with service claimed in both the British and American armies, who had 'been through many cavalry engagements during the European War' and had 'organised and trained the National Army's first Cavalry Corps'. However, in September of 1922 McGreal was arrested, and on 12 October was tried at Portobello Barracks on charges including embezzlement and attempting to desert; he was promptly dismissed by the Army Council. While he was acquitted of all charges, Commandant General Diarmuid O'Hegarty (Director of Organisation) reported that McGreal had been 'engaged in very shady transactions in connection with the purchase of horses' and for those reasons alone it seems his cards were marked and his services would, most likely, have been dispensed with sooner rather than later anyway.[17]

While McGreal had no direct involvement in the event himself, the proceedings against him precipitated the men of the Mounted Services to mutiny against the appointment of their new commanding officer (CO), Colonel Commandant Michael Dunphy. The Chief of Staff, General Seán Mac Mahon, appointed Dunphy as Mounted Services CO for a period of one week, in order that he could write a report on the unit's efficiency given the previous issues with McGreal. On Monday 1 October, the men of the Mounted Services were paraded and informed that Dunphy would be assuming command. Following rumblings of discontent Dunphy called a parade of the unit, at which they were given the opportunity to speak freely and air any grievances, which they duly did. They said that they were not prepared to serve under a 'Post-Truce' officer (one who had joined after the 11 June 1921 Truce in the War of Independence, often referred to by the pejorative term 'Trucilliers') and particularly a former British officer (Dunphy had served with the Royal Dublin Fusiliers). This is ironic given McGreal's similar British Army service, though it had transpired at his court martial that he had deserted. Another grievance they expressed was their resentment that they, as men of the Regular Army, would fall under the command of an officer of the Volunteer Reserve. The NCOs also spoke in favour of their own officers, who 'had not been proved incompetent' and objected to being 'dictated to by an infantry Officer' who, as Dunphy conceded, 'knew nothing about Cavalry work'.[18] While mutiny is strictly considered taboo in professional armies, an internal report acknowledged that there was 'a certain jealousy in all Armies between mounted and infantry services' and that the appointment of an infantry officer as commander was 'indiscreet'.[19]

Dunphy, in response, put it to the men that the Commander-in-Chief (Mulcahy) was an infantry officer, and would they not obey him? To this, the men replied with a resounding no. Two other NCOs informed Dunphy that he was not welcome as he was 'too strict'.[20] As one participant recalled the origins of the episode:

> On the 2nd October, Sergeant Major Kinsella [the acting Adjutant of the Mounted Services] came into the Officers Mess, Ponsonby Barracks, and reported to Captain Donoghue that the men would not serve under Colonel Commandant Dunphy, that they were armed, and that they wanted him (Capt. Donoghue) to address them with reference to their intended objection. Captain Donoghue replied 'I wish I were a Trooper today' and also remarked that he would not serve with Colonel Dunphy, 'either under or over him.' He made no attempt to dissuade Sergeant Major Kinsella from his declared intention of objecting to Colonel Commdt. Dunphy. Later Captain Donoghue declared that 'if the boys go to clink, I'll go with them.'[21]

While some of the ringleaders stated that their action was incorrectly termed a mutiny 'as we did not take up or down arms, it was meant as a complaint or protest',[22] another member of the unit stated that Sergeant Major Kinsella informed the NCOs and privates:

> That should a parade be called 'they,' meaning Sergeants, would not comply with this order and instructed us to do likewise or words to that effect. Immediately afterwards, Sergeant Major Lamphier entered and distributed arms and ammunition to us, giving us instructions to stand by our rifles in case of being attacked. Quarter-Master Sergeant Bracken [one of the four signatories of the previously quoted statement claiming that no arms were involved] also informed us that in the case of a shortage of ammunition plenty

could be got in his bunk, and should troops advance on us we were to take positions in Barrack rooms and open fire thus holding our position safe. Sergeant Maher my troop NCO gave orders to the effect that no orders from Colonel Dunphy were to be complied with. I and all men at present confined in Prison at the Curragh openly believe that Kinsella received orders from higher authority and we also consider Captain O'Donoghue is directly the cause of this trouble.[23]

The majority of the men recanted, distancing themselves from the ringleaders and submitting a joint letter to the GOC of the Curragh Camp, pleading that they be allowed to remain in service. In the end, forty-eight of the men were recommended for retention by the Army Council and thirty-nine for dismissal. Shortly afterwards, the unit itself was disbanded; though this had already been in train (the Armoured Car Corps, the predecessor of the modern Cavalry Corps, was formed in September of 1922, effectively rendering mounted cavalry obsolete except for ceremonial purposes); the mutiny no doubt hastened its end. There was insufficient evidence to implicate Captain Donoghue, but nine NCOs were remanded for general court martial on 25 October, facing three charges, namely: conspiring to cause a mutiny; endeavouring to persuade soldiers to join a mutiny; and failing to inform their commanding officer after coming into knowledge of an intended mutiny.[24] All were found guilty on at least one charge.

Following Davitt's review of the court martial findings, Kinsella was found guilty on all three charges, and five others on the first and third. The death sentence was eventually commuted in all cases, something strongly advised by the Law Advisor to the Provisional Government, Hugh Kennedy, with the men receiving sentences of penal servitude or imprisonment without hard labour. In relation to the remaining three, Davitt adjudicated that the findings could not be confirmed and they were discharged.

BROADER IMPLICATIONS

While serious, the mutiny of the Mounted Services was not an isolated incident. Cahir Davitt said at the time that he could not help concluding that these cumulative instances of indiscipline and insubordination upon the part of the Regular Forces represented 'progressively serious symptoms of something gravely wrong' at the Curragh.[25] One aspect of this Davitt identified as jealousy between the Regular Forces and the Volunteer Reserve – in fact Dunphy had suffered an act of drunken insubordination by a Captain Thomas Buckley of the Mounted Services the previous month, prior to his posting to the cavalry.[26] Davitt believed that this was only part of the problem though, and that disciplinary proceedings against the men would only further exacerbate the situation without a root-and-branch investigation into the causes of ill-discipline at the Curragh.

This case proved unexpectedly significant for another reason, not only to the young Army but to the young state, with the potential to challenge not only the Army's legal system but the constitutional basis of the National Army itself. On 31 October, Davitt forwarded to Mulcahy a letter from the defendants' solicitor, P.J. Byrne, stating that he intended to apply for a writ of *habeas corpus* in respect of the accused. The implications were that:

> The question which will be decided upon the hearing of such an application will simply be this: Whether we have any right to try

any soldier or officer of the National Forces, by Court-Martial or otherwise for any offence whatever, or to inflict any punishment. In other words the whole question of the constitutional position of the National Forces will be reviewed … The charges upon which the accused were tried involve the death penalty, and the importance of the matter in every respect can hardly be exaggerated.[27]

This necessitated Davitt seeking advice from Hugh Kennedy. While the writ of *habeas corpus* was not pursued to the end, not without some obfuscation and heel-dragging on Byrne's legal requests by the Army Legal Service, it impressed upon Mulcahy and GHQ the need for the formal legislative underpinning of the Army. This legislative pitfall was symptomatic of wider challenges to maintaining law and order faced by the Provisional Government. Seosamh Ó Longaigh, for example, has written about this peculiar situation whereby the Provisional Government's legislative powers were unclear, and it did not have the right to implement new legislation without royal assent during the interregnum period between the signing of the Treaty on 6 December 1921 and the establishment of the Free State on 6 December 1922. In the subsequent more high-profile trial and execution of Erskine Childers, Ó Longaigh notes, a request had been made for a writ of habeas corpus based on the argument that the Provisional Government was prohibited from establishing military tribunals. While this was subsequently dismissed by Lord Justice O'Connor, who declared that the Provisional Government was both de facto and de jure the ruling authority and was obliged to administer the law and suppress attempts to subvert or overthrow the state[28] (the reason Byrne's application was eventually withdrawn too), it demonstrates the precarious legal ground being trodden on matters that concerned not only discipline but life and death.

Nor was the tactical use of *habeas corpus* to attack and undermine the legal basis of military courts unique to the defence of the Mounted Services mutineers. Seán Enright, for example, has noted that very shortly after the Civil War, Michael Comnyn KC, an anti-Treaty barrister who used his profession to discredit the Provisional Government's actions by means of inquests into deaths in state custody, sought a writ of *habeas corpus* in the case of Jock McPeake, a National Army man who had changed sides and stole the Slievenamon armoured car for the IRA. The National Army had continued the questionable practice of holding military courts after the conclusion of the Civil War, when it was no longer justifiable, and in June 1923, anti-Treaty detainees initiated a sequence of *habeas corpus* proceedings against the Army, contending that with the war concluded, there existed no legal authority to detain them.[29]

ARMY DISCIPLINE AND GENDER-BASED VIOLENCE

Gender-based violence was not a systematic or generalised aspect of the conduct of the Irish revolution. As Gemma Clark has identified, 'the genocidal aims underlying conflict-related G.B.V. [gender-based violence] elsewhere in the world were absent in Ireland, where gendered power structures, shored up by Catholic authority, remained largely unshaken by the revolution'.[30] Research by Ciara Breathnach and Eunan O'Halpin concurs that there is nothing to suggest the tactical employment of sexual violence during the Civil War, and with reference to the War of Independence period they have pointed out that 'while females experienced a range of gender-determined threats and actions such as armed raids on their homes, the "bobbing" of hair and other means of "shaming", rape, accepted as the most serious act of sexual assault, was regarded by all combatants as beyond the pale'.[31]

That said, regardless of its prevalence or absence of systematic use, contemporary scholarship has demonstrated that gender-based violence was inflicted to some degree by combatants on all sides during the 1919–23 period, be they military, police, paramilitary or separatist. While rape was its worst expression, gender-based violence ranged from forced haircutting to transgression of the domestic sphere. Arguably, it extended after the Civil War into the structural violence of denying women pensions for military service that would have incurred remuneration had they been male. Perhaps the most well-known example is the case of Margaret Skinnider. Despite being a member of the Irish Citizen Army and receiving a gun-shot wound during the Easter Rising, she was refused a wound pension on the tenuous grounds that the term 'soldier' in the 1923 Army Pensions Act referred to men only. It is only in recent years that the concept of 'rape culture' – a 'social environment that allows sexual violence to be normalized and justified, fuelled by the persistent gender inequalities and attitudes about gender and sexuality'[32] – has entered the public and academic discourse. If this phenomenon manifests in discernible ways in peacetime, it is only logical to expect to find an increased prevalence of sexual policing and opportunistic misogynistic violence within conditions of militant revolution; a time during which, as Michael Laffen described it, 'old scores were settled in the name of principle or patriotism [and] warfare produced thugs as well as heroes'.[33] Linda Connolly, who has been influential in bringing historical cases of violence against women to light, has noted that 'influential texts have therefore defined the violence of the Irish Civil War and War of Independence as gendered by focusing primarily on men's experience, or have presumed that because these conflicts are considered "low rape" wars there is little to address in the arena of sexual assault in particular'.[34]

The fact that women experience war and conflict in many ways unique to their gender and that this had, for a long time, been overlooked, is now an indisputable and fundamental issue in disciplines ranging from feminist academia to military doctrine. The National Army was not unblemished by incidents of gender-based violence. Two of the most insightful in terms of the attitudes of the most senior officers were among the most notorious: the multiple-perpetrator rape of Cumann na mBan member Margaret Doherty in Foxford, County Mayo, and the violent assault on the McCarthy sisters in what became known as the 'Kenmare Incident'.

MARGARET DOHERTY

So seriously was the Doherty case taken that it was dealt with by the Army's Commander-in-Chief (Mulcahy) and the Commissioner of the Civic Guard (O'Duffy). Margaret Doherty reported being raped by three National Army officers in May 1923. Her parish priest, Canon Henry, sent a statement[35] on the matter directly to Mulcahy, who contacted O'Duffy the same day. Shortly afterwards, the Adjutant General (O'Sullivan) sent two officers to arrest the three suspects (Lieutenants J.J. Watters, J. Benson and H. Mulholland, 61st Infantry Battalion, Ballina) in order that they would face court martial at Claremorris. This direct intervention was supported by the Judge Advocate General's assessment that there was no investigation necessary – 'that the important thing is to have action taken on the P.P.'s [parish priest's] report'.[36]

70

O'Sullivan was acting on Mulcahy's direction, who was extremely keen to have the men court martialled and, due to either his gut instinct or some other information to which he was privy, was unsympathetic towards the three accused. The following letter gives an insight into both Mulcahy's attitude as well as a certain reticence among officers of the Claremorris command:

I feel strongly that there should be a Courtmartial in this case.

There are three Officers here under a particular cloud. They appear to have made no statement of their whereabouts themselves during the time in question – there is a considerable amount of contradictory evidence. One of the Military witnesses on whom most reliance appears to be placed, gives evidence to the contradictory to the evidence of an outside person, no doubt brought in by the Officers in question.

I feel that the Officers should be charged with a view to seeing them on their defence; and also with a view to clearing out of the Army anybody whose evidence was not satisfactory at the Courtmartial.

It seems a very extraordinary thing that there has been no confidential report by any responsible Officer in the Command on this particular case. I think the only way to make everybody face the situation in a manly and responsible way is to have a Courtmartial.[37]

The trial, held on 23 July, resulted in the three accused being honourably acquitted. In a further twist, 'owing to an oversight'[38] the court martial was held and concluded without the Department of Defence and, by extension, the Civic Guard, being advised. Mulcahy was unimpressed, requesting the Adjutant General's 'personal views ... of the Officers themselves' and of 'the possibility of clearing out of the Army any of those who did not give their evidence in a satisfactory manner'.[39]

Margaret Doherty never recovered from the incident. Her mother, Catherine, who had been dependent upon her, made an application under the Army Pensions Act in relation to Margaret's Cumann na mBan service 1918–23 as well as work on attachment to the IRA. In her application, she recorded that Margaret, 'prior to 31st May 1923 … was in perfect health and had never been ill. After that date she gradually failed, physically and mentally' as a result of having been 'dragged from her bed, stripped naked outside and raped'.[40] Margaret eventually succumbed to her ordeal and 'died in the Mental Hospital, Castlebar, on the 28th December 1928'. As the work of Linda Connolly has demonstrated, a century later this event still resonates strongly and painfully with Margaret's family and local community.

THE KENMARE INCIDENT

During the Kenmare Incident, which occurred on 2 June 1923, three members of the National Army's Dublin Guard unit (deployed to Kerry during the Civil War) raided the house of Dr Randall McCarthy, pulled his two daughters, Jessie and Flossie, from their beds and, dragging them out into their garden, beat them severely with their Sam Browne belts and doused their hair with motor grease. Their motivation, according to Cahir Davitt, 'appeared to arise from the belief that in the period prior to the Truce the girls had been friendly with some members of the British Crown forces',[41] that the men 'bore an intense dislike for some reason or other against the Misses McCarthy' and that this had some connection to Captain Niall Charles Harrington.[42] Harrington had apparently been romantically involved with one of the sisters, while General Paddy O'Daly had been rejected. Harrington had also been at the centre of another outrageous incident in the vicinity around the same time, the burning of the home and family business of Noel Hartnett.

O'Daly, along with Captain Ed Flood and Captain Jim Clarke, had in fact been involved in the attack on the McCarthy sisters. O'Daly, a veteran of the War of Independence who had been in the thick of the fighting, had been the Officer Commanding the first National Army troops in uniform, the Dublin Guard. He is also remembered as having been responsible for the notorious Ballyseedy Massacre, a revenge attack that took place in March of that year, when nine IRA prisoners were tied to a landmine which was then detonated, killing eight and injuring one.

Following a court of inquiry (an investigation to determine the facts of an incident and the existence of grounds for further disciplinary action), it was Cahir Davitt's categorical opinion that the three officers should face court martial. A parallel inquiry by the Civic Guard recommended the same. Davitt advised O'Sullivan that:

> It is possible to take the view that to save the scandal of trying a distinguished [O'Daly] general officer and the G.O.C. of a command that all three should be given the alternative of resigning their positions or standing their trial. This however would savour of weakness and an attempt to cloak matters and besides would not avert the scandal of the McCarthys themselves instituting civil or criminal proceedings ... The whole affair is horrible and distressing, but a straight and courageous course is bound to be the best in the long run for all concerned. If 'irregularism' within the Army is not checked at once it is good bye to any hope of ever making anything out of the army.[43]

For Davitt, 'one of the main reasons justifying the commencement of the Civil War was the necessity to stop unlawful interference by

73

force with the rights of ordinary citizens'.[44] This failure to comply with democratic norms by National Army officers was something he considered more closely characteristic of the spirit of the anti-Treaty IRA ('irregularism') and entirely unacceptable. While there would always be a minority who abused authority and, as in this case, used the cloak of Óglaigh na hÉireann for malevolent purposes, it was by the standards of that very same organisation that their misconduct was condemned by men like Davitt.

Following the intervention of both Mulcahy and Cosgrave, however, this case was not acted upon. O'Sullivan, in response to Davitt's call for prosecution and firm belief that there was certainly a prima facie case for it, objected that they could not try someone as high ranking and highly regarded as O'Daly.[45] Mulcahy also second-guessed Davitt's opinion, as he 'felt' O'Daly was innocent, had 'a high opinion of his character' and referred to O'Daly's 'distinguished and honourable military and national record'.[46] Davitt recalled that:

Not long afterwards O'Sullivan told me that there was going to be no Court-Martial or disciplinary action of any kind; that [Hugh] Kennedy had advised Mulcahy that the evidence against the three officers was not strong enough to justify their being put on trial. I was surprised – to put it mildly – but I was not shaken in my confidence that my own opinion was correct. The three officers were never proceeded against in any way. I was told that at a meeting of the Government at which the matter was discussed, [Kevin] O'Higgins expressed himself vehemently; and had some very bitter things to say about [Hugh] Kennedy [the Attorney General] and his opinion; but correct or not it sufficed to prevent a prosecution of any kind; and, since no civil proceedings were ever instituted by the Misses McCarthy, the disgraceful business never became public.[47]

With the passage of time, perhaps the most damning insight into this case and wider attitude towards the conduct of the Civil War comes from Ernest Blythe, an unendearing man who would later come under the suspicion of the Irish security services for his far-right leanings. Blythe described himself as far less exercised by Army excesses in Kerry than Kevin O'Higgins had been. As far as he was concerned, it was understandable that soldiers who had seen their comrades shot or blown up:

> … by men who quickly surrendered when brought to fight, took the law into their own hands and quite a number of Irregulars were put to death in a criminal and unjustifiable way, sometimes being forced to remove land mines which, according to the suspicions which prevailed amongst members of the Government had been deliberately planted.[48]

O'Higgins was far more exercised by the conduct of the war in Kerry, which was why, according to Blythe, 'he made up his mind to bring it to a test in the Kenmare case'. As Blythe described it to the Bureau of Military History:

> Apparently, the girls were dragged out of their beds and were beaten with belts. No great harm was done to them, and the outrage was more an indignity than anything else. O'Higgins was for having drastic action, for having the Commanding Officer dismissed, and for having those who were suspected, or who might come under suspicion as a result of further investigations, brought before a

courtmartial. Mulcahy, of course, resisted this very strongly, and there were bitter exchanges between himself and O'Higgins. Cosgrave was anxious to prevent dissension going further, and suggested that all the documents be referred to Hugh Kennedy, who was then Attorney General.

The meeting was adjourned till next day, and Kennedy produced a written report in which he pointed out the lack of evidence and various other factors that would have made a courtmartial difficult. He also, as well as I remember, brought out the fact that the suspicions which Ministers entertained were the result of rumour and particularly of Irregular propaganda, and could not be made the basis of legal proceedings. Personally, though I was never in favour of outrages and was strongly in favour of the removal of O'Daly from the Kerry command, largely because he was not prepared to stand up to the necessary business of carrying out executions when they were justified, I did not agree with O'Higgins in feeling particularly revolted, at what seemed to me to be merely a case of a trouple of tarts getting a few lashes that did them no harm. [It is unclear why he said 'trouple' instead of 'couple'.] Even Desmond Fitzgerald, although more in agreement with O'Higgins than I was, did not feel that we could proceed to produce an Army crisis over a matter which was essentially only an ordinary war incident.[49]

O'Sullivan directed Davitt to deal with the Hartnett case first and wait until its conclusion before pursuing the McCarthy case, with O'Sullivan subsequently instructing that charges against Harrington be dropped. The result of this delay meant that the McCarthy case would not be dealt with before the Defence Forces Bill became law, after which time it would become impossible to try anyone subject to military law for an offence committed before the passing of that Bill.[50]

DIFFERING ATTITUDES?

These two cases form interesting counterpoints. In the case of the multiple-perpetrator rape of Margaret Doherty, Mulcahy recommended forgoing a court of inquiry in favour of immediate court martial. Even when the men were acquitted, he wanted to pursue the matter and even dismiss any members of the Army who did not give evidence in a satisfactory manner.

In the case of the serious assault of the McCarthy sisters, not only did he second guess the court of inquiry and the Judge Advocate General, but the extant records also demonstrate both his and O'Sullivan's pre-determination that Paddy O'Daly would not face charges due to his own reputation and the potential damage it would do to the reputation and morale of the National Army.

So what was the difference? In general, court records from the 1920s and '30s demonstrate that it was difficult for victims of sexual assault to get justice, something 'underlined by the high number of acquittals in relation to rape and carnal knowledge cases in particular'.[51] While both of these cases are the subject of much contemporary interest and scholarship across several disciplines, it could cautiously be inferred that the difference was that the Doherty case was of an overt, sexual nature, as described previously by Breathnach and O'Halpin as the crime 'regarded by all combatants as beyond the pale'. When analysed with respect to wider attitudes and biases towards women (later chapters will describe Mulcahy's attitude towards 'unmarried wives' and 'illegitimate' children, Military Police patrols watching 'women of ill repute', the weighting of responsibility for venereal disease among soldiers against the women with whom they had sex, etc.) it could be argued that rape's unacceptability (compared to hair cutting, tarring or beating women) lay in its representing a demeaning of the *perpetrator* as much as of the victim, something unmanly and un-Catholic, and that this was a significant contributing factor to it being considered 'beyond the pale'. This may be a contentious proposition, and certainly one open to argument (both the Foxford and Kenmare cases were raised before the Army Inquiry Committee in 1924 as events of the utmost seriousness), but it is not an untenable hypothesis either. On the other hand, the principle of Occam's razor may be most appropriate – O'Daly had a highly distinguished revolutionary career and was, like Mulcahy, a member of the Irish Republican Brotherhood (IRB). Perhaps Mulcahy's loyalty made him unavoidably blind, or wilfully ignorant, to O'Daly's character and shortcomings.

A CASE STUDY: THE CLAREMORRIS COMMAND

As a case study of the general privations of military-social conditions in the immediate aftermath of the Civil War, the Claremorris Command (the jurisdiction within which the Doherty case occurred) is as illustrative as any, with Mulcahy regularly receiving letters pleading for an increased military presence there. In September 1923, Minister for Industry and Commerce, Joe McGrath (TD for North Mayo), forwarded a petition to Mulcahy from several notable Cumann na nGaedheal supporters, to establish a military post at Ballycastle, in the northwest of County Mayo[52] to protect them from IRA violence and intimidation. Besides the fact that post-Civil War demobilisation was ongoing and the establishment of new posts was not an option, the Army had intelligence to suggest that Dr John Crowley, an anti-Treaty TD, was driving this petition for some reason, perhaps acting as an agent provocateur to reignite hostilities against the Free State.

Following the death of a National Army soldier, Corporal Hogan, Army patrols had increased in the area.[53]

Fr O'Hara, the parish priest at Ballycroy, Westport, also wrote to McGrath in late 1923 to take up what was basically a matter of slander. A 'notorious blackguard' and 'Captain of the Irregulars' named Cleary had stood up during a Confirmation in June 1921 accusing him of 'bringing the Black and Tans to the parish'. Having initially raised the matter with Cathal Brugha in 1921, Fr O'Hara raised it anew with McGrath, certain that had Brugha lived 'and if there were no split in your ranks' he had 'reason to know he could have these fellows civilised'.[54]

In the aftermath of the Civil War, IRA criminality, including looting, intimidation, house-breaking, theft, arson, poteen distilling and attacks on police stations remained common practice. One report on conditions in Galway during late 1923 noted in relation to an attack on the Civic Guard that it 'was on a Fair day when certain people had drink in'.[55] An intelligence report from August 1923 on 'enemy electioneering activities' identified Cumann na mBan members as prominent in house-to-house canvassing as well as in an 'organised scheme for interfering with meetings held by Government supporters'.[56]

The National Army were not covering themselves in glory either. The Military Police had to be deployed to the command area and were credited by their efficiency with bringing about 'a noted improvement in the conduct of our troops'. Conditions for National Army troops were poor in the area, with one report to HQ that a significant number of troops' uniforms were so badly worn that they were unable to attend Mass because of it. This was described as 'having a very bad effect, generally, as there is nothing so shabby as a badly dressed soldier'.[57] Another report drew attention to the 'lack of courtesy displayed by many Officers of the Army when coming into contact with civilians in the course of their duty'.[58]

One of the most damning, and indicative of the need for widespread demobilisation and professionalisation of the Army after the Civil War, was the report of an inspection of the 52nd Infantry Battalion in Ballinrobe, County Mayo, conducted at Mulcahy's direction in late 1923. The 52nd Battalion was subsequently disbanded with troops transferred to other units. The following extracts from the report speak for themselves:

Officer Commanding. Commandant Michael Brannock:

Dull-witted and uneducated. Has no conception of duties of Battalion O.C. or of any Officers for that matter. He made no effort to supervise Departments. Is too familiar with all Officers and men. Does not visit posts often and is out of touch with Battalion as a whole.

Second in Command. Captain James Ruane:

Is a 'stranger among strangers in a strange land.' Has made no effort to remedy affairs, but I believe that he is powerless to do anything. Fairly well educated.

O.C. L.M.G. [light machine-gun] Company. Captain Michael Corliss:

Ignorant and uneducated. Knows nothing at all about Company Administration or training, and evidently makes no effort to learn anything. Was connected with the Irregulars up to the end of June 1922. Joined National Army 2/1/23. Was immediately promoted Captain through influence of Commandant Brannock. Gazetted on G.R.O. 30. I was unable to trace his movements between June 1922 and 2/1/23, but they are open to grave suspicion.

2nd Lieut. Wm. 'C' Company

Is a first cousin of Commandant Brannock. A big uneducated unbalanced country boy who would never make a good Officer.

Barracks:

A partly-burned workhouse, in a very bad state of repair. Men most uncomfortable. Heaps of garbage lying in close proximity to barracks. Some of rooms untidy – old uniforms, sheets etc. lying about.

Cookhouse:

Dirty. Cooks filthy.

Guard:

NCO i/c [in charge] absent when I visited.
I found that the Clerk of the Union has his office still in the Union. The Board of Guardians still meet in the Union and pass anti-Government resolutions. This is the laughing stock of the district.

CHAPTER 6

DANGEROUS WOMEN

As the Civil War came to an end, the Military Police were keeping tabs on another prevalent enemy of Army propriety – 'girls of ill repute'. During one particular week in September 1923, this campaign was led by Captain John Marius Brophil of the Office of the Provost Marshal (the senior Military Police officer). From Mullingar in County Westmeath, Brophil had attended St Finian's College, a school which had a particularly religious emphasis and was considered a preparatory school for the National Seminary in Maynooth. Brophil had served as an officer in the Leinster Regiment and British Indian Army from 1914–21, joining the National Army in 1922.

Based out of GHQ, between 23 and 29 September Brophil deployed a team of hand-picked Military Police lieutenants to the streets of Dublin to gather information on the threat. Brophil was tasked with overseeing this 'special duty' by the Adjutant General (O'Sullivan) and it was to him that he reported directly. O'Sullivan had, in turn, been tasked by Mulcahy with investigating the problem of 'public immorality' by the officers and men of the Army.

Lieutenant A. Murphy, of the Office of the Assistant Provost Marshal, was instructed to take up duty at eight in the evening at different locations throughout Dublin. On 23 September, he first called to O'Connell Street, the city's main thoroughfare. Here he 'passed two officers in uniform talking to two girls' who were, in his opinion 'of ill repute'. Another fifteen soldiers also passed by 'with girls of this class'. The next leg of the journey took Murphy down North Earl Street towards Amiens Street where, in his opinion, the very specific figure of '7 out of every 12 women were of ill repute and were out for the purpose of picking someone up'. At 10 o'clock it was on to Fleet Street, where he passed a further six soldiers in the company of girls who were also, in his opinion, of ill repute. The more salubrious areas of Grafton Street and Dawson Street offered Murphy no respite from the moral deficiency either – here he counted eighteen women who, in his opinion, 'were of ill repute and trying to pick up Officers or men'. As he headed back down Westmorland Street at half past eleven that night, he counted a further twenty-five women who were also of 'ill repute' and 'waiting to pick up passers-by'. Murphy even provided Brophil with his analysis of the 'types' of women he encountered: 'About 55 of those girls I mention in my opinion were prostitutes, different other classes numbered at 30.'[1]

Lieutenant J.F. Farrell, based at the Hibernian School in the Phoenix Park, reported with admirable statistical precision on the numbers of 'girls of ill repute' active on his patrol route and their variance over time.

In O'Connell Street about 8:30 I saw two Officers in uniform standing with two girls who were in my opinion girls of ill repute. From 8:30 to 9pm three out of every five girls were trying to pick up soldiers. From 9 to 10 about two in five were trying to pick up soldiers. The falling off in numbers from 9 to 10pm being in my opinion due to the fact that the large number had picked up soldiers and left the streets with them.

From about 10 to 11pm three out of every five were trying to pick up soldiers. After 11 about four out of five were trying to do so.

While standing in Amiens Street, 10 women passed, seven of whom made advances, and who were in my opinion women of ill repute. In Westmorland Street, about 11:30, I noticed about 25 women who appeared to be prostitutes. Up to 11:30pm I passed about 50 women who were in my opinion prostitutes.[2]

Lieutenant J. Feeney, based at Collins Barracks, took a more qualitative approach to reporting. It was Feeney's assessment that four out of ten women he encountered were 'of the immoral class' and that he also noticed 'a couple of Officers gossiping with some of those women'.[3] Lieutenant L. Lacey was 'convinced' that half of the women he saw while out on patrol were 'immoral' and were 'trying to draw the attention of soldiers'.[4] The Phoenix Park was, according to Lieutenant P. Geogh of the Assistant Provost Marshal's office, a hotbed of illicit activity for soldiers. Here, accompanied by Lieutenant Kavanagh, in a single, very small area of the park, he 'found 40 soldiers in company with girls not respectable characters, and about fifteen of them were of a younger age'.[5] It is the report of Lieutenant I.J. Foley, also of the Assistant Provost Marshal's staff, that provides the most direct insight into why the Army authorities viewed the threat of 'immoral women' so seriously:

While in O'Connell Street I saw at least 5 girls of ill repute with soldiers. There were about ten girls, from what I could see, out for the purposes of soliciting men, for immoral purposes. At least six of those 10 *had the appearance of being infected with disease* [italics own] … The most dangerous of these women frequent the Quays and afterwards adjourn to the Phoenix Park.[6]

The evidence from these reports very strongly demonstrates that, for women, the Free State certainly fell short of the aspirations to equality espoused in the 1916 Easter Proclamation. Taking a broader perspective, Mary McAuliffe, for example, has described why, for this reason, the 1916 Proclamation was a key document for the women of Cumann na mBan, whose membership voted vastly to reject the Anglo-Irish Treaty. As McAuliffe described it, they put 'their militant energies behind the anti-Treaty cause, and would endure the trauma and anti-women legacies of this decision on into the Irish Free State'.[7] Quoting Margaret Ward, in his study of the Irish Civil War *Between Two Hells*, Diarmaid Ferriter described the double standard applied to anti-Treaty women and men: 'While the Catholic Bishops decried "decent" Irish boys who had "degenerated" by taking up arms against the new state, the women who rejected that state were frequently dehumanised.'[8] Looking back at the intervening period in her electoral address of 1943 while running for a seat in Dáil Éireann, Hannah Sheehy Skeffington observed that 'under the 1916 Proclamation, Irishwomen were given equal citizenship, equal rights and equal opportunities. Subsequent constitutions have filched these or smothered them in mere "empty formulae."'

This double standard was reflected in the attitude of the Army and Church hierarchy to men who had contracted venereal disease and the women who ostensibly gave it to them. James M. Smith has described the mutually beneficial, collusive relationship between the Free State and Catholic Church, through which the former abdicated responsibility to the latter for matters of sexual knowledge, constructed an idealised and objectified identity for Irish women, exclusively in domestic terms, that conformed to the prescribed national paradigm,[9] particularly regarding their purity and virtuousness. Ferriter has described how during the decade following the creation of the Irish Free State, 'it was frequently maintained that sexual morality was in decline and that perceived moral failings needed to be tackled by a joint alliance of state, Catholic Church and voluntary lay Catholic groups in an effort to recover a historical (or mythical) Irish chasteness'.[10]

The women being watched by Brophil and his team were described as being 'immoral', 'of ill repute' and 'dangerous'. These terms were rarely applied to the men who consorted with them. They were generally described as being, at best, victims of the lure of immoral women or, at worst, negligent. As is elucidated in Lieutenant Foley's report, this equivocal moral panic was inextricably connected with venereal disease, which was of serious concern to both the Army and the entire country at the time.

During August of 1922, in a very early report from the Director of the Army Medical Service to the Commander-in-Chief, the Chief Sanitary Officer, Major Donal Carroll, included his observations of recently acquired cases of venereal disease among members of the force. These, Carroll connected with prostitution and assessed the percentage of infection amongst prostitutes as being very high. Among the recommendations, made both on moral and physical grounds, were encouraging the establishment of 'special police to prevent women assembling near barrack gates or camps', the deportation of all known foreign prostitutes, and promoting abstinence among the men.[11]

Brophil was of similar outlook to Carroll in these matters and took part in the investigations along with his lieutenants. Brophil encountered girls he 'knew' to be of 'the prostitute class' and others 'of the servant class', who although, as he described it, were not openly prostitutes, 'parade the streets' to pick up Army men 'for immoral purposes'.[12] The streets were not the only place that the men of the Army were participating in this 'public immorality' either.[13]

On the night of 25 September, it rained heavily in Dublin. As a result, Brophil and his team reported very few girls on the streets – instead they had taken shelter in the picture houses and theatres, which proved conducive to immorality due to their dimly lit rear aisles. At the Theatre Royal, Brophil spotted 'eight well known prostitutes' drinking in the company of three officers, and at La Scala Dance he estimated that half of the girls were 'immoral, if not prostitutes'.[14] Other licentious venues included The Broadway Soda Fountain and many of the tea shops in O'Connell Street.[15] Lest it should seem that the entire city was a den of iniquity, Lieutenant Gough did, however, manage to find some girls who he deemed to be 'respectable' at the Myra Carnival.[16]

Brophil consolidated the reports daily and forwarded them to O'Sullivan, who in turn forwarded them to Mulcahy. Towards the end of the week, Brophil saw fit to contribute some analysis and suggested some austere solutions to the Adjutant General. It should be noted, however, that these solutions were not of his own creation, but had been taken from an earlier memorandum by the Director of the Army Medical Service, Major General Maurice Hayes.[17]

It would seem to me that the danger to the soldiers does not lie so much from the professional 'prostitutes' as from the young girls who are out for the purpose of 'picking up' or being 'picked up' and who could be termed 'amateurs.' I would venture to say that the statistics would prove that the 'amateur' is the cause of more men in hospital than the Professional.[18]

Brophil's proposed solution to O'Sullivan was that an Army Medical Officer (MO), upon diagnosing venereal disease in a member of the force, should be under obligation to contact the Assistant Provost Marshal's (APM) office 'by phone if possible' (most likely to expedite the matter). The APM would then proceed to the hospital and take the full details of the woman from whom the patient had contracted the infection or, if unknown, a full description, including where he had met her and if she was known to habitually frequent that location. If/once apprehended, she would be brought in front of the man to be identified. Upon being identified, Brophil recommended, she would then be medically examined to see if she also had the disease. Afterwards, he said:

> Some proceedings should be taken against her, and if possible sent to prison for a period where she could be cured of the disease. If the latter course was not possible, she should if possible be got out of the country.[19]

The imbalance between the consequences for the man and the woman in the scenario are strikingly clear. It is also noticeable that the matter of consent to medical examination for venereal disease is not considered, as well as the sort of moral policing of women implied in advocating the imprisonment of those Brophil himself identified as more likely not being 'professional' prostitutes (leaving aside modern debates and sensibilities on the legalisation or decriminalisation of prostitution). Under the Contagious Diseases Act, 1864, any woman charged with being a prostitute and diseased could be summoned before a magistrate and face committal to a hospital or prison. This was repealed in 1886. What was being suggested was arguably even more draconian, facilitating the imprisonment perhaps even of women who were not prostitutes.

Most conspicuous and sinister, however, is the implication that, if it was 'not possible' for the woman to be jailed, she should be 'got out of the country'. Is this an inference to pregnancy? Upon analysis, it could hardly refer to deportation – these were Irish citizens and it was not as if Ireland had colonies to which it could 'transport' convicts as the British had done. There had, of course, been calls for the deportation of 'alien' women, so while this inference is by no means conclusive, the practice of sending unmarried pregnant women out of the country to maintain that fundamental social element of 'respectability' (as described by Foster and discussed previously) was a regular occurrence throughout much of the twentieth century. Unfortunately, Brophil's report does not elaborate further. Brophil's suggestions obviously carried some weight as the Chief Sanitation Officer (Carroll) included them practically verbatim (omitting the recommendation about getting women 'out of the country') in a confidential letter to the Head Chaplain in October the following year.[20]

UNMARRIED WIVES AND ILLEGITIMATE CHILDREN

Aside from 'professional' and 'amateur prostitutes', there was another kind of woman who was considered problematic to the Army. During the autumn of 1922, O'Sullivan wrote to Mulcahy on the paradoxically-sounding subject of 'unmarried wives' to clarify the matter of what, if any, claim they could have on the Army resulting from the loss of their 'unmarried husband'.[21] Mulcahy was of the opinion that 'unmarried wives and illegitimate children' should not be regarded as dependents and, should it be proven that a member of the Army had such, he should face dismissal.[22] Things were even harder for such women and children following the establishment of the Free State, as the provisions for the maintenance of illegitimate children provided for in the Bastardry Act 1863 were not continued from the British administration.[23] Diarmuid O'Hegarty (Director of Organisation at the time) advocated adhering to the practice that had prevailed in the British Army, that the state should not pay for illegitimate children but that a deduction should be taken from the soldier's pay as a form of maintenance allowance. O'Hegarty's views were more measured and humane than Mulcahy's:

> This Memo opens up a very peculiar social question on which I hold rather strong views. The law, as you are aware, provides for the maintenance by the father of his illegitimate children where paternity is established and if the law so provides, it would be rather peculiar for the Army to take steps which would, in effect, be a violation of the spirit of this provision.
>
> The fact that a soldier endeavours to provide for the maintenance of those for whose maintenance he is both legally and morally responsible, should not, in my opinion, be regarded as a reason for discharging him from the Army; it should in fact be welcomed as a recognition of the responsibility on his part. Apart from this consideration, it is hardly to be justified on moral grounds that support should be denied to a child because of circumstances over which, it, at least, has no control.
>
> The question of unmarried partners is somewhat less clear, but I feel we have enough trouble on our hands without raising thorny problems of this nature. The more so as we have hitherto followed established practice in most cases, and the established practice in every Army would appear to be, that if a woman is depending upon a soldier for maintenance, whether she be his wife according to legal standard or not, she is regarded as being entitled to receive Separation Allowance.[24]

Mulcahy's opinions on the matter was more austere and uncharitable:

No person with illegitimate connection will be recruited. It has always been understood that this is a type of people not wanted in the Army, and very probably there is no case where a man having admitted dependents of this nature being accepted as a recruit. Where he is recruited after disclosing the information, the cost is to be deducted from his pay; and if the case arises after recruiting, he will be dismissed from the Army. This is the general decision as the result of the Staff Meeting, but each case is to be considered individually.[25]

The prevailing attitudes to providing for the dependent partners and children of unmarried soldiers can be traced from policy to real-life implication in cases such as that of Private Patrick Perry. Perry was killed in action in Cork on 8 August 1922, aged twenty-four. He had not been married, but soon after his death it was brought to O'Sullivan's attention by a Dr Marshall Day that he had been living with a woman, May Perry (née Mooney), for the previous four years with whom he had two children. For her part, she was a married woman who was living apart from her husband and whom Perry had met while in Glasgow some years previously. Her husband had joined the Royal Dublin Fusiliers in 1915 and never returned to her. Rose had been in the House of Recovery and Fever Hospital in Cork Street, Dublin, with their two children who were suffering from whooping cough, when she heard of Perry's death fighting in the Civil War. They had been admitted there from the South Dublin Union (a complex of workhouses for the destitute and infirm) the previous month.

The Army Finance Officer, Thomas Gorman, the Secretary to the Minister for Defence, C.B. O'Connor, and Captain H. Carney of the Army Pay Corps, all shared the professional assessment that

Rose constituted Patrick Perry's dependent for pension purposes. Gorman informed O'Sullivan that the basis on which dependence was assessed in such cases included any woman who has been 'dependent on a soldier for maintenance and who has been supported regularly by him on a bona fide permanent domestic basis'.[26] While a counter claim of dependency had been submitted by Perry's mother, Gorman stated that 'it appears clear that the man did not support his mother and sister before enlistment. If, therefore, it is fully established that the man did maintain the woman and children referred to by Dr. Day, these people are the dependents.'

However, the General Staff disagreed, and on 22 October they informed Gorman, via O'Sullivan, that it was their opinion that 'these women could not be recognised as dependents'.[27] Irked by the supercilious tone, Gorman requested clarification from O'Sullivan and that he 'kindly state the case and be good enough to let me know what precisely the General Staff decision was on the case'. O'Sullivan's subsequent letter was as terse as his first – a single line stating that 'The decision of the General Staff is that persons in this category cannot be recognised as rightful dependents.'

While initially it seemed that she could have received something, in 1925 the Army Pensions Board assessed that she was not entitled to any dependent's pension. A small allowance was proposed to be granted for each of the two children to be paid to 'the institution or person having charge' of them –in this case, St Brigid's Orphanage, Eccles Street, Dublin. Following legal advice, however, they too were precluded. His mother, Mary Perry, received a partial dependent's gratuity of £50, a claim supported by her local priest, Fr M.M. McCarthy, of St John's, Blackrock.

LIFELONG SHAME AND BASTARDRY

There is, within the departmental correspondence on the matter of developing a policy on 'Unmarried Wives', a handwritten draft suggesting that any man, who is unmarried with a partner while in the Army, 'should be tactfully approached with the view of putting his position aright by marriage'. In another case from March 1923, the moral and social propriety of marriage was conspicuously intertwined with the spirit of the Army and its revolutionary antecedence, when Cavan solicitor G.V. Moloney wrote to Private Patrick Lavery at Belturbet Barracks as follows:

> I have been consulted by the parents of Miss Elizabeth McCormack, of Barrack Hill, Cavan, with reference to your promise to marry her under which she was seduced by you.
>
> My client instructs me that you kept company with her and made love to her for a period of about two months from the month of October to the month of December last and during that time promised time and again that you would make her your wife and provide a home for her.
>
> I am further instructed that all your friends knew you were keeping her company during this time and that it was expected that you would marry her. In view of this your change in attitude once she told you of the conception of your child is most painful to anyone who has respect for the uniform you wear.
>
> This case has now come into my hands and in the first instance I appeal to your sense of chivalry to see this girl right as far as you are concerned. My association with the members of the old I.R.A. and the spirit which animated them leads me to believe you will not do a cowardly turn to a poor girl abandoning her to a lifelong shame and your own child to bastardry.

I make this appeal to your sense of honour as it is with the greatest reluctance a case of this kind is taken by me. The bona fides of the poor girl cannot be questioned by anyone who considers the matter and if you hope to brazen it out in Court I can promise you that I will use every effort in my power to see she gets the last farthing that both she and your child are entitled to.[28]

By November of 1924, Elizabeth McCormack had 'died in her confinement'.[29] Lavery had left the Army, and the case for an allowance for their child had been taken up by Elizabeth's mother, Annie. When the Eastern Command Chaplain (Fr Casey) visited the officiating clergymen to the troops in Clones (County Monaghan) and County Cavan, Fr O'Daly (Clones) denied any truth to reports that soldiers had been responsible for some illegitimate children in the area. The previous year, while the Special Infantry Corps had been posted there, there had been some 'cases' but in all of these, he assured Casey, 'the parties had been married in time, i.e. before any baby was born'. The fact that, on the day of his visit, Casey noted that over 33 per cent of the entire garrison strength had been at the church to attend Confession, was presented as evidence of the general moral standards. Fr Comey (Cavan) conceded that there had been some such cases in his parish but that these were also attributable to troops who had been temporarily posted to the area with the Special Infantry Corps. There had, of course, been the case of Elizabeth McCormack, and one other woman in Ballina (County Cavan) 'who has to work hard to support her illegitimate child' but that besides these two he could not recall any other cases and had only the highest praise for the troops based in Cavan at the time. A hand-written annotation on this letter records that some civil servant had, at some time, asked if this letter belonged in a 'VD File?' Even though the sacrament of marriage could divinely intervene to 'legitimise' women and children, venereal disease remained agnostic to its influence.

CHAPTER 7

VENEREAL DISEASE

Susannah Riordan has described how, in the wider context of Europe in the nineteenth and early twentieth centuries, the discovery of Salvarsan in 1910 as a treatment for syphilis contributed to the transformation of the moral context of venereal disease policy-making. The various Contagious Diseases Acts of 1864, 1866, and 1869 had met with such strong opposition due to their regulationist, stigmatising and compulsory aspects that they were repealed, and subsequent governments were reluctant to revisit the debate. The availability of a treatment for syphilis which was gender neutral and did not differentiate between 'guilty' and 'innocent' patients facilitated conditions for the establishment in 1913 of a Royal Commission on Venereal Disease. Three years later, the Commission's recommendations included the establishment of clinics for the provision of free and anonymous treatment, the cost of which would be heavily subvented by the exchequer. While this was quickly implemented throughout the rest of the United Kingdom, it had limited effect in Ireland because of legislative delay, the disarray of local government after 1919 and local government health cuts being focused on venereal disease treatment schemes. Such was the dysfunctional state of things in relation to the treatment of venereal disease at the time – the Irish State, and by extension, the Army, had 'inherited a treatment mechanism which reflected the determinedly anti-regulationist thinking of the British state, but it was not operating as had been intended'.[1]

Venereal disease in the Army was seen as much as a problem of morality as one of health. That its prevalence was of significant concern was apparent from shortly after the commencement of the Civil War. When hostilities ceased, cases became even more numerous.[2] In early 1923, it was the opinion of the Director of the Army Medical Service that this group of diseases was making such headway amongst all ranks of the National Army that 'immediate steps' were 'imperative' to 'stem the ravages'.[3] Until the beginning of the Civil War, the Army Medical Service had had no proper organisation, operating on an ad hoc basis and relying entirely on civilian medical personnel and facilities. Soldiers were being recruited with little or no medical inspection. Overcrowding was rife and hygiene and sanitation were almost universally bad. Michael Collins, upon assuming the rank of general and the role of Commander-in-Chief of the National Army at the outbreak of the Civil War, was quick to see the defects and dangers of this and in July of 1922 established an Army Medical Council, entrusting it with the establishment of a formal Army Medical Service. Dr Maurice R.J. Hayes was appointed as its first Director General and appointed to the rank of Major General on 14 August 1922.

In the previously mentioned report from Hayes to the Commander-in-Chief of August 1922, venereal disease not only had its own section but an appendix on policy relating to it. In October, the *Temporary Orders for the Army Medical Corps* – the first formalisation of its remit and responsibilities – was issued by Hayes. It included instructions relating specifically to venereal disease patients, including that sheets, bed linen and other materials used by venereal disease patients be marked with a 'V' and steeped in creosol solution before being laundered.

Brophil's 'special duty' of 23–29 September 1923 had originated from correspondence between the Minister for Defence and the Adjutant General the previous week. On 17 September, O'Sullivan wrote to Mulcahy on the matter, attaching a memorandum on venereal disease in the Army, and informing him that he had called a meeting between the Command Chaplains, the Director of Medical Services and himself for the following Thursday, 20 September. O'Sullivan had also begun consultation with the Army's Inspection Staff with a view to adopting measures to eradicate venereal disease from the force.[4]

The Memorandum on Venereal Disease in the Army, authored by Hayes, gives a multidimensional insight into the contemporaneous views of its causes and effects. Venereal disease, it warned, had increased at an 'alarming' rate among the troops, cautioning the generals not to be lulled into a false sense of security by 'parade evidence of increased efficiency amongst the men'. From a practical perspective, venereal disease was a threat to the combat effectiveness of the Army, rendering men ineffective for longer than any other contagious disease. A case of venereal disease rendered a soldier inactive for a minimum of nine weeks. During the first half of 1923, there had been 537 men admitted to hospital with venereal disease (the lowest month being February with 51, and the highest month being April with 124). From 1–31 July, the numbers remaining in hospital peaked at 189, and peaked at 196 for August. These numbers represented an annual rate of 35.1 in 1,000 members of the Army; in the British Army it was 33.66 in 1,000. The fact that it was decreasing in the British Army while increasing in the Irish Army with 'fearful rapidity' was specifically noted for consideration.

As for the patients themselves, the report described them as being 'of an unruly type, and the difficulty of hospital administration where they are admitted, is great'. Conditions within the Army, however, were also blamed. Alcohol, of course, was identified as a key aggravating factor. The report was categorical about this; as it described, 'intemperance and venereal disease go hand in hand'. In tackling the general monotony of army routine, the report advocated the:

> Provision of amusements, recreation rooms, reading, writing, and billiard rooms, in camps; athletic activities and social meetings are to be encouraged. Many soldiers, when barrack life becomes monotonous, or when subject to a dreary routine in outposts, migrate to public houses and the streets, and come in contact with public and private prostitutes.

The use and abuse of alcohol was a prevalent national issue during the early 1920s and certainly not exclusive to the Army. The 'extremely serious and wholesale demoralisation' that the 'almost universal use of poteen'[5] was having in the west of Ireland rang alarm-bells among the Executive Council. The Ministries of Finance and Agriculture identified the possibility of restricting or banning the importation of treacle and other key ingredients through an Act of the Oireachtas as one solution. The other, more direct method, was for the military to deal with it.[6] This was necessary given that the IRA were involved in a number of the illicit distilling operations.[7]

Regulations issued in October 1922 had provided for 'civilians found to be in breach of any general order or regulation made by the Army Council'[8] to be tried by court martial. Invoking these powers, in May 1923 the Army Council issued a proclamation prohibiting the illicit distillation and manufacture of spirits. This allowed for a sentence of penal servitude for those found guilty and empowered National Army officers to seize and destroy stills.[9] While this pertained to the wider civilian population, some commanders expressed their keenness to see the introduction of these measures with a view to the speedy termination of the sale and distribution of illicit spirits to soldiers of the National Army.[10]

The Memorandum on Venereal Disease also presented moral imperatives. Marriage should be encouraged among soldiers, it recommended, as well as the 'maintenance of an excellent moral and physical standard among the troops' which would also serve to 'make valuable propaganda for anti-venereal campaigns in the civilian community'. This echoes Mulcahy's and Devane's previously mentioned aspirations that the Irish soldier would be an example of the kind of 'manly loyalty to God' necessary for 'genuine loyalty to country', and Liam Lynch's (pre-Civil War) aspiration that 'the regular soldier would be an example to be always looked up to by all classes of the community in Irish life'.

The report also made pragmatic recommendations. It noted that practical experience had shown that better conditions in barracks for soldiers attended a diminution in venereal disease, and that prostitution and venereal disease had been allowed to flourish by 'the hypocritical assumption that they did not exist in Ireland'. The Army needed to employ all practical measures, and to do so urgently, if it was to tackle venereal disease. 'Moral prophylaxis' (abstinence) was insufficient, the report warned, and provision was necessary for the personal treatment of soldiers after any 'suspicious intercourse'. Sanitation stations (chemical prophylaxis) should be established in all barracks and posts, where a soldier could carry out the 'necessary disinfection'. This would mean that severe penalties could be applied, not because a man had contracted venereal disease, but because he had neglected to avail of the preventative treatment at his disposal. For those infected and needing hospital treatment, the establishment of a central hospital in an isolated part of the country was urged, in order to 'obviate the possibility of sexual or alcoholic excess'. Haulbowline, off the coast of County Cork, was recommended for this purpose.

Haulbowline had, in fact, been recommended previously by Colonel Thomas F. Higgins, the Adjutant (Director from 1924) of Medical Services. It was, as much as for the medical treatment, for the advantages that a remote location offered in terms of removing temptation (i.e., women and drink) and enforcing propriety through the sheer isolation of the place. His reasons were based on the same logic that the British Army had used previously, in designating it as a location for treating venereal disease: alcohol and venereal disease were considered natural bedfellows; if such a hospital were in a public place, questions would be asked by the public and it was undesirable to advertise the number of soldiers suffering from venereal disease; and the absolute removal of contact with the opposite sex was, of course, one of the cardinal points identified for successful and speedy recovery. Higgins informed O'Sullivan that, had Haulbowline been available as a venereal disease hospital for the previous year, since June of 1922, the cases amongst troops would have been 80 per cent less than they were at his time of writing.[11]

The memorandum was practical and, in some ways, progressive. Mulcahy, however, took a more severe approach. He wrote back to O'Sullivan, looking for his views, and those of the Director of Medical Services, on a proposal that an order should be issued that all officers and men found to be suffering from venereal disease would be immediately discharged from the Army, and that all commanding officers would arrange for the immediate medical examination of all under their command for that purpose.[12] Mulcahy could easily afford to discharge offenders following the end of the Civil War. In a May 1923 memorandum, he had proposed demobilising 20,000 men between July and December of that year, and re-enlisting 8,000, publishing formal procedures to this end in Defence Order No. 20 of 30 July 1923.

Hayes told Mulcahy that he considered this impractical. For one thing, he stated, men suffering from a contagious disease could not be discharged from the Army to become a menace to public health. They first had to be cured. For another, from his experience, universal medical examination was an impossible task. The way to deal with it was as he had described in his memo – education, provision of disinfectant stations and the isolation of patients. 'The fact that Venereal Disease is inevitable in an Army must be realised,' he told Mulcahy, 'and provision made for dealing with it by regulations, like any other infectious disease.'[13]

On 20 September 1923, the same day that Hayes provided him with his opinion on Mulcahy's proposal to deal with venereal disease by discharging anyone who contracted it, O'Sullivan met with the Army's chaplains. The Memorandum on Venereal Disease in the Army was read for their consideration and, while O'Sullivan did not allow the chaplains to come to any formal decisions there and then, he listed what he described as the 'feelings of the meeting' for Mulcahy's consideration. These were: that no decision regarding the establishment of prophylactic stations be come to before 1 January 1924; that the remaining three months be utilised for a 'moral drive' against venereal disease, its causes, and general 'loose-living' in the Army; that all ranks be advised of the dangers of 'immoral intercourse' by the chaplains; that officers be especially advised of their responsibilities in relation to the health and well-being of the men under their command; that every effort be made to increase living standards and comfort in barracks; that both the military and civilian police apprehend prostitutes; that men infected and cured not be re-attested into the Army; that temperance be encouraged; and that the sale of spirits would cease in Army canteens (beer was fine). While these were the general feelings, some of the individual suggestions were even more ascetic – there was a suggestion from one chaplain that only total-abstainers should be re-enlisted into the Army as part of the ongoing demobilisation and reorganisation.[14] Arising from this meeting, the following text for a General Routine Order dealing with offenders was recommended by O'Sullivan. It was subsequently published as General Routine Order No. 51 on 2 October 1923 with direction that it was to be republished in command and battalion routine orders and read to troops on parade every three months:

> Any soldier who finds himself suffering from venereal disease must report at once to the Medical Officer. After the date of this order, disciplinary action will be taken against any officer or man, suffering from a Venereal Infection, who has not reported the fact.

As discussed previously, the symmetry of Army discipline and Catholic morality, representing the corporeal and spiritual realms, characterised the approach to instilling in soldiers loyalty to both God and the Army. From October 1923, the General Staff had observed a marked improvement in the religious life of the Army. This was credited in no small part to demobilisation, which had 'removed undesirables, and the stability of barrack life in contrast to promiscuous war-time billeting'.[15] As the Army began its first full year as a peacetime force in 1924, this same dualist approach would continue to be invoked in the struggle against venereal disease, and the ill-discipline and immorality identified as its root cause.

Blessing of the colours at Griffith Barracks, 1922.

Curragh Camp
Sept 10th 1924

My dear Dr. Ryan

I have already reported to you "re" the sale of English Sunday papers in the Camp. I asked Eason's to discontinue the sale of these objectionable periodicals but their reply was an adamant refusal. I have now placed the matter in the hands of the G.O.C, who will in turn ask the adjutant-General to interfere. I should be thankful; if you, also, could take up the business with the A.G. For your own information I enclose you three cuttings taken from one issue of one of these papers – "Reynolds news".

I may add that Eason's sale of English weekly papers is about 3600 per week. The highest sale during the days of the British occupation was from 300 to 400 per week.

Sincerely yours
P. Donnelly.

Some of the correspondence between Charles Eason of the well-known eponymous bookseller and newsagent, the Department of Defence, Curragh Command Headquarters and the Head Chaplain, regarding the sale of certain English newspapers, described as 'objectionable' publications, by Fr Donnelly, Curragh Camp chaplain, left and overleaf.

PUBLISHERS OF
CATHOLIC PRAYER BOOKS,
LOCAL VIEW POST CARDS,
CHRISTMAS CARDS.

BOOKSTALL AND
ADVERTISING CONTRACTORS
ON IRISH RAILWAYS.

EASON & SON. LIMITED.

79-82 MIDDLE ABBEY STREET,
DUBLIN.

TELEGRAPHIC ADDRESS:
"EASON, DUBLIN"

TELEPHONES:
DUBLIN.
COUNTING HOUSE, 721.
NEWS AND BOOKS, 7988.
STATIONERY, 2133.

WHOLESALE NEWSAGENTS, BOOKSELLERS, MANUFACTURING STATIONERS & PRINTERS.
FANCY GOODS DEALERS.

OUR NO.	YOUR REF.
CE	-

12th January, 1925

- O'Connor Esq.
Secretary,
Ministry of Defence,
Portobello Barracks,
DUBLIN.

Dear Sir,

We are enclosing herewith a copy of the letter which we
are sending to Colonel Dunphy in reference to papers at the Curragh,
and we also send you copies of Peg's Paper" and "Womans Friend"
the two papers which we think are hardly worth interfering with.
We are only sending 9 "Peg's Paper" and 6 "Womans Friend" in all.

Yours faithfully,
FOR EASON & SON, LTD.

Charles Eason
Director.

This is a sample of our "Spur" Bond Paper.

Copy/

CE

12th January, 1925

Col. Dunphy,
Headquarters,
CURRAGH.

Dear Sir,

We have received from our Manager at the Curragh your
letter of the 10th inst, and we have instructed him to carry out
your directions and not to sell the papers mentioned in your
letter until further notice. We beg to assure you that we quite
recognise that you are entitled to decide such matter, but at the
same time we should feel obliged if you would give us notice
beforehand so that we may have an opportunity of putting our views
before you, and we would ask to write to us direct as our manager
cannot act on his own responsibility. We can understand the
objection to such papers as "News of the World" & "World's Pictorial"
and in a less degree to "Reynolds" & "Thompson's Weekly".
We may say we are not selling "Sunday News" at present.
With regard to "Peg's Paper" & "Woman's Friend", the total
supply sent to the Curragh is 9 copies "Peg's Paper" and 6 copies
"Woman's Friend". We send you copies of recent issues and will
be obliged if you would look into them and mark anything in them
which you think objectionable. We would suggest that it is
hardly worth while to take steps with regard to these papers.

Yours faithfully,

(Sgd) Charles Eason

BIRTH CONTROL.

"SANITY AND DISCRIMINATION IN THE CONTROL OF PARENTHOOD."

A book for Married People and Those About To Marry. Specially written for working-class parents in PLAIN SIMPLE LANGUAGE; it tells you FACTS about BIRTH CONTROL from which thousands of working-class parents have obtained definite information and benefited greatly. Only supplied to the married and those about to marry. (Declare which when writing). 2s. 6d. post free in plain sealed cover from Sec. No. 7, The Parents Clinic, 199 Plashet Rd, London, E.13.

The Clinic is open daily from 10 to 6. Principal and qualified nurse midwife in attendance. Consultations and ADVICE FREE.

Wholesale agents to the Trade: Messrs. F. J. PRICK & SONS, 4½0, Green-street, London, E.13.

MARRIAGE

AND ITS MYSTERIES.
SURPASSES ANY OTHER BOOK ON BIRTH CONTROL.

THE most Wonderful Book ever Published. 100 editions issued, and over 600,000 copies sold during the past 40 years. It is still selling all over the world. Several foreign Editions have been published. On the limitation of families there is no other work in the world to compare with it. The present up-to-date Edition contains some wonderful and sensational facts. For those married or about to marry, don't fail to get this celebrated work at once. It is important; don't delay. Three times this work has been seized and prosecuted by the Police. On all occasions the author scored a victory. We have received some hundreds of thousands of valuable testimonials from all parts of the world, stating that their eyes have been opened through its sensational disclosures. Sent Post Free, 2/-. Address:—

C. J. WELTON,
MEDICAL DEPOT, NOTTINGHAM.

WONDERFUL BOOKS.

DR. STOPES' Celebrated Works. "Married Love," 6/-, and Wise Parenthood, 3/6. Aristotle's Complete Works, Coloured Plates from Grand Paris Edition, 6/-. Man: His Diseases and How to Cure Them; the most wonderful book ever published on Contagious and Venereal Diseases; thousands of testimonials received, only 2/-. Man, Know Thyself, 2/-. Girlhood and Wifehood, sensational revelations, adults only, 5/. The New Man, 2/-. The Book to Cure You, 1/6. 500 Valuable Receipts, 1/6. Sexual Physiology, 7/6. Sterile Marriages, 7/6. Startling Revelations, 6d. Boyhood, 2/9. Manhood, 2/9. Wise Wedlock, 6/-. Poor Man's Hell, 6d. The Bride, 2/-. Decameron, 5/-. Balzac's Droll Stories, 5/6. "Jeanette," adventures of abandoned life, remarkable true story, 1/3. Night Side of Paris, 1/9. Night Side of London, sensational, with 60 illustrations, 1/9. Grand Love Scene, from the Great Painting, "Abode of Love," 9d. Post Free.—Address:—

C. J. WELTON,
MEDICAL DEPT., 24, DRURY HILL,
NOTTING

Newspaper clippings forwarded by Donnelly to the Head Chaplain, illustrative of some of the 'objectionable material' appearing in the English papers being sold to soldiers and their families at the Curragh.

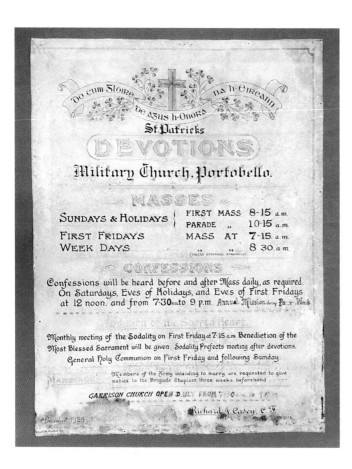

Poster bearing details of Masses, Confessions and meetings of the Sodality of the Sacred Heart, Portobello Barracks, Rathmines, December 1924.

The Eucharistic Congress medal awarded to Colonel Dan McKenna, who became Chief of Staff in 1940.

DEFENCE ORDER No. 3.

AIREACHT CHOSANTA,

9th November, 1922.

PAY—CHAPLAINS.

1. It is notified that the following temporary rates of pay will be issuable to Army Chaplains :—

(i.) *Chaplains Resident in Barracks :*—

    (*a*) Chaplain in charge : £1 per diem with free quarters, fuel, light and an allowance of £36 per annum for a housekeeper.

    (*b*) Chaplains serving under a Chaplain in charge : 17/6 per diem with free quarters, fuel and light. If living in quarters separate from the quarters of a Chaplain in charge, an allowance of £36 per annum for a housekeeper will be admissible.

(ii.) *Local Clergymen appointed as Officiating Clergymen :* When the total number of officers and other ranks under the Clergyman's care on the Sunday at the commencement of the week—

	but does not	£	s.	d.	
Exceeds 9	exceed 50	...	0	10	0 per week.
,, 50	,, 100	...	1	0	0 ,,
,, 100	,, 200	...	1	12	6 ,,
,, 200	,, 300	...	2	0	0 ,,
,, 300	,, 500	...	2	10	0 ,,
,, 500	...	...	3	0	0 ,,

2. (i.) When, in the case of a post ministered to by an Officiating Clergyman, accommodation at the usual services with the ordinary congregation cannot be provided, and a separate service therein is consequently performed specially for the troops, an additional sum of 10/- for each separate service shall be granted upon the certificate of the Commanding Officer that such service is necessary, provided that the number of officers and men actually present at the service is not less than 50.

(ii.) Should the place at which troops are stationed be at such distance that the Church cannot be conveniently be made use of, the Officer Commanding may request the Officiating Clergyman to hold a service at the place in which the troops are stationed. An extra payment of 10/- will be made in respect of each Sunday, or Holiday of Obligation, on which such service is held.

3. A Chaplain or Officiating Clergyman who is remunerated under the terms of paragraph 1 above, shall not be entitled to fees for the performance of any ministerial duties for officers or other ranks or their families, nor for furnishing them, if required, with copies of certificates of baptism, marriage or burial.

4. Arrangements for the appointment of Chaplains will be made through the Adjutant General.

Signed,

Risteárd Ua Maolicísic

Aire Chosanta.

M.P.W.—Wt.2595.—2,000.—11/'22.

Defence Order No.3 of November 1922, which formalised the payment of both full-time chaplains and 'officiating clergymen.'

The Eucharistic Congress Guard of Honour. Colonel McGauran, who was invited to sit beside Éamon de Valera at the formal dinner following the Mass held at the Phoenix Park, is front and centre.

Steward's armband from the Eucharistic Congress.

A member of the Mounted Escort, more commonly known as the 'Blue Hussars.'

An Air Corps aerial photograph of 6 Avro Cadets (incorrectly lables as Vickers Vespas in this slide) flying in cruciform formation, which escorted the Papal Legate, Cardinal Lauri, as he arrived by ship from Holyhead to Dún Laoghaire for the Eucharistic Congress. Dated 20th June, so perhaps a rehersal?

Army chaplains, photographed in December 1924 and appearing in *An tÓglach*. Left to right: Front row: Fr Fahey, Baldonnel; Fr O'Neill, Collins Barracks, Cork; Fr Ryan, Head Chaplain; Fr Clavin, Gormanston Camp; Fr Casey, McKee Barracks. Back row: Fr Byrne, St Bricin's Hospital; Fr Traynor, Portobello Barracks; Fr Pigott, Collins Barracks, Dublin; Fr Drea, Kilkenny Barracks; Fr McCarthy, New Barracks, Limerick; Fr O'Hart, Finner Camp, Donegal; Fr Feeley, Custume Barracks, Athlone.

National Army soldiers, 1922. The soldier in the back left of the photo wearing predominantly civilian attire, the soldier in the front row second from the left with no leather gaiters, and the man beside him with his finger resting on the trigger instead of on the trigger guard, all suggest the initial rapid and ad hoc nature of the establishment and organisation of the Army.

Kit laid out for inspection. The rigours of inspection were grounded in very practical concerns. Instilling discipline in a soldier in how he cleaned and took care of his clothing and equipment was essential to ensuring standards of hygeine and sanitation while living in close confines and often under conditions of privation. While the equipment has advanced significantly, this image will still be familiar to anyone with professional military service today.

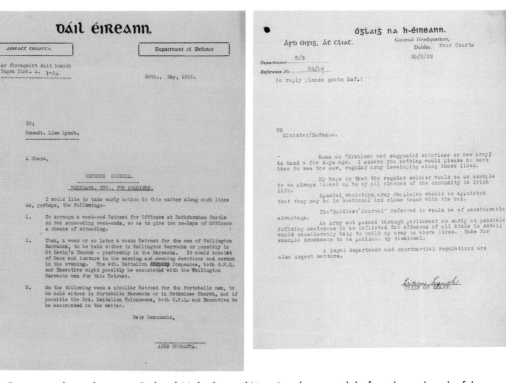

Correspondence between Richard Mulcahy and Liam Lynch, a month before the outbreak of the Civil War. Lynch strongly supports Mulcahy's recommendations, including the recruitment of full-time chaplains, as well as suggesting the passing of an Army Act by the Dáil, the establishment of an army legal system and issuing of court martial regulations.

Note on Lynch's reply the heading 'General Headquarters, Four Courts, Dublin,' and the appointment 'Chief of Staff' under his signature.

Sport was identified early on as an essential part of army life, forming in the soldier an ethos of physicality, teamwork and discipline. Such organised physical activity, keeping the men active and busy, was also identified as an excellent means of keeping them away from the temptations of women and drink. Chaplains were heavily involved in sport and recreation, with several attending the inaugural meeting of the Army Athletics Association at Portobello Barracks in 1924.

The Broadway Soda Fountain – one of several venues identified by Captain John Brophil where 'illicit behavour' between soldiers and 'immoral women' took place in Dublin. In this photo, a National Army Rolls Royce armoured car is having its tyre changed.

Spartan conditions awaited the solder who found himself in military detention.

Above left: A Sacred Heart medal bearing a bar with the words 'Military Confraternity.' From the earliest days of the Army the chaplains were keen advocates of devotion to the Sacred Heart and a strong sodality network was developed around devotion to it.

Above right: The Papal Legate, Cardinal Lorenzo Lauri. Photograph from an invitation to a garden party organised by the Irish National Teachers Association as part of the Euchatistic Congress, held at Blackrock College.

Below: From the same invitation – Very Reverend John Charles McQuaid, president of Blackrock College, de Valera's *alma mater*. McQuaid would go on to become Archbishop of Dublin and the man most synonymous with years of pervasive Catholic authoritarianism.

Fr Patrick Donnelly, chaplain to the Curragh Camp. *Image courtesy of Mr Reggie Darling.*

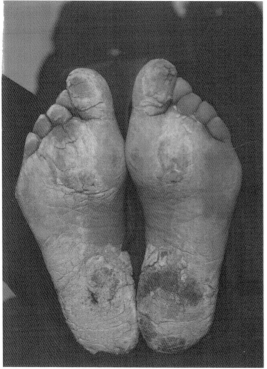

They say an army marches on its stomach, but in reality it marches on its feet. This Medical Corps instructional photograph demonstrates the importance of strict personal discipline in the field.

In 1923, a cenotaph dedicated to Michael Collins and Arthur Griffith was erected on the lawn of Leinster House. This forty-foot Celtic cross bore a medallion on either side depicting portraits of Collins and Griffith, and featured an inscription which read 'Do Chum Glóire Dé agus Onóra na hÉireann' (For the glory of God and the honour of Ireland.)

President of the Executive Council, WT Cosgrave, at the dedication of the cenotaph.

Above: A National Army soldier escorts a woman and child in a donkey-drawn cart across O'Connell Bridge.

Below: A chaplain visits with the troops at dinnertime.

CHAPTER 8

THE MORAL TONE

The National Army, having cut its teeth and emerged victorious in the Civil War of 1922–23, entered its first full year as a peacetime force in 1924. Stepping down from a war footing, with demobilisation and reorganisation in progress, the Army was in a position to be more selective about its membership. The new year represented an opportunity to press home the advantage and develop the force along lines appropriate to a 'young Army of a Christian State'. The year 1924, however, turned out to be a turbulent one. Firstly, having gone from being untenably bloated at the end of the Civil War, by April of 1924 the Army's strength stood at 13,306 – difficulty attracting new recruits meant that it was 4,624 men below the number provided for in its new scheme of organisation. This meant that troops were significantly over-tasked, which had a knock-on effect on morale.[1]

On top of the previously standing moral challenges and campaigns, the very loyalty of the Army came under scrutiny during and after the Army Mutiny of that spring. One very significant outcome of this was the appointment of General Eoin O'Duffy to the concurrent positions of General Officer Commanding the Forces and Inspector General, to restore order and discipline in the wake of the mutiny. While he held this position for less than a year, it gave him 'near-dictatorial powers'[2] within the military. This power, combined with his own conservative, Catholic principles, which he would impress further in his service as Commissioner of An Garda Síochána, could not but make an imprint on the moral and disciplinary development of the Army during this year.

With the Civil War behind it, it was time to replace the existing force with the more formalised structures and professional ethos of a regular, peacetime army. Mulcahy had addressed the National Army's anomalous, unlegislated position when he introduced the Defence Forces (Temporary Provisions) Bill to the Dáil in July of 1923. Formally enacted the following month, this legislation ensured that 'all powers to establish, maintain, organise, discipline and control the Defence Forces must be sought from the Oireachtas in the ordinary way', thereby subordinating it to the will of the state's democratically elected representatives.[3] The act vested the powers of Commander-in-Chief in the Minister for Defence, who would exercise them on behalf of the government. It also removed the previous aberrant situation whereby the Minister of Defence could simultaneously hold executive military command, as Mulcahy had as both Commander-in-Chief and Minister for Defence. This regularised the roles and remit of the National Army and made provision for the formal designation of the Irish military as the 'Defence Forces'. This particular provision was brought into effect on 1 October 1924 by proclamation of the Executive Council.

Of particular relevance to discipline, as part of the post-Civil War reorganisation, a new establishment for the Army Legal Service was authorised in April 1924 by the Army Finance Office. It consisted of a Judge Advocate General (JAG) holding colonel rank, two deputy JAGs holding major rank, five District Legal Officers and HQ Legal Officers holding commandant rank, six Brigade Legal Officers and six temporary Legal Staff Officers holding captain rank.[4] Cahir Davitt (JAG) deemed this the minimum strength necessary to meet the Army's post-Civil War needs, but also one that would leave sufficient space for promotions and encourage unqualified men to take up legal studies with a view to pursuing an appointment with the service.[5] While the act and regulations further codified standards and enforcement of discipline, the issue of moral standards was firmly in the sites of the Head Chaplain.

THE HEAD CHAPLAIN ADDRESSES 'THE PREVAILING IMMORALITY'

The year 1924 began with *An tÓglách* reminding the men of the Army of their duty as exemplars of Irish values, asking them about their New Year's resolutions: 'But, as an Officer, N.C.O. or Private of the Army, what about a little Resolution for the good of the Nation? It is your duty as a Soldier of the People to be the best soldier you can.'[6] This same month, the Head Chaplain wrote to Mulcahy suggesting that the moral direction he had envisioned for the Army was falling short of the mark. 'The religious atmosphere and moral tone is not what it should be.' And the chief culprit was, according to Ryan, alcohol. The first step to remedying this was 'a vigorous campaign against intemperance and the use of drink', which Ryan considered to be both indirectly and directly at the root of the 'prevailing immorality'.[7]

These points had been formulated in much more detail earlier that same month, in Ryan's first report to the bishops in his role as Head Chaplain.[8] As O'Duffy would also identify in the succeeding months, Ryan was conscious of the detrimental post-war listlessness that accompanied demobilisation and pay reductions. This, he said, exhibited itself in an attitude of religious inconsistency among the troops and 'a careless atmosphere' that had 'created a spirit of discontent in which the habit drink had converted into recklessness'. Specifically, this was a reference to instances of venereal disease among soldiers. He noted, however, that the 'moral drive' advocated the previous September as an alternative to the installation of disinfection stations, was bearing fruit and case numbers were starting to decrease. It remained a serious concern though, and the fact that venereal disease was being diagnosed in soldiers in all parts of the country, not just Dublin and other urban centres, was both a surprise and an indication of 'a lower standard of morality than is generally acceptable' to Ryan. There was still something of a double standard in his warning to the bishops of the dangers posed to their flocks by a cohort of recently demobilised soldiers who had not been cured. Venereal disease was not exclusive to the Army, but this misconception remained prevalent until refuted by the findings of the Interdepartmental Inquiry into Venereal Disease two years later.

In his assertion that the 'moral drive' was bearing fruit, Ryan's assessment clashed with that of the Director of Medical Services, Colonel Thomas Francis Higgins.[9] Higgins described the instances of infection during 1924 as 'remarkably high' and informed the Minister for Defence that this was unsurprising given that the repeated advice from his department had been ignored. His department recorded almost 400 cases in 1924, numbers he categorically asserted that neither he nor his staff could accept responsibility for, having been prohibited from treating venereal disease as they would any other infection:

For the past 18 months this department has been asking for a free hand in dealing with venereal disease, and protesting against the policy of discharging soldiers from the Army who are not guaranteed to be cured. Further, we have been advocating the installation of preventative disinfection centres in barracks. These suggestions have been repeatedly turned down, with the result that our whole policy regarding venereal disease has been a negative one, not one positive action has been taken to combat the disease.[10]

While Higgins was vehemently critical of the moralistic constraints on the medical treatment of venereal disease on the one hand, in his defence of the men of the Army he demonstrated the practically unanimous gender bias that blamed contagion on female immorality:

It is nothing short of criminal to issue an order to the effect that the unfortunate soldier who has fallen into the clutches of a diseased woman, must be denied all facilities for disinfecting himself, and must be given no possible chance of escaping a foul disease ... that he must be discharged from the Army, deprived of his livelihood and thrown on the roadside.

As of early 1924, venereal disease was proving both a financial and administrative strain. To remedy this, the Adjutant General proposed that Tallaght Camp, which was due to see a reduction in staffing under the ongoing reorganisation, be partly converted into a venereal disease hospital. O'Sullivan's intention was to propose to the upcoming Council of Defence meeting that it be used as 'an internment camp for all V.D. cases in the Army, thereby ensuring isolation and avoiding the presence of patients in populated areas and access to public houses, which prolongs and encourages re-infection'. Financially, the employment of a triplicate venereal disease treatment staff – at the Curragh, Cork and Dublin – was proving a heavy strain on the Army's funds. As thing stood, any member of the force who contracted venereal disease was treated in hospital until cured and then discharged from the Army. O'Sullivan proposed that using the camp in this way, for a period of six months, would enable the Medical Services to virtually eradicate venereal disease from the Army.[11] How exactly he anticipated that this would prevent further instances of infection going forward is unclear. By the end of the year, the Army would find itself central to the Interdepartmental Committee of Inquiry into Venereal Disease in the Irish Free State.

THE CHAPLAINCY AND RELIGIOUS LIFE

In January 1924, the Dublin Command Chaplain, Fr Gleeson, wrote to the Head Chaplain to express his concern that GHQ had not issued a formal instruction on the furnishing of Church Parade Statements from all barracks and posts, resulting in laxity and failure in sending him these attendance records. Such statements, he said, 'if they were strictly enforced and interpreted … would go a long way towards having the fullest possible attendance … at Divine Service on Sundays and Holy Days'. So while both the Free State and the Army had made overtures to the integration of other denominations, a definite element of compulsion for the Roman Catholic majority was becoming evident.[12] The Parade Statements, official army forms (abbreviated to AF followed by a number, in this case AF107), contained one column for 'Catholics' and one for 'Other Denominations', so it can be assumed they would have a very practical purpose in calculating the remuneration of 'officiating clergymen'. Gleeson's proposal, however, was to use these documents to give an idea of who and how many were *not* attending Mass.

This resulted in the further formalisation of church parades in the Army. Some chaplains exercised more informal approaches ('whichever of us was free went around and saw that all hands were in for Mass'[13] / 'I think that it would not be wise that the Church Parade interfere with those going out on week-end passes, especially married men.'[14]) Others were more rigid, such as Fr Pigott at Collins Barracks:

> The Church Parades here have been very good for several weeks back, and I am pleased with the results. It is to be regretted however that to ensure success, and make it permanent, means that the Chaplain has often to use rather high-handed methods …
>
> … No one except married Officers and a few senior Officers named in Camp Orders shall have permission to leave Barracks to hear Mass without a special Pass from the Camp Commandant to which the Chaplain has consented …
>
> … Soldiers of all denominations shall be obliged to fall in on the Major Church Parade. Non-Catholics shall be ordered to fall in on the left and sent to their own places of worship.[15]

The administration and structures of the Chaplaincy Service continued to evolve in tandem with the Army during 1924. With numbers falling during this year and a new scheme of organisation introduced in April, the position of Command Chaplain was abolished and replaced with positions at each Brigade HQ as well as the new Army School of Instruction (opened in April 1924), St Bricin's Hospital and the Air Service at Baldonnel. Just as the other branches of GHQ developed their own policy directions, the Head Chaplain had very definitive ideas for the spiritual and moral direction of the force. Church attendance was vital, and certain services could not be left voluntary. Ryan was unimpressed that many senior officers in particular never attended church parades and was concerned that some officers missed Mass without 'genuine' cause. He considered religious life vital to the Army and the good example of officers in this regard was essential. To this end, Ryan wanted to make church parades a semi-ceremonial affair. This would have both spiritual and corporeal benefits and this is illustrative of how realms of state and Church jurisdiction could prove reciprocal and mutually beneficial. On the one hand, he proposed that it would engender a religious spirit and remind all ranks of their brotherhood before God. On the other, the military ceremonial aspect would reinforce military authority and the significance of rank.

The matter of military sodalities, first raised in 1922 by Fr Devane, was one that Ryan believed would find fertile ground. In particular, the Devotion to the Sacred Heart was one that he had observed as the most marked during the War of Independence. Initiated by a general retreat during Holy Week, so as to ensure simultaneous organisation throughout the force, this would involve a morning offering, daily decade of the Rosary and monthly sacraments of Confession and Communion. Regarding the latter, he suggested to the bishops that GHQ should leave the first Friday morning of each month free before breakfast to facilitate a 7:15 Mass.

While the matter of the sodality was optional, his ideas on daily devotions demonstrate how the Catholic ethos permeated Army life:

The Angelus should be sounded at traditional times by a special bugle call, Military discipline requiring all troops to stand to attention. Night prayers should be encouraged in the Chapel especially during the month of May and October, and during Lent. At other times Night prayers, or the Daily Decade required by the Sodality Obligation may be recited in the Barrack Rooms. Each Barrack Room and sleeping billet and each Officer's room should be supplied with a Crucifix and Holy Water Font. Each man's kit should include a copy of an Official Army Prayer Book.

An article from *An tÓglách* that year suggests the depth of religious zeal within the Army. In February of 1924 it reported the tragic death of Lieutenant Timothy Nevin of the Air Service, who had died in a flying accident the previous month. It made a particular point of noting that he was a man who had attended Mass daily and regularly served at it. His religious observance and 'making the Nine First Fridays Devotion' meant that 'the Sacred Heart gave him ample time to prepare for death in accordance with the 12th Promise to those who make the Nine Fridays'. While 'everyone in the camp regretted that this brave young pilot was cut off in the prime of life' they were 'consoled by the thought of his exemplary religious life and happy death'.[16]

Addressing troops in Ennis, County Clare, in January 1924, the Bishop of Killaloe, Michael Fogarty, paid tribute to the part played by the Volunteers of Clare in achieving and maintaining national independence. Drawing on the lineage from the Irish Volunteers to the National Army he expressed his opprobrium towards those who took the anti-Treaty side in the Civil War and the evils their dissension had wrought. 'As the victory at Clontarf over the Danes was rendered fruitless by internal quarrels, so was the freedom so dearly won from England in 1921 well-nigh lost through the action of some of our own countrymen.'[17]

Sunday 13 April 1924 saw the first visit of a Church of Ireland (COI) Archbishop to the Curragh Camp since the foundation of the Free State, when the Most Reverend Dr John Gregg visited the COI church there in conjunction with a Confirmation ceremony.[18] Unsurprisingly however, as a predominantly Roman Catholic force it was the Catholic Chaplaincy that came into the ascendency during this year. Building on the momentum of Fr Ryan's Holy Week general retreat, a spiritual drive during Lent and Easter saw retreats and missions get a serious boost. The Curragh bi-annual retreat saw 'the vast majority of officers and men fulfil their Easter Duty'. Over 700 officers and men received Holy Communion during the mission week at Portobello Barracks. Over 400 officers and men from GHQ and the Remount Depot, Arbour Hill, were present at St Bricin's Hospital oratory on Good Friday when the stations of the cross were devoutly performed. Ninety per cent of the officers and men at Griffith Barracks attended the general Communion on the first Fridays during Lent. At Keogh Barracks, Fr Casey presided over a very successful Triduum (a three-day observance recalling the passion, crucifixion, death, burial, and resurrection of Jesus) with over 500 receiving Holy Communion during the month. As a special feature at Keogh Barracks, each man was 'presented with a little cross as a souvenir of his promise to approach the Sacraments once each month' attached to which was a 'Plenary Indulgence until the hour of death'. Similarly successful religious ceremonies took place at Baldonnel, Limerick and Kerry.[19]

As the Army had become increasingly professionalised, the functions of the Chaplaincy Service had become formalised. While some soldiers considered it a 'soft job', one contributor took to the pages of *An tÓglách* to explain how 'few have a more arduous task' than the chaplain. For one thing, conducting religious retreats for the welfare of the Army required 'tremendous energy', not least given the 'lack of inspiration of the average layman'. The chaplain was also the last port of call when trying to deal with a problem soldier when all disciplinary avenues had been exhausted. It was the chaplain whom the soldier called, along with the doctor, if his comrade took severely ill after hours in the barrack room, and the chaplain who was a ubiquitous nominee on welfare and recreational committees as an advocate for the troops. The chaplain indeed had no 'soft job' but it was considered 'a grand job nevertheless, for every C.F. [chaplain to the forces] has the friendship of his fellow men, and the friendship of one's mankind is invaluable'.[20]

TEMPERANCE AND CLEAN LIVING

Alcohol maintained its place as the root of all (or at least most) evil. With reorganisation and recruitment ongoing and a new cohort of young Irishmen donning the uniform, this had to be nipped in the bud. Ryan was no puritanical teetotaller though. While he did recommend a Lenten campaign against intemperance, the rest of his recommendations were practical and geared towards creating social and living spaces for all ranks that did not centre around a culture of alcohol without advocating prohibition. Canteens should only sell beer and stout – no wine or spirits. Bar areas should be separate to the mess room, and dry canteens (ones that do not sell alcohol) should be well furnished, well equipped and attractive places 'where the soldier may obtain all his requirements'. Ryan saw a role for the chaplains in the supervision and oversight of recreation and living quarters – outdoor games and physical activities were comfortable and natural territory for the Army authorities; the realm of indoor amusements, recreation and lectures he considered as that of the Chaplaincy Service.

CHAPTER 9

HOPE FOR THE FUTURE

In September of 1923, a Defence Order was issued providing for the demobilisation of officers by March of the following year. This was a major contributing factor to the Army Mutiny and explains why it was an officer-centric crisis. The short-term Civil War contracts of the other ranks meant that there was less friction in reducing enlisted numbers. The mutiny took place when a minority group within the Army known as the Irish Republican Army Organisation (IRAO), with support from a faction within government led by the Minister for Labour, Joe McGrath, issued an ultimatum to the government 'to suspend, and establish an enquiry into, demobilisation and reorganisation and to give the IRAO a say in it'.[1] Their grievances were centred on the perceived favouritism being shown to former British Army men over IRA veterans, the revival and influence of the IRB, and their perceived abandonment by the government of Michael Collins' conception of the Anglo-Irish Treaty as simply a stepping-stone to fuller independence. While it could be argued that the pre-Truce service of some of the leaders was being disregarded in the reorganisation of the Army for pragmatic purposes, some had been identified for removal from important positions due to their track record of violent and unpredictable behaviour, not least the mutiny ringleaders, Liam Tobin and Charlie Dalton.

On 19 March, Mulcahy ordered the arrest of the conspirators, who were drinking in Devlin's public house, 68 Parnell Street, Dublin. This was done without the authority of General Eoin O'Duffy, who had recently been given the new appointment of General Officer Commanding the Forces in order to restore order and discipline. In response, the Executive Council called for the resignation of the Army Council – the Chief of Staff (Lieutenant General Seán Mac Mahon), the Adjutant General (Lieutenant General Gearóid O'Sullivan) and the Quartermaster General (Lieutenant General Seán Ó Murthuile). They also asked that the Commander-in-Chief, General Richard Mulcahy, be requested to resign as Minister for Defence.

The mutiny, and subsequent inquiry, initially had negative implications for public and political perceptions of the loyalty and discipline of the Army. However, its outcome copper-fastened the subordination of the military to the democratic process, vindicated the Army and ultimately showed the discipline of the force in a positive light. October that year saw the introduction of the oath of fidelity to be made by officers which, among its requirements, required that the officer swore 'not to join or be a member of or subscribe to any political society or organisation whatsoever, or any secret society whatsoever'.[2] This is a direct reference to Mulcahy's revival of the IRB, a contributing factor to the dissatisfaction of the mutineers. The prohibition on secret societies in the Army also piqued the interest of the Catholic Church hierarchy, being 'morally interested' and seeking assurances in early October from the Minister for Defence, via the Head Chaplain, that this would be implemented.[3]

The mutiny also contributed to government and civil service neurosis in Irish defence policy-making and preoccupation with civilian control. This has been described by numerous historians and journalists as having kept the force starved and on life-support, unfit for any truly meaningful role in national defence and neutered of a proper system of military command. During 1924 specifically, of the most significant occurrences for the formation of the character of the force was the previously mentioned appointment of O'Duffy as General Officer Commanding the Forces and Inspector General.

O'DUFFY'S INFLUENCE

The wake of the mutiny and subsequent resignations saw new appointments to the General Staff. Colonels Hugo MacNeill and Felix Cronin became acting Adjutant General and Quartermaster General respectively. Seán Mac Mahon refused to tender his resignation and was replaced as Chief of Staff by Peadar MacMahon. W.T. Cosgrave, the President of the Executive Council, replaced Mulcahy as Minister for Defence as an interim measure.

On 10 March 1924, the government temporarily appointed Garda Commissioner Eoin O'Duffy as General Officer Commanding (GOC) the Forces, in a bid to ensure its control of the Army during the mutiny crisis. This position had not existed previously but was, for all intents and purposes, the equivalent of the previously extant appointment of Commander-in-Chief. The Defence Forces (Temporary Provisions) Act 1923 had, however, vested the power of command-in-chief in the Executive Council, to be exercised by the Minister for Defence, but the Minister was prohibited from exercising executive military command. This new appointment of GOC the Forces was intended to strengthen the personnel of the HQ staff of the Army according to Cosgrave.[4] Though his exact remit was initially vague and undefined, it placed O'Duffy in overall command of the entire force, answerable directly to the Minister. In addition to this, on 14 March, the new position of Inspector General of the Defence Forces was created by order of the Executive Council and O'Duffy held both appointments concurrently. The role of the Inspector General was defined as to 'inquire into and report to the Minister on the organisation and administration of the Forces and the suitability and efficiency of their personnel and equipment'.[5] During his tenure as GOC the Forces, O'Duffy presented a catalogue of recommendations to the government to improve discipline and morale, from overhauling the chaplaincy to reducing rates of venereal disease. The combination of O'Duffy's position within the Army and his personality made him the most influential figure on the disciplinary and ideological trajectory of the force during that year.

O'DUFFY'S REPORTS TO THE EXECUTIVE COUNCIL

From early April 1924, from his headquarters at the Royal Hospital, Kilmainham, O'Duffy submitted regular reports to the Executive Council of Dáil Éireann. In his first, he described the general standard of discipline and morale in the Army as good. He noticed, however, 'a certain amount of slackness and want of "click" which makes an unfavourable impression' which he attributed to the want of proper training.[6]

Taking the week of 7–14 April as a snapshot, O'Duffy reported that the principal offence among NCOs and privates had been short periods of absence without leave, and drunkenness – in fact there had only been twenty-four charges of absence, two of insubordination and eight of drunkenness. Representing 0.3 per cent of the NCOs and privates in the Army, this was not a bad situation. There remained significant dissatisfaction in the Army, however.

Compounding the over-tasking of soldiers with duties because of the shortfall between the actual and established strength of the Army (there were instances of exhausted sentries being found asleep at their posts in the middle of the day), discipline and morale were being undermined by the deduction of 9d a week from soldiers' pay for hair cutting and laundry. Not only was this in contravention of defence legislation, but it was also excessive when measured against the actual cost of those services, services which were met from public funds in the British Army. O'Duffy presented the need to remedy this unfairness in no uncertain terms. In fact, throughout his tenure, O'Duffy demonstrated the utmost concern for the welfare of the men of the Army.

That said, it was more vital than ever at this time that discipline be enforced and a high standard set within the Army, and his sympathy did not stretch to those who did not meet the standard of conduct considered befitting of an Irish soldier. These were volatile times. In the aftermath of the mutiny there was a potent mix of dissatisfied ex-officers, uncontrolled arms on the streets, a 'very considerable leakage of munitions … from the Army' and the allure of the Republican side.[7] In relation to the latter, Frank Aiken had instructed that no demobilised or resigned National Army officer was to be taken into the ranks of the IRA unless he could show good reason that he was acting on principle and not from any motive of self-interest. Ironically, as Minister for Defence in 1934, Aiken would announce the establishment of a Volunteer Force as a reserve element of the Defence Forces, which was in no small part an effort to offer the allure of military adventure to young men as an alternative to joining the IRA.

During February of 1924, the physical standard of soldiers was described as deplorable by the Adjutant General due to their not being medically examined upon entry. In relation to venereal disease, while it had seen a reduction towards the end of 1923, it was beginning to rise again steadily from the beginning of 1924. Despite initially beginning the year with 'energetic measures' to patrol the city of Dublin, O'Sullivan noted that this had waned and implied that the Military Police Corps themselves may have succumbed to temptation, commenting that 'the Corps itself is not immune from disease' and 'more energetic supervision' was apparently required.[8]

To address the standard of men coming into the Army, O'Duffy submitted to the government a draft proposal for recruitment which addressed the significant ongoing problems – physical standards were to be enforced and the Garda Síochána and Dublin Metropolitan Police (which still existed at that time, being amalgamated into An Garda Síochána in 1925) would hold sole responsibility for providing references for those who wanted to join. In relation to recruitment, O'Duffy noted that the Army had not received a single enquiry from the public as to when it might resume – a problem he categorically attributed to the poor pay offer.

Unsurprisingly, O'Duffy paid particular attention to the reconstitution of the Military Police, a corps for which he had a particular affinity. This was the section of the Army responsible for the enforcement of discipline and investigation of breaches of military law, and its strength dropped from 719 to 385 between 24 March and 5 April 1924. O'Duffy informed the Executive Council that he intended to be personally involved in bringing the corps back to full-strength.

Into May, O'Duffy continued to report that discipline in the Army remained good across all ranks, with the Military Police reporting just 124 cases of ill-discipline in the fortnight from 21 April to 7 May; the majority (54) being for the charge of 'absence without leave' and thirty-five for 'conduct to the prejudice of good order and discipline', one that remains a sort of catch-all charge under military law to this day. Only seven charges were for drunkenness. Perhaps this was unusual given the Head Chaplain's concerns about intemperance in the force, but more likely attributable to, and demonstrative of, the 'non-overlapping magisteria' of secular and spiritual law. Perhaps they were drinking too much in the Head Chaplains' opinion, but this was not translating into overt breaches of military law. The other charges during this period were for returning late from pass (9), breaking bounds (11), the attempted appropriation of government property (1), disobedience (2), leaving post (2) and being improperly dressed (3).

O'Duffy was tentatively optimistic and positive about the formation of a disciplined, professional force. With a new scheme of organisation for the Army having recently been approved by the Executive Council, a resumption of recruitment and the issuing of commissions to officers, O'Duffy believed the desired effect could be achieved of countering the unrest and unease within the Army in the aftermath of the mutiny by fostering an environment conducive to 'the intensive training of Officers and men' and allowing officers to 'settle down to work on clearly defined lines'. However, until sufficient time had passed to allow these improvements to run their natural course and take effect, the conditions in the Army were not conducive to ensuring the long-term respect and loyalty of the troops, as the Executive Council were not showing any respect and loyalty to the troops themselves. This primarily manifested itself in underinvestment. O'Duffy informed the Executive Council that:

> Presently the barracks are unsanitary owing to the want of proper Engineers or proper tradesmen. The arrangements for issue of clothing, boots, etc. are bad; the food allowance, particularly bread, is altogether inadequate; the cooking arrangements are not satis-

factory, and the men are not receiving military training. All these things can be remedied immediately the Scheme of Organisation is put into operation and the Army brought up to strength.[9]

O'Duffy was explicit and candid in his motivations for the need for the Army to grow into a professional, capable, disciplined force, one with backbone that would provide an example of loyalty and leadership to the rest of the nation. The reality in the immediate aftermath of the mutiny was stark – if the Army did not step up and fill the void in public confidence in it as a military force, the IRA would:

> There is no doubt that the only political party in the country with any driving force is the Irregular or 'Republican' organisation. Force of circumstances – more than anything else – have given these people wonderful opportunities of building up their organisation, and full advantage has been taken of the recent political and military development, which have seriously shaken the confidence of the people in the existing order of things ... The ominous feature of the situation is that while 'Republicans' are active and enthusiastic, almost everyone else is apathetic, and Cumann na nGaedheal, as a political factor, is pretty hopeless.[10]

When recruitment finally resumed on 26 May it promised a much-needed respite for soldiers from excessive working hours and monotonous duties. During the second week of May there had been four cases of desertion by men who had just had enough of excessive duties, the number of which was bordering on ludicrous. The National Army was rostering and arming 40 per cent of its members for guard duties daily, while in the British Army the figure was 2 per cent. This could only have a detrimental effect on the morale, and by extension, the discipline of the Army in the long run, as it would in any army.

By the end of May, the new scheme of organisation had come into effect and there had been a significant interest in the new recruitment drive in Dublin. The men were of a poor standard however, and although exigencies were great, O'Duffy was 'very much opposed to admitting undesirables or the loafer or corner-boy type'. O'Duffy was satisfied with the 'good type of young soldier' that already existed in the Army and recommended quotas for Dublin combined with careful selection procedures – to this end he had enlisted the assistance of An Garda Síochána (of which he was Commissioner), Dublin Metropolitan Police, the Ministry of Industry and Commerce, and the Postmaster General.[11]

O'Duffy himself took personal interest in maintaining and encouraging discipline. During May, he paraded 350 officers at the Curragh Camp and the recently established School of Instruction in Kildare to explain exactly what was required of them as the Army left the mutiny behind and began to organise on evermore professional lines. From June however, his assessments began to take a sharper and more forthright tone. There was something missing in the overall formation of the soldierly character that irritated him:

> Discipline in general continues satisfactory, inasmuch as all orders are obeyed promptly and carried out conscientiously. Causes for complaint are however apparent as regards detail in case of Officers. There is not that outward sign of respect for superiors or scrupulous regularity or smartness in dress and personal appearance that I would like to see in the junior officers. I have noticed this principally among the officers serving at GHQ where good example should be shown to the whole Army. It is the senior officers and not the junior officers to whom the blame must be attached for

this. The system that has prevailed has, in my opinion, also been wrong. The great majority of Officers at Headquarters never went through the mill down the Line – they have been working at GHQ since the formation of the Army, with the result that they have developed into quite good clerks but lack even the appearance of soldiers.[12]

To remedy this situation, O'Duffy recommended that all staff officers undergo a training course at the School of Instruction and afterwards be posted to line units (in military terminology, 'line units' are those that don't have a specialist function). Their appointments at GHQ would be filled by officers who had already undergone training at the School of Instruction and who had previous experience in the infantry battalions or other corps.

The discipline of the NCOs and privates, on the other hand, O'Duffy considered as 'very good indeed' and reported to the Executive Council that:

The number of NCOs and men in detention barracks[13] is only 18 or 0.1% of the total NCOs and men in the Army. It affords me great pleasure to pay tribute to the good conduct of the NCOs and men of the Army. I have not seen a single drunken soldier during my three months in the Army, and only one case of disgraceful conduct has occurred. This was in Galway where an ex-British soldier serving in the National Army is charged with the crime of sodomy. While 12,000 self-respecting youths can be brought together, and under rather undesirable conditions in many cases, there is hope for the future of the State.[14]

It is telling that O'Duffy had chosen to include the descriptor of the man who had been charged with 'sodomy' as having had ex-British service. There is also an echo of Fr Devane's warning to Mulcahy two years previously, of the dangers of vice inherent in large bodies of men living in close quarters, and the aspiration that their upstanding moral conduct would reflect upon and influence that of the nation.

It became clear to O'Duffy during June that the recruitment campaign was proving to be a disappointment. Many men were failing on medical grounds, and while he understood the necessity of a medical standard, O'Duffy contacted the Director of Medical Services to discuss his intuition that it was perhaps too high. While 621 recruits had been admitted, 527 had been rejected. Combined with the number of serving soldiers who had sought their discharge upon completion of contract in the same period, the Army had only increased in strength by 488 men. Those soldiers still in service were growing tired of working twenty-four hours on, twenty-four hours off, or conducting extensive patrols and escort rosters, and their only relief was the anticipation of new recruits coming along to lighten the load. At the same time as the Army was 5,000 under strength, there were 6,000 applications for a very small number of places in An Garda Síochána. O'Duffy had instructed the Garda recruiting sergeants to recommend to them the Army as an alternative route of employment.

By the beginning of July, when the total figure of recruits accepted, recruits rejected and soldiers taking their discharge was tallied, the Army's strength was still only increasing slightly. However, even this slight increase was having something of a steadying effect as anticipated by O'Duffy. In conjunction with this, the provision of an additional stipend of 3d a day, after a year's satisfactory service, for ex-Army men who returned to the force, was attracting 'a very fine type of recruit' which he considered 'the best type of ex-soldier'.[15]

Discipline continued to improve. O'Duffy was satisfied with the Army's Discipline Branch with the exception of the Military Police Corps – 'the material' of which he regarded as 'first class' but 'its state of training and smartness' left 'much to be desired'. Part of this disarray was due to the existing uncertainty regarding the definite locations of several Army services and decisions on the closure of several barracks in and around Dublin city. For O'Duffy, the Military Police Corps was essential to building a disciplined force. In July 1924 he informed the Executive Council that:

> A code of Police Regulations is also being drafted. It is my intention to make this force the 'Corps d'Elite' of the Army, by transferring unsuitable men, recruiting desirable types from other services, putting Officers and men through an intensive course of training, tightening up discipline, and generally making the Military Policeman realise that he belongs to a Corps that demands big things of him.[16]

It is easy to envision O'Duffy as an authoritarian caricature, some sort of fascist cartoon, particularly given his later descent into alcoholism, notoriety as leader of the 'Blue Shirts' and his lacklustre service in the Spanish Civil War. Maurice Manning, giving the keynote address at the launch of Eoin Kinsella's *The Irish Defence Forces 1922–2022: Servant of the Nation* in 2023, commented that, had O'Duffy not disgraced himself in his latter years, he would have secured a proud legacy for himself for his contribution to the Defence Forces during turbulent years. He certainly displayed authoritarian tendencies, but also pragmatism. For example, at this time, he encouraged the government to release all political prisoners – sentenced and unsentenced – and to grant amnesty to republicans who were on the run. He did, however, temper this with the recommendation that 'it should be made very clear in the Dáil, before the leaders are released, that a second Army or a second Government will not be tolerated, and after the country has settled down from the effects of the releases, and the consequent "victory" meetings, very firm – even severe – government may be necessary'.[17]

By the beginning of September, O'Duffy was satisfied that discipline was continuing to improve gradually and that the officers were striving not just to maintain it but to exceed it. Progress with the Military Police Corps remained incomplete, but a syllabus of training and a code of regulations had been prepared and these were awaiting a government decision on the location of a corps depot before being fully progressed so that training could begin.

What discipline there was existed despite the generally unconducive conditions. The lack of access to a service vehicle, a mileage allowance, or even provision of petrol from Army stock to the Battalion Medical Officers in order to inspect the various outposts, resulted in desperate physical conditions. In the Southern Command, for example, the proportion of cases of lice among the troops had risen from 28 per cent to 32 per cent during August 1924. Scabies was rife, and an epidemic of virulent fever was feared. Conditions were apparently so dire that a General Staff report later that decade reflected that soldiers at this time were 'a potential disseminator of disease and a menace to public health'.[18] O'Duffy advocated that the government introduce a monthly travel allowance for Medical Officers and submitted a scheme along the same lines as that approved for District Officers of An Garda Síochána.

At the same time, the Chaplains' Branch came under severe scrutiny from O'Duffy, who informed the Executive Council that:

I am not entirely satisfied with this Branch. Up until recently the clerical and administrative work was carried out by a Staff Officer in the Adjutant General's Office. This was not, in my opinion, correct. The Chaplain General was not in that close contact with his branch that he should be. I am arranging a conference of the Brigade Chaplains to examine into the working of the Branch in detail throughout the various units. I only saw the Chaplain General once since my appointment, and, on that occasion I sent for him. He had very few suggestions to offer, and so far as I can learn, takes very little interest in the troops in their outdoor games or indoor amusements, libraries, etc.

One or two Brigade Chaplains are working very hard for the men, but they inform me they are getting very little encouragement from GHQ. While I do not pretend to be an authority on morals, I believe that unless troops get sufficient outlet for their energies in properly organised strenuous outdoor games, and mental exercise in the form of indoor amusements, reading room, libraries, etc. they soon fall into habits of vice.[19]

The Army School of Instruction, which welcomed its first students in April of 1924, had been a key contributor to professionalising the Army. By the time of O'Duffy's final report to the Executive Council, at the end of September, the mandatory training at the school was beginning to yield a gradual improvement in the general standard of officers. These intensive courses covered the full range of military skills necessary to infuse professionalism. The course was not without need of improvement, however. As O'Duffy noted at a meeting held on 5 September 1924, attended by the Chief of Staff, Adjutant General and GOC Curragh Command amongst others, musketry skills were lacking in some vital areas and particularly in relation to the pistol –

especially worrying 'in view of the number of accidents which have taken place in handling revolvers'.[20] Similarly, the absence of any training on bombs and mines was concerning in light of the number of lives that had been lost theretofore 'owing to the want of knowledge on the part of our Officers' in that regard. Similarly, arrangements were made for an elementary exam for all NCOs, to weed out 'a number of surplus NCOs and a very large number of inefficient and indifferent NCOs in the Army presently'. Successful NCOs would have the opportunity to avail of advancement and specialist training at the Curragh. The unsuccessful ones would be returned to the ranks, but again, demonstrating characteristic fairness, consideration would be shown to those who had pre-Truce service or who had displayed exceptional ability in their National Army service.

While the syllabus was comprehensive, if deficient in certain areas, Kildare Barracks was considered by O'Duffy as categorically unsuitable as a School of Instruction and he was of the opinion that the Curragh would be a more suitable location. The reasons for this included widespread reports of ill-discipline at Kildare Barracks, a wholly unsatisfactory environment for a course intended to train those with overall responsibility for instilling and maintaining the standards and discipline of the Army. The litany of incidents included:

NCOs and Privates being supplied with drink from the Officers' Canteen; stout passing out from the Officers' Canteen to the Orderly Room at night; undue familiarity between Officer students and troops; condonation of students' misdeeds by School Staff; officers allowed to pass out of the School improperly dressed; no wall around the camp, meaning that ingress and egress is quite easily effected; proximity to Kildare town where opportunities are many to distract the student from their work; and malingering

– with 20 out of 100 officers having reported sick on the 1st of September.

Among the prime offenders on the School Staff were the Quartermaster, Major Bishop, who associated with the students too much and was generally unsatisfactory, and the Assistant Chief Instructor (O'Neill), who was 'given to drink and indiscipline'.

In this, his final report to the Executive Council, O'Duffy also wrote in detail on the development of esprit de corps within the Army. It is a lengthy passage but worth including in its entirety as it gives a tremendous and fascinating insight into his aspirations for the Army's ethos, values and place within Irish society. It demonstrates a genuine desire for the betterment of the Army and for its members. Unlike any other entry in his series of reports to the Executive Council, this entreaty is quite philosophical in aspect – in the sense, as described by Bertrand Russell, that it exists in the no-man's-land between the theological and the scientific. Through this expedition into no-man's-land, O'Duffy wanted to stake a claim to the soul of the Army and its men. At the same time, it is worth being cognisant of O'Duffy's propensity for long and alarmist memos. There is clear disillusionment here too, and nationalist overtures foreshadowing his later ventures with the 'Blue Shirts' and alignment with the fascists in the Spanish Civil War. Evident too is what Diarmaid Ferriter has described as O'Duffy's characteristic 'customary self-importance, stridency and alarm':[21]

I would like to draw attention to a matter connected to both the Esprit de Corps in the Army, and incidentally the national education of our troops. At the present time, I fear that our Army is Irish in name only, and that any sign of Esprit de Corps is confined to a few scattered Units. I mention these two things together as, in my opinion, the development of one is closely allied to the promotion of the other. You can not have Esprit de Corps without patriotism, and unfortunately, patriotism in the Army is conspicuous by its absence. To be frank, we have a mercenary Army pure and simple. This is really not to be wondered at when we consider the composition of the Forces. Our Officers are mainly drawn from the ranks of the old IRA, our NCOs from the British Army, while the majority of the rank and file served in neither Armies.

The problem before us to my mind is to succeed in welding these three elements into one composite mass, and then to install into the whole that old pride of Nationality that our Officers presumably once held, but seem to have forgotten. Most people seem to think this impossible owing to what they call 'the lack of tradition'. They point to the British, French, German and other foreign Armies with their famous Regiments whose name and fame go back for centuries. If we go with this argument, we must wait for centuries before we can attempt to nationalise our Army – to make it really Irish in all its essentials. Personally I do not agree with this argument. I hold we have our traditions as glorious and old as any foreign Army. Unfortunately, however, we are allowing them to be wrested from us. Day after day for the past few years, we have listened to the Irregulars declaring that they are the rightful successors to every Irish soldier that ever fought in the Nation's cause, to every military force that ever battled for Irish freedom; while the first regular Army since the days of Sarsfield or Eoin Ruadh, remain silent, apparently admitting the fact.

I would therefore make a plea for recapturing our tradition, and using it to cultivate the proper spirit of Nationality among our soldiers; and nearly as important, to promote that most essential of military virtues – Esprit de Corps. To begin with, we could allot an historical name to every Battalion. I would let them select the name themselves, but would make GHQ the approving authority in case of duplication, or unsuitability for any reason. The main point is to ensure that the name selected must be that of some notable Irish soldier of the past, who actually served in Ireland in the ranks of an Irish Army – either Regular or Insurgent. I would then make it a regulation that a portrait of the Regimental patron would be hung in every Officers' or Sergeants' Mess, and in every Men's Institute; that his name should be inscribed in the Battalion Colours, if these are provided; that lectures be delivered to all recruits on joining, on his life and achievements, just as the British recruit is 'sponsored' on the glories and traditions of his Corps on joining. I would also make it compulsory for every Officer or NCO going forward for promotion to give at least a brief summary of the life of his Regimental Patron. In addition, a suitable anniversary would be set aside annually, on which the Battalion would have a special Ceremonial Parade, and would otherwise be regarded as a holiday for the men.

Eventually we will reach a stage when the soldier will be proud of the name his Unit bears, and will boast about it to his friends in other Battalions. They, anxious to uphold the honour of their own Corps, will insist on the boaster listening to the deeds of their own particular Patron. And when we reach this stage, we will have achieved a great deal. We will have succeeded in instilling some of the old ideals in our young troops, and at the same time will have done a great deal to promote Esprit de Corps among them. At present the average soldier knows no more about the deeds of Irish soldiers than what he hears of the work of the 'Munsters' in France or the 'Dublins' in Gallipoli, from the lips of some ex-British NCO and the narration of such deeds is not calculated to promote a healthy Irish spirit in our men.

I believe if we adopt this scheme, we shall have succeeded, not alone in proving to the country that our Army is something more than a third rate imitation of the British Army dressed in green uniforms, but also, in giving our troops some higher ideal to fight for than the Pay Envelope. And some day we may be very thankful that we did cultivate such a spirit.

CHAPTER 10

GERMS AND SOULS

Both before and after O'Duffy's tenure, the blurring of the lines between the respective spheres of spiritual and temporal responsibility was most evident in the dialogue between religious and secular military authorities in relation to venereal disease. In this regard Major Carroll, as Sanitation Officer, ranked as highly as any of the military hierarchy for conservative and austere moral zeal. In October 1924, he wrote directly to the Head Chaplain with his recommendations for combatting venereal disease.[1] This letter not only straddled their respective remits within the Defence Forces but stretched into the wider civilian realm, aware that this information would make its way to the bishops as well as the generals. This was most blatant in two of his recommendations in particular: the first was for the recruitment of female civil police to help 'cleanse the Phoenix Park, streets and back lanes of Dublin' – a matter that the Minister for Defence had asked be put to Kevin O'Higgins for consideration as the Minister for Home Affairs; the second was a request that the Catholic hierarchy be appraised of the problem of 'country girls' coming to Dublin and being 'left to their own devices instead of being sought out and encouraged to join sodalities'. These, he suggested, were a serious cause of the spread of venereal disease. He also restated Captain Brophil's suggestion from the previous year relating to the Military Police investigating diagnosed cases of venereal disease in soldiers and apprehending the women 'responsible'.

Other recommendations intruded on the realm of the General Staff and were arguably over-reaching his remit as a medical officer. These included recommendations that battalions be centralised and not split between posts, in order to avoid the 'moral inertia' that this allegedly evoked in the men. In contrast to his counsel as it related to the policing, both literally and socially, of women, for the men of the Army he recommended increased indoor and outdoor recreation, compulsory sport on Wednesdays and lectures from medical officers.

Carroll also sent regular statistical reports to the Head Chaplain, which were compiled based upon the questioning of soldiers admitted for venereal disease treatment. The fact that the medic reported to the cleric is telling but unsurprising. What gives even greater suggestion as to their world view were the categories used in these reports: 'Prostitutes' and 'Amateurs' were the primary descriptors, both of which were sub-divided into whether they were from 'Dublin' or 'Country' women. 'Wife', 'Outside Saorstát' and 'Insufficient Information' constituted the remaining columns.

Carroll made recommendations on the increased staffing and professionalisation of the Isolation Hospital[2] on Infirmary Road, Dublin. These included two 'Irrigator Orderlies' responsible for the urethral irrigation of gonorrhoea patients, a 'useless if not dangerous' practice if carried out incorrectly, and a 'Theatre Orderly' to assist with the daily 'arsenobenzol injections, circumcisions and urethroscopic examinations'. As of October 1924 these, as well as the roles of storeman and NCO in charge of the maintenance of discipline, were all being undertaken by one private soldier. That this private had been highly recommended for promotion to NCO rank is hardly surprising given the nature and scope of his duties.

Carroll also highlighted a glaring inconsistency in how military discipline dealt with venereal disease. NCOs and privates who contracted venereal disease were docked 25 per cent of their pay while ineffective. There was no such policy for officers. Carroll believed that they should suffer similar financial penalties but urged against the threat of discharge. Pitfalls to the propriety of officers (both patients and MOs) were, of course, to be attenuated as this would encourage concealment:

> ... with disastrous results ... or that there will be cases where considerable pressure will be brought to bear on the Medical Officer to prevent notification. Such a Medical Officer might even attempt treatment, which, as he would not have adequate facilities, would lead to endless complications. This has happened.

The Army's regulations surrounding venereal disease did indeed result in attempts at circumvention and concealment. In one such cautionary example that occurred in July 1924, the Deputy Judge Advocate General recommended charges be brought against a Private Murray, for attempting to conceal an infection of venereal disease contracted by a Private Hynes, both of whom were based at Collins Barracks, Dublin. The particulars of this case illustrate the lengths and desperation to which some people went to avoid the repercussions of venereal disease. As Hynes described it himself:

> About a fortnight ago I went with a woman in the Phoenix Park. About the 30th of June I noticed a stinging pain on the top of my penis. I told Private Murray of the MT [motor transport] Corps. He said he understood all about these things, or words to that effect. He said first he would cure me for four pounds. We arranged between us to pay it weekly, I then gave him ten shillings.

Each morning at any time he would get a chance, he rubbed in some watery liquid stuff which smarted when put on. It was getting worse and I began to get nervous so I reported sick on the morning of 8th June 1924.[3]

Murray had agreed to treat Hynes for venereal disease for payment. The recommendations of the Sanitation Officer to the Director of Medical Services, in this case, reflected the dysfunctional system for the treatment of venereal disease that the state had inherited (as most notably discussed in the work of Susannah Riordan referenced earlier). Under the Venereal Disease Act of 1917, Murray's actions could have incurred imprisonment with hard labour up to two years or a fine of £100. However, as Carroll lamented 'the Local Government Board of Ireland never applied this act, as I am informed by the Public Health Department of the Ministry concerned'. They were, at that time, planning on enforcing it in Dublin, but that would have been too late for this particular case.

On the day that Murray reported sick, and Hynes was interrogated on the matter by the Brigade Medical Officer, the latter then absconded, and was not apprehended until 31 August. He was subsequently tried by court martial and sentenced to twenty-eight days' detention that October.

THE ADJUTANT GENERAL'S PERSPECTIVE

Towards the end of 1924, on the direction of W.T. Cosgrave, the Department of Local Government and Public Health tasked one of their experienced medical inspectors, Dr Robert Percy McDonnell, with making 'suitable inquiries from Army Medical Authorities, Chaplains, Hospitals, and other authorities as to the incidence of

Venereal Disease and the steps necessary to secure improvement in the general position regarding it'.[4] The reply on behalf of the Army was submitted by the Adjutant General, Major General Hugo Mac Neill. As the year drew to a close, the Director of Medical Services noted that the instances of venereal disease were 'the one big blot on the Army's balance sheet'.[5] However, while one could be forgiven for thinking that venereal disease was a problem exclusive to the Army, this was not the case. In defence of the Irish soldier, Mac Neill began his report informing the Minister for Defence of his concerns over this misconception. The two reasons for it, he explained, were that Army members were naturally inclined to confine their attention to cases within the Army, and because the Army were the only people furnishing statistics of any description on the matter.[6]

Mac Neill believed that in the absence of figures from other sources, the public were inclined to believe that venereal disease did not exist to any significant extent among the Irish civilian population. He informed the Minister for Defence that he considered this to be, in fact, a national problem, requiring the coordinated action of three Departments: Defence, Justice, and Local Government and Public Health. Describing it in military terms, he argued that:

> Any one of these Departments acting alone is only attacking the enemy from one side, leaving him two other avenues of escape. From the purely military viewpoint this is a wretched tactic; and yet we are pursuing an even more unsound plan in up to this leaving one small section of one of these departments to tackle the problem.

After consulting with the Head Chaplain and Director of Medical Services, Mac Neill submitted a proposal for a cooperative action by all three of the aforementioned departments of state – a scheme that, perhaps for the first time, addressed the confusion between cause and effect, one that would 'eradicate V.D. from the country and, incidentally, from the Army'. Mac Neill proposed that the matter of venereal disease in the Army was one that had to be dealt with by the Minister for Defence and the General Staff, *assisted* by the Medical and Chaplaincy Services – the latter two having been left theretofore to bear the brunt of tackling venereal disease while the former two did not shoulder the responsibility themselves. Mac Neill's recommendations relating specifically to the Army were in concurrence with the recommendations of the International Army Medical Congress of 1923, which had been held in Rome and attended by Mac Neill and the Director of Medical Services.

For the Army's part, it would tackle the problem on multiple fronts. The first was by ensuring that soldiers had reasonable comfort and recreation in barracks, Mac Neill noting that even 'the lowest criminals in any of our prisons have access to well organized libraries but nothing is done to extend the same privileges to the defenders of the State'. Discipline, of course, was essential, but perfect discipline was deemed impossible under the present situation of short-service enlistments. Lectures, from both medics and chaplains, were not only essential but proven to be effective. Mac Neill informed the Minister that soldiers who knew the dangers and results of infection avoided the causes, as was evidenced by the NCOs and men of the Medical Corps. They had all been instructed and lectured on venereal disease and 'while no better morally than the soldiers in the other branches of the service' only experienced one case of infection among a strength of 500 during a twelve-month period. Medical inspections had to be weekly and 'absolutely air-tight' so that no NCO or private could avoid them. Echoing his predecessors proposed intentions for Tallaght Camp, Mac Neill believed that a central treatment station remained necessary in Dublin. This should also function as a central registry, educational centre, and records office for venereal disease treatment. Special case-cards, he recommended, could be given to all patients upon returning to their units with which they would report weekly to the Medical Officer, allowing every individual case to be tracked. Finally, serious consideration would have to be given to the evacuation of small posts, which Mac Neill described as 'the ruination of discipline and, in many cases, breeding places of immorality' as well as providing logistical difficulties in carrying out efficient and regular medical inspections.

Mac Neill qualified all of these proposals with the statement that it was 'useless to think of purifying the Army unless some steps are taken to purify the whole country', insisting that even enforcing all of his recommendations simultaneously and with immediate effect would be useless without the co-operation of other departments of state and the acceptance that venereal disease was not simply an Army problem:

> I believe that if a census of cases amongst the civilian population was available the figures, to say the least of it, would be startling. In the Army the figure is as high as 30 per thousand per annum, and yet the soldiers know that they will forfeit their pay and risk the danger of demobilisation. The ordinary civilian has not to face such penalties.

He recommended that the Department of Local Government make venereal disease notifiable and create a central state registry of infected people. This would demonstrate, as Army records did already, that the prevailing opinion that venereal disease was confined to Dublin was false, as soldiers had become infected 'in practically every village in the country'. Mac Neill demonstrated pragmatism and insight in his recommendations that:

If the disease were made notifiable, as suggested, provision would also have to be made for a Treatment Centre in every County. With the exception of two hospitals in the city of Dublin there are no centres competent to deal with this disease in a scientific and up to date manner. The result is, of course, women get contaminated, the acute stage subsides, and they become chronic carriers of the disease for the rest of their lives. They pass it to various men who, in their turn, transmit it to other women.

This was contested by the head of the Department of Local Government's Public Health Section, Dr Stephenson, who believed it would be counter-productive and result in concealment.[7]

Mac Neill also recommended that lighting in public parks and similar dimly lit locations that facilitated furtive liaisons should receive more attention than it did. He suggested that the recruitment of female police could be worth considering (as had been touted since 1922) and, perhaps somewhat progressively for his time, he recommended changes in the law to allow for the arrest of men found engaging with prostitutes as well as the women, though this was with a view to deterring them by 'fear of public scandal'.

McDonnell, with assistance from Carroll, produced the 'Report on the incidence of venereal disease in the army and amongst a section of the civil population in the Free State' later that month. Its recommendations ultimately led to the establishment of an interdepartmental committee of inquiry on venereal disease which submitted its report in 1926.[8] However, in framing terms of reference for this inquiry the Army was still viewed with suspicion. On 9 December, a confidential memo from the Secretary of the Department of Defence (C.B. O'Connor) to the Secretary of the Department of Local Government (E.P. McCarron) stated that:

I am directed by the Minister for Defence to state for the information of the Minister for Local Government and Public Health
that he is seriously concerned regarding the prevalence of the
disease in the Defence Forces. He is of the opinion that the circumstances of the evil should be investigated by an Inter-departmental
Committee with a view to framing measures for their prevention
as far as possible.[9]

THE DIRECTOR OF MEDICAL SERVICES' PERSPECTIVE

The Director of Medical Services produced his own memorandum
on the subject. In this, Colonel Higgins emphasised the benefits
of preventative disinfection and advocated the installation of early
treatment centres – which had been advocated in September 1923
but which had been declined in favour of a 'moral drive'. Higgins
was critical of this. His expressed opinions demonstrated the first real
friction between the respective realms of the clerical and the medical
in the moral and disciplinary formation of the Irish soldier. It also
demonstrated the customary proportioning of blame to 'contaminated' women into whose 'clutches' many unfortunate soldiers (all
too readily) fell. Reflecting on his previous and continuing advocacy
for taking a practical medical approach and its rejection by the chaplains as 'encouraging soldiers to indulge', Higgins wrote that:

I pointed out that experts from all the civilized armies in the world
meeting in conference advocated the installation of prophylactic
centres as the essential element in combatting V.D. in armies. Since
then I have sent further communications advocating positive action
on the above lines.

Now to review the results of all this volume of correspondence and highly expert advice on a technical question – the result of all these communications is 'NIL', it is worse than 'Nil', in so far as we have positive ruling from the Military forbidding us to take any active steps to combat the spread of the disease and ordering us to discharge solders from the Army when they are rendered non-infective, that is before they are cured. [In late September 1924, the Adjutant General received a verbal order from General O'Duffy, which he assumed had emanated from the Minister for Defence, instructing him to retain these men in the Army. This was transmitted to the Director of Medical Services but, as of the end of the year, had not been confirmed in writing.[10]]

A moral drive has no germicidal effect, preaching and sermons have no terrors for the Spirochaete [a spiral-shaped bacteria causing diseases including syphilis] but disinfectants have. I know the value of sermons and I appreciate the very big work that is being done by the Chaplains, but by itself it is not sufficient, the Medical Service must be allowed to attend to the germs, with as free a hand as the Chaplains have in attending to the souls. We must be allowed to have Disinfectant Centres and the soldier who has the misfortune to keep company with a contaminated woman must be given an opportunity of escaping the disease …

… I wonder if those who withhold authority for allowing us to kill the germs of V.D. understand their responsibility and what, in fact, they are doing. It means that 'by order' they decree that the unfortunate soldier who falls into the clutches of a syphilitic woman must develop the disease and that he must not get a dog's change of escaping it. I wonder if they understand that they are sentencing subsequent generations, to come into this world, hopeless objects for sympathy, deformed etc., suffering from hereditary syphilis.[11]

THE HEAD CHAPLAIN'S PERSPECTIVE

On 16 December 1924 the Head Chaplain met with the Minister for Defence to give his own opinions on the proposals of the Director of Medical Services. He objected to the suggestion of the establishment of treatment centres, agreeing that from a medical point of view they were 'ideal' but 'while you will have less disease, you will have more immorality'. He did, however, agree with the Adjutant General's proposal for the establishment of an interdepartmental committee. Nor did he share the national bias that the Army was a unique and exceptional source of infection, concurring that if there was a census of infection among the wider civilian population it 'would surprise everybody'. The Head Chaplain continued to emphasise the merits of spiritual and bodily discipline, combined with the need for providing for both the comfort and dignity of the men of the Army. As the memorandum on the meeting between the Head Chaplain and the Minister for Defence recorded:

The Chaplains' remedies are – besides the purely clerical (Church Parades, frequentation of the Sacraments, Missions, and the Army Sodality) – that the lectures by the Medical Officers would be continued and more frequent; as he is firmly of the opinion that if the men realized the seriousness of the matter, we would have much fewer delinquents; that the Medical Inspection would be more strict. It has not been possible to do this owing to the scarcity of medical officers and the number of scattered posts; that more attention would be given to recreation and indoor amuse-ments for troops – the Adjutant-General will put up proposals in this connection – gyms, libraries etc., and see that the 'messing' arrangements for the men would receive more attention from the Battalion Officers. He particularly stresses the fact that in almost every post the men, though under strict disciplinary control while on parade are not under discipline when going to their meals; that they are lined up in a queue, and when the doors are opened that there is a tumble and scramble for the food, which is 'messed up' to them as if they were animals.[12]

From late December, the plans were in motion to establish a committee of inquiry. On 23 December 1924, O'Connor wrote to McCarron confirming Colonel T.F. Higgins as the Minister for Defence's nominee, also offering that arrangements could be made for the Head Chaplain to attend any of its meetings at which they may wish to solicit his opinions or observations.[13] The committee would begin its work in 1925 and would present its final report in 1926.

SANITATION AND DISCIPLINE

Good discipline was not only linked with the prevention of *venereal* disease however. It was, and remains, a basic and ubiquitous tenet of military life that discipline, attention-to-detail, cleanliness and hygiene are inextricably linked. It was also inextricably linked to masculinity, as *An tÓglách* described in terms of 'manly conduct' how:

Soldiers must be made to understand that the manly virtues which are developed in them by their military training, because they are essential for military efficiency, cannot be strongly built into their character unless they are constantly practised by every individual of his own accord in all his dealings as a private citizen. They are taught, for instance, that scrupulous cleanliness of body, clothing and surroundings is essential for the health of the troops in barracks, in training camps, or in the field. They must therefore be clean, smart and tidy as a matter of habit at all times.[14]

The tropes of the sergeant inspecting the recruits' quarters for dust with white cotton gloves, the epitome of soldierliness with not a button or thread loose, or the officer on parade with gleaming shoes, razor-sharp trouser crease and not a hair out of place, are derived from the realities and exigencies of military life. Where soldiers are living in close confines, under conditions of privation, or at least without many of the comforts of civilian life, discipline is critical to ensuring that clean habits become automatic. It was not just venereal disease that rendered soldiers unfit for duty.

Higgins was critical of the number of soldiers who were ineffective through illness, which averaged around 3 per cent at any given time, throughout 1924. While this was low in comparison to other armies, something Higgins himself acknowledged, it was his opinion that it should have been lower. Suspecting that this was a disciplinary matter more so than a medical one, with a significant quantity of those attending the daily sick parade (the formalised military procedure for reporting sick) guilty of malingering, Higgins recommended soldiers be stopped 10 per cent of their pay on admission to hospital.[15]

The authority and remit of the Sanitation Officer, therefore, is not surprising. One memo from 1924 noted that 'troops in occupation must keep their quarters clean. The responsibility rests on the Commander; but the Medical Officer is his adviser and it is up to the Medical Officer to see that proper instructions are given and carried out.'[16] Of particular concern in Ireland at the time was the disease typhus, which is spread by lice. Direction was given on how soldiers were to fold their bedding each morning so as to prevent lice, and on how running a hot iron over the seam of their trousers would kill the eggs that were prone to deposit there and not killed by other means. While many will be familiar with the motifs of soldiers having their beds particularly and perfectly made up in 'bed blocks' for 'room inspections', and the razor-sharp crease in their trousers on parade, many may not know that the origins of these practices are extremely practical.

Directions on how soldiers should clean urinals, for example, were very detailed and very specific:

> Urinals must be scrubbed daily –if malodorous and made of earthenware, they can be cleaned perfectly with commercial hydro-chloric acid. If made of slate they can be treated with a coat of tar – or alternatively swilled down with buckets of water and the crude petroleum applied with a stiff brush. Once the latrines and cubicles are properly cleaned, they should receive a scrubbing with Creosol Solution 2½% daily.

Tuberculosis was another disease of serious concern, so much so that spitting was prohibited and incurred severe disciplinary penalties. As well as these two, poor sanitation and over-crowding posed a risk of other particularly nasty diseases common at the time including typhoid, cerebro-spinal fever, diphtheria, measles, mumps and scarlet fever.

A total of 10,000 copies of the final draft of *Notes on Military Sanitation* were printed for distribution throughout the force. As well as the examples just mentioned, the overlap between discipline and remaining disease-free is clear in this handbook with direction given in detail: barrack rooms were to have appointed daily order-lies to ensure cleanliness; windows were to remain open at least 3 inches at night and at least 3.5 feet maintained between beds; troops were to clean their eave gutters every autumn to prevent dampness and whitewash walls frequently; and 'dry scrubbing' was prohibited because of the danger from the dust it kicked up – solders were directed instead to rub floors with a damp cloth or sprinkle them with tea leaves or damp saw dust before sweeping.

It is clear from this that sanitation and medical officers had a very important role in keeping the Army functioning, and the reason for their remit bleeding into that of military discipline becomes apparent. While it was considered a matter of great importance, it is interesting, as a side-note at least, that an application by a medical officer, Commandant Green-Foley, for expenses relating to a proposed visit to the British Army School of Sanitation at Aldershot was not considered favourably at an Army Finance meeting the following year, attended by the Minister and Chief of Staff. It is also telling that the British Army put so much store in the importance of hygiene and sanitation that it had a school devoted entirely to the subject.

CLEAN-LIVING IRISHMEN AND DECENT, RESPECTABLE GIRLS

The twin vices of drink and venereal disease cropped up again in December of 1924, when the Adjutant General corresponded with the Minister for Defence (Peter Hughes, who had replaced the interim minister, Cosgrave, the previous month) about the Minister's previously expressed opinion on the need to improve welfare conditions for soldiers. Mac Neill noted that, while there had been some specific examples of positive efforts in relation to soldiers' welfare, the general condition was such that 'the general welfare and comfort of the soldier off duty has been scandalously neglected'. When a private soldier was dismissed from parade in the evening, there were generally two sources of amusement open to him, namely, 'loose women or public houses and shebeens'. The natural consequence of this was, of course, the spread of venereal disease.

As for the blame, Mac Neill laid this at the feet of both junior officers, whom he opined had neither realised nor bothered with the fact that the welfare of their men was their responsibility, and the state itself, which had 'not recognised any financial liability in such matters' so even with the best will, proactive officers were ham strung without the money to bring their will to bear.

It was from this impetus that Mac Neill initiated the Soldiers' Welfare Scheme. In many ways it was predictable, but perhaps it is more accurate to say that the solutions were well known but had never been properly implemented. Mac Neill recommended that the welfare of troops be rigorously inculcated in officers and requested the necessary funding from the Minister. A wide range of sporting activities were naturally included, given the physicality and demographic of the men concerned. In relation to wintertime amusements, the matter of dances came in for particular attention, as a potential moral pitfall. The matter was discussed at length, and 'it was decided that large Battalion or similar dances were out of the question, but that short Company dances could receive considera-tion'.[17] Keeping these dances parochial and among relatively small, closely frequented groups of soldiers, 'would at once let the soldier – and the country – see that he is recognised as a decent, clean-liv-ing Irishman, who can be depended on not to abuse a privilege when he gets one' and would 'encourage him to seek the com-pany of decent, respectable girls, whom he need not be ashamed to "show off" before his comrades, Officers and Chaplains'.

***

Whereas, since 1922, matters of morality and discipline had been negotiated against a backdrop of turmoil and the labour pains of the new independent state, as 1924 drew to a close the rhythm of life in the Defence Forces was beginning to regularise and find its equilibrium. The turmoil of the Army Mutiny had passed without detriment to the morale of the men, the Defence Forces had come through it intact and the Free State had not failed. Religion was a contributory factor in this and to the credit of the chaplains, in part at least. As they described it themselves, 'after the Annual Retreat of 1924, a healthy religious tone was founded in all ranks. The disturbance caused by the crisis of March 1924, failed to affect the morale of the men, a fact which in no small measure is due to the Chaplain's influence.'[18]

By the end of 1924, the Adjutant General, the Director of Medical Services and the Head Chaplain had evolved into the pre-eminent triumvirate in the moral direction of the Army, representing martial, corporeal and spiritual discipline respectively. The next couple of years would see the Defence Forces trying to establish and specify its functions as a peacetime military as it wrestled with the development, for the first time, of a formalised (albeit vague and loose) defence policy within which it would operate.

CHAPTER 11

COMPLETE CHANGE

CHANGING CONTEXTS 1925-26

The 1925–26 period was a key juncture in the internal development and national direction of the Defence Forces. During this time, as David McCullagh has deftly described, it became abundantly clear that the Cumann na nGaedheal government had little gratitude to show to the Defence Forces, despite owing its existence to it.[1]

In October 1924, the National Army had been officially designated the Defence Forces, a title that encompassed the Air Corps as well as the Army. While symbolic in some ways of a new venture into more peaceful and stable times, it retained the official moniker of Óglaigh na hÉireann, as it does to this day, illustrative of its direct lineage to its antecedent organisation, the Irish Volunteers and the fight for independence. In September of 1923 Ireland had joined the League of Nations, indicative of the country's wider international and multilateral ambitions. The Defence Forces had endured the tribulations of demobilisation and mutiny and by 1925 it had the breathing-room to undertake a comprehensive review of the state's defensive needs.

There was now a pressing need for the General Staff to build on the momentum in getting the Army functioning professionally and living up to the aspirations placed upon it. Since 1922, the

Army had been in a state of flux with no stated defence policy to give it direction, so in May of 1925 the Chief of Staff, Lieutenant General Peadar MacMahon, established the Army Organisation Board. The Board's role was 'to examine into, and report on, the necessary modifications in the organisation of the Defence Forces to enable them to fulfil the functions of a modern army in relation to National Defence'.[2] In November of that year, the government produced a vague memorandum on defence policy, confirming a commitment to neutrality but also confirming that the Irish military should be capable of full integration with the British armed forces in defence of the Irish Free State should the necessity arise.[3]

The subject of Irish neutrality remains one inextricably linked with conceptions of anti-colonialism and national virtue. As has already been discussed, the 'Irishness' of the idealised Irish soldier was very often defined as much by his non-Britishness as any other metric; this had manifested repeatedly, be it in the form of the resentment of Irishmen with previous British service being pro-moted over IRA veterans, or expressed in more ideological terms in the pages of *An tÓglach* ('Ireland cannot be said to be free while her children's language, amusements and customs are those of the British'[4] etc.). Now, just under three years since independ-ence, Cumann na nGaedheal had conceded that its policy for the defence of the state was contingent on British military intervention and interoperability.

In relation to Irish neutrality itself, this has been an ide-ology inaccurately represented in several ways for rhetorical purposes over the years: an ostentatious display of post-colo-nial virtue; independent defiance of the great world powers and their neo-colonial ambitions; and even moral deficiency. The real origins of Irish neutrality, however, lie in *realpolitik* and the pragmatism of a small, newly independent, and often cash-strapped state. From the end of the Civil War in 1923 until the outbreak of the Second World War, this neutrality was born of necessity, driven by the obligations of the Anglo-Irish Treaty and Commonwealth membership, rather than any position of idealism or virtue.[5]

The Army Organisation Board presented its report in mid-1926, cognisant of both economic realities and public opinion. It proposed a military based on three interdependent components: a Regular Army, a Volunteer Force (second line reserve), and a Reserve Officers' Corps. This was a proposed military structure designed to safeguard the country against both invasion and internal disturbance and was based on the principle of gradually reducing the number of permanent soldiers and increasing the number of reservists. Starting from its current strength of approximately 11,000 all ranks with about 550 other ranks posted to the Reserve, the predicted end-state was that by 1940 the Army would have reached approximately 5,000 all ranks, with a Regular Army Reserve of 25,000 and a Volunteer Reserve of 20,000. While it looked good on paper to politicians and civil servants, this parsimonious approach resulted in an underfunded and underequipped force. The absolute naivety of this plan became obvious with the outbreak of war in Europe.

To expand upon the work of the Army Organisation Board, it was immediately followed by the departure of six officers to the USA to study their military system with a particular focus on education and defence legislation. The Military Mission to the USA demonstrated the ideological disposition of the Army as firmly within what would later become known as the Western Bloc. In more immediate terms, the lessons learned by the Military Mission contributed to the establishment of the Military College in the

Curragh in 1930 – a key institution in the training of NCOs and officers to this day.

By the beginning of 1925, the demobilisation of NCOs and privates from the Army was 'having a good effect on the [discipline of the] remainder' and the officer support for the IRAO was petering out, with those who were 'usually disaffected and disgruntled' becoming 'particularly silent'.[6] Throughout 1925 and 1926 the Chief of Staff reported to the government that discipline and morale were high and the health of the troops was good.[7] The former was due in no small part to the ongoing courses of professional training for officers and NCOs at the Curragh Camp.

The first Senior Officers Course of Instruction finished in January 1925, with results that were deemed satisfactory by the Chief of Staff, while training continued similarly at the Army School of Instruction. In general, both discipline and morale were good throughout the force. While IRA activity was generally increasing and they remained a threat, intelligence suggested an ever more aimless, disorganised and dis-unified force. At the same time, Sinn Féin was becoming progressively more organised, the significance of which, the Chief of Staff said, could not 'be overestimated in face of the chaos prevailing in the Cumann na nGaedheal ranks'. They were making progress in gaining influence in public bodies like the GAA, with prominent leaders proclaiming their position in this regard as 'fairly satisfactory'. Even the Catholic Church they described as 'coming around ... and ... not so outspoken on the side of the Free State'.[8] With a split becoming evident, the following year de Valera would form Fianna Fáil, taking the gunman further out of anti-Treaty politics. It was against this background of increasing normalisation that the Army entered 1925.

As peace and normality grew, the former status and prominence of the Army in Irish society quickly diminished. Its strength fell by several thousand during this period, hitting 12,016 by December of 1926. One of the most prominent changes at this time was the handover of responsibility for domestic intelligence to An Garda Síochána during 1926, resulting in the Defence Forces' role in domestic espionage and security being eroded to the point where the Chief of Staff remarked that the handover of responsibility and records left 'the General Staff … in complete ignorance of the activities of Irregulars in the country'.[9]

Regardless of its deteriorating status and prestige within the state, day-to-day life went on for the men of the Army. So too did the struggles to keep their bodies healthy, their minds disciplined, and their souls saved.

'DISCIPLES OF THE GOSPEL OF PERSONAL CLEANLINESS'

In 1925, the Army Medical Corps became structured along more formal military lines and the NCOs and privates were graded into three classes, according to their medical ability. While claims for service and wounds during the 1916–23 revolutionary period under the Army Pensions Act had accounted for a considerable amount of their work, this eased up during 1926. As a result, a greater emphasis could be placed on preventative hygiene and sanitation.

This emphasis on the discipline of personal hygiene was reflected in the improvement of the general health of Irish soldiers. During 1923, the health of the Army had been deplorable, with diseases rife due to 'dirt and ignorance', including 51,138 cases of lice, 2,038 cases of scabies and 1,250 cases of 'other preventable diseases' reported. By 1926, cases of lice had fallen to 2,139, scabies to 148 and 'other preventable diseases' to 357. Even accounting for the reduced numbers in the Army, on a per capita basis this represented a reduction in lice from 1,278 per 1,000 men (obviously individuals suffered repeat infestations) to 178 per 1000, scabies from 51 per 1,000 to 12 per 1,000, and 'other preventable diseases' from 31 to 28 per thousand.

The efforts of the Medical Corps to inculcate the Army with the principals of cleanliness, hygiene and sanitation had achieved no meagre degree of success. Thorough weekly inspections meant that the stats for 1926 were extremely accurate, while those for 1923 were regarded as 70 per cent accurate at best, implying even greater rates of disease among the force. As the General Staff reflected:

> The complete change has been affected in three years, so that where the Army and the soldier of 1923 was a potential disseminator of disease and a menace to public health, the Army is now a model in cleanliness and sanitation, and the soldier is a disciple of the gospel of personal cleanliness.[10]

'OBJECTIONABLE MATERIAL' ON SALE AT THE CURRAGH

In late 1924, Fr Donnelly, the Catholic chaplain to the Curragh Camp, wrote to both the GOC and the Head Chaplain to express his grave concern about the sale of Sunday newspapers in the camp and the 'incalculable harm' being caused by these 'objectionable sheets'.[11] While, as he observed, these papers had a weekly distribution of 300–400 during British occupation, they were currently selling about 3,600 copies. Donnelly had contacted the distributor, the well-known Irish newsagents and book-sellers Eason and Son, who were 'impervious to Christian appeals', and left him dismayed that they did not acknowledge his right to interfere in the matter. To this end, Donnelly now petitioned the GOC and Head Chaplain to request the intervention of the Adjutant General. Donnelly attached, for their information, clippings of three such examples of the scandalous content in question. These contained references to birth control, a book on venereal disease and how to cure it, and a photo collage featuring two bare-legged dancers. The GOC duly forwarded the letter to the Adjutant General for direction. The Head Chaplain was more proactive, suggesting that 'foreign Sunday papers' be either prohibited or, as a minimum, limited to only those reviewed and passed as suitable by the GOC.[12] The scandalous papers in question were named as the *News of the World, World's Pictorial, Reynolds News, Thompson's Weekly, Sunday Weekly, Peg's Paper* and *Woman's Friend*.

The real movement on the issue started in January 1925, when the matter made it as far as the Minister for Defence himself, who had ruled that the GOC should make direct representation to Eason and Son. If the diplomatic approach did not work, the Adjutant General informed the GOC that he could take the necessary steps to enforce his 'request' including declaring the shop out of bounds to troops.[13]

Charles Eason himself replied on 12 January 1925 to both Curragh HQ and the Department of Defence. While he conceded the matter that Army authorities were 'entitled to decide such matters' he requested the opportunity in future to put his own views across. While he bowed to pressure to stop stocking the first five papers listed previously, *Peg's Paper* and *Women's Friend* had a total circulation of fifteen between them, so Eason suggested it hardly worth interfering with those two.[14] Colonel Dunphy, the Curragh Camp Administrative Officer, agreed to 'temporarily waive the objection to these papers' but informed Eason that 'in the meantime I shall have them censored and will call your attention in the event of any objectionable feature being discovered'.[15] Censorship, which would become a social control apparatus inextricably linked with the Irish state for decades to come, was legislated for under several acts during the decade of Cumann na nGaedheal govern-ment – while the Censorship of Publications Act (which prohibited the advertisement of contraceptives though their sale remained legal) and the Censorship of Publications (Amendment) Act would not be passed until 1929 and 1930 respectively; there had already been the Censorship of Films Act (1923) and the Censorship of Films (Amendment) Act (1925) passed at the time of Donnelly's campaign against 'objectionable material' being sold by Curragh newsagents. The episode between Fr Donnelly and Charles Eason at the Curragh was, of course, symptomatic of wider national mores.

MARRIED MEN MAKE BETTER DRIVERS

The year 1924 had seen an alarming number of traffic accidents involving soldiers. So much so that W.T. Cosgrave himself requested a report on the cost to the public purse of the resulting compensation claims.[16] On 1 July 1924, the Director of Transport, Major J.P.M. Cotter, initiated a traffic accident register to keep track of them.

In March 1925, formal procedures in relation to the investi-gation of traffic accidents were codified in an Adjutant General's Memo,[17] and reviewing the previous six-months' data in April, Cotter was shocked to discover that there had been 105 accidents reported. These involved 98 of the total 337 drivers (29 per cent) belonging to the Army Transport Corps. The discrepancy of seven was the number of drivers who had been involved in two accidents during that two-month period. Twenty-six of these had resulted in disciplinary action being taken, and in seven of these, alcohol was proven to be a contributing factor. While the Director of Transport noted that in several cases the drivers were not themselves culpable, 'the extraordinarily large number of accidents … was due to a lack of a sense of responsibility and balance on the part of the drivers'. The statistical analysis proved something else of interest – married men were far less likely to be involved in traffic accidents than their single counterparts.

Of the seven men who had been involved in two accidents, all were single. Of the total of ninety-eight men who had been involved in traffic accidents, twenty had been married and seventy-eight single. Of the overall total pool of 337 drivers, ninety-seven were married and 240 single. So, only 20 per cent of married men had had accidents while this was 30 per cent among the single men. Furthermore, of the twenty-six drivers who faced disciplinary action, only four were married while twenty-two were single, or 4.1 per cent of the total number of married men and 9.1 per cent of the total number of single men.

To address the problem, the Director requested that a specified number of driver appointments be formally allocated to married soldiers, and that pay rates be increased so as 'to attract the more experienced class of drivers' – something he said would cost less in the long run when balanced against 'the heavy payments which occasionally have to be made to injured parties'.[18]

Perhaps modern sensibilities may view as naivety bordering on the absurd the focus on encouraging married men to take appointments as Army drivers rather than, for example, providing increased training. And perhaps this is reminiscent in its logic of the chaplains' advice that men be encouraged to marry in order to reduce venereal disease infections, while obstructing the establishment of chemical disinfection facilities within barracks. There is, however, some merit in the actuarial logic that married men were, by virtue of their age, station and family responsibilities, generally more steady pairs-of-hands statistically speaking. In this regard, Cotter's suggestion was a logical one grounded in the sensibilities of his time. Yet again, this time through the unexpected lens of the Transport Corps, the interplay between military discipline and moral aspirations is revealed.

CHAPTER 12

SEXUAL VICE

By 1925, the Chaplaincy Service had matured and settled confidently into its place within the military system. On a very practical level, for example, the Head Chaplain secured £1,200 from the Army budget for the provision of church seating.[1] On an intellectual level, the Chaplaincy Service developed a formally approved military syllabus for educating troops on the perils of venereal disease. This provided set headings to ensure some level of uniformity but gave the lecturer leeway regarding their arrangement. The Memorandum on Venereal Disease in the Army had stated that 'moral prophylaxis by itself is insufficient' and that provision ought to be made in barracks for disinfection measures, and that the chaplains, due to the nature of their position and their work, had an important role to play in countering venereal disease. However, the Chaplaincy's military syllabus contradicted the Director of the Medical Corps, advising lecturers that 'the question of prophylaxis [in this case to mean physical and chemical prophylaxis] is intentionally omitted' as 'a dangerous one to discuss in such audiences as those to which the lectures will be delivered'. Despite this, the Chief of Staff gave sanction in February 1925 to initiate a compulsory chemical prophylactic treatment programme, initially in the Dublin barracks. The results amply justified their expectations, leading to a 70 per cent drop in venereal disease cases in the Dublin area and 50 per cent within the total force.[2]

Despite the categorical evidence, the Chaplaincy preferred its own methods, with the Army syllabus covering the following ten, almost baroque-sounding headings:

1. Self-restraint – described as 'the basis of civilisation.'
2. The Evils of Promiscuity – including 'loss of self-respect' and the 'degradation of women.'
3. Chastity – described as 'possible for all' and 'not unmanly.'
4. Definition and Variety of Venereal Disease:
   Gonorrhoea – 'Cause of sterility in both sexes and blindness in children.'
   Syphilis – 'Causes many deaths of children and adults, and much insanity.'
5. Prevention – 'Only safe method is continence' and that venereal disease was not only caused by 'mercenary prostitutes.'
6. Cure – Interestingly noted that curing venereal disease was 'only possible by medical means' and that soldiers would 'be cured, not punished', somewhat ironic considering the objections to chemical and physical prophylaxis.
7. 'IT IS CRIMINAL to infect a healthy woman. IT IS BASE to seduce a virgin. IT IS DANGEROUS TO HAVE TO DO WITH A PROSTITUTE.'
8. Safeguards – including temperance, exercise, avoiding 'filthy literature and lascivious thoughts and conversation.' It also noted that 'nocturnal emissions are harmless, and should not cause mental anxiety; it is nature's relief.'
9. Importance of preventing all diseases in the Army, particularly V.D. as a 'common cause of invalidity in soldiers.'
10. Temptations – both in camps and at home.[3]

A sample lecture, provided for chaplains to use as an example for drafting their own, demonstrates clear echoes of the ethos espoused by Mulcahy and some of the more hard-line conservative politicians, with its focus on masculinity and appeals to manliness, and their role, not only in pioneering the new Irish state, but vouchsafing Irish Catholic civilisation itself.

> You will all be aware of the possession of sexual powers and passions which are given to you for the begetting of children, and for the continuance of the life of the nation. You will all feel instinctively by nature that those are high and important powers; it is in fact the possession of these powers that makes you men, and gives you all those high qualities of body and mind which we call manly. But like all high powers, they are capable of gross misuse; and such misuse is always harmful. The sexual functions operate by means of a delicate mechanism, which is especially liable to damage or even destruction by particular infections which are very common both in this country and elsewhere. A sensible man, who understands these things, will restrain himself and curb his desires. Health in every way is largely a matter of self-restraint, and this is especially true in matters of sex. Indeed, when you come to think of it, civilisation, as opposed to barbarism, is mainly a matter of the exercise of self-restraint, and of the keeping under control of our natural desires and lusts.
>
> ... Self-indulgence of any kind is not manly; and if, in seeking pleasure for yourself, you do harm to anyone else, especially a woman, you are then acting in an unmanly way. If you wish to be strong and rule others you must first learn to rule and restrain yourself ... Sexual vice is entirely harmful both to the man, the woman, and the State ...[4]

The language was unflinching and may seem uncharacteristically direct to those with misconceptions of the sensibilities of the last century as twee, coy and euphemistic. The medical descriptions of symptoms were anatomical and accurate. The consequences of venereal diseases were not sugar-coated.

> The first child of syphilitic parents is seldom born alive; later children may survive but run the risk of being blind, or deaf, or feeble-minded, or deformed in face or body. Such is the case of an uncured syphilitic, but that is not all; a special form of insanity sometimes follows, mostly in cases which at first seemed slight. It is called 'General Paralysis of the Insane.' To the patient its only redeeming feature is that his or her miserable existence does not last more than three years after onset. Another nervous disease due to syphilis is 'Locomotor Ataxy' which makes a man or woman a useless burden to friends for the rest of his life.

The potential impotence associated with gonorrhoea would leave a soldier 'deprived at one stroke of that power which is of the greatest importance to him both as a man and a citizen'.

Regarding the dangers posed by venereal disease to the family unit, it lamented how pitiful it was to see 'otherwise healthy children blind from infancy the result of the father's Clap [gonorrhoea]' but 'worse with the Pox [syphilis], for the Pox affects the whole constitution' resulting in 'wretched specimens of humanity, poor and wizened, with deformed face or body, and damaged brains' who were 'a misery to themselves and their parents, and a burden to their country'.

In advising the soldier directly, the chaplains were not naive to the ways of the world, acknowledging that the threat of future issues fathering children was not one on the immediate horizon of young, adventurous, virile men. They appealed, therefore, to the soldier's pride in keeping himself fighting-fit in order to be able to do his duty. Nonetheless, the doctrine was clear in relation to contraception or chemical prophylaxis and the troops were advised that 'the only safe way to prevent disease is to keep clear of women'. In relation to this, abstaining from drink, avoiding 'dirty books and pictures' and engaging in rigorous physical exercise were advised as the three best means of avoiding the troubles of venereal disease.

The chaplains' language in relation to women remains congruous with those expressed in documents cited in earlier chapters from the Military Police and the Medical Services. They were, by way of caution, divided into 'innocent' and 'not innocent' women. The 'innocent' ones where those the soldier had a duty not to take advantage of and to protect 'from others, and even from themselves' lest he 'inflict an irreparable loss on her dignity and future'. The 'not innocent' where those who 'may look ever so attractive and yet may be diseased'.

A final warning to the attending soldier was that the wickedest thing he could do would be to touch any woman if there was even a suspicion of disease upon himself, an act regarded as nothing less than criminal. Here, the chaplain warned against the 'terrible but common superstition which says that the way to cure a man's disease is to cohabit with a virgin'.

THE ARMY CONFERENCE ON VENEREAL DISEASE

Colonel Higgins, as discussed previously, had been appointed as the Army's representative to the Interdepartmental Committee on Venereal Disease in December of 1924. As the time to begin approached, the Adjutant General and the Minister for Defence decided that it would be beneficial to precede the interdepartmental conference with an internal conference, in order to discuss the matter from an Army point of view and as 'an invaluable guide to our representative [Higgins] at the Interdepartmental discussions'.[5] The Minister for Defence (Peter Hughes), Chief of Staff (MacMahon), Adjutant General (MacNeill), Director of Medical Services (Higgins) and Head Chaplain (Ryan) met at 3pm on Thursday, 8 January 1925 at the Minister's Room, Portobello Barracks.

There was general agreement with Higgins' suggestions except when it came to 'direct methods' – i.e. treatment stations, chemical and physical prophylaxis, etc. Higgins described the steps taken by the American and European armies and pointed out that 'it was neither today nor yesterday that this problem engaged the attention of the army authorities in every civilized nation in the world'.[6] In all cases, he explained, these other armies had started with 'indirect methods' and in all cases they had failed, leaving 'direct methods' as the only effective solution. His comment, however, that it was with considerable reluctance that he had to fall back on 'direct methods' – a hint at the moral exceptionalism of the idealised Irish soldier as conceived by Mulcahy or O'Duffy previously. Still, he pointed out to the conference that in the cases of the German and US armies, the introduction of prophylactic treatment had reduced venereal disease practically to a minimum and that if it were introduced throughout the Irish Army he guaranteed 'the disease would to all intents and purposes disappear'. (In reference to the use of the singular – 'the disease' – it should be noted that in much of the contemporary correspondence, venereal disease was often used synonymously with syphilis.)

Despite the potential to virtually eradicate from Irish soldiers a disease with severe consequences to both themselves as well as their wives and children, Ryan objected on the grounds that Higgins was looking at it simply as a medical matter and that there was 'a larger aspect to the matter' as in other countries 'the religious aspect of the problem was not looked on in the same light as it would be in the Irish Army'. Ryan toed the usual line of the 'moral drive', lectures and indoor recreation. His logic was both conservative and paternalistic. He explained that canonically there was no objection to the 'treatment' but that his opinion was that while the disease would be diminished, immorality in the Army would be increased. He was convinced that the resulting immunity that some of the soldiers would feel towards venereal disease would break down their morals and expressed his concern for the shock that the ordinary innocent-minded soldier would receive at the suggestion of 'treatment'.

Higgins stood his ground, retorting that when syphilis came to prominent notice in the Army two years previously, it had been agreed at a meeting of their preceding appointment holders, after 'considerable pressure' and 'considerable discussion', that the Medical Services would not press for the disease to be dealt with by 'direct methods' on the understanding that if the chaplains' 'indirect methods' did not work then they would be revisited again after twelve months. Eighteen months had now elapsed and instances of the disease had not decreased. As a shocking illustration, Higgins 'showed that the casualties from this disease alone in the army were more than those inflicted during the whole of the "irregular" struggle, together with casualties from every other disease taken together'. Furthermore, this was costing the state £13,000 per annum at the current rate of infections.

After considerable discussion, it was accepted that the 'indirect methods' had failed and that it was time to engage 'direct methods' against syphilis. Higgins proposed compulsory treatment at all barracks and posts, starting with the Dublin barracks. Despite conceding that 'indirect methods' had failed, Ryan was still primarily concerned with the moral and spiritual welfare of the Irish soldier, suggesting that treatment be voluntary. Higgins objected on the grounds that this would render the scheme useless, and so a three-month trial of compulsory prophylactic disinfection of all troops was agreed upon as an experiment to run from 1 February to 1 May 1925.

While the theory was sound, the methodology was slightly baffling and arguably implies other moralistic biases. All troops returning to Dublin barracks after 9:30 p.m., except Beggars Bush (as Army Headquarters it was not deemed appropriate 'for obvious reasons'[7]), would be administered the treatment by the medical officer on duty. Those returning prior to 9:30 p.m., however, would not, except upon request. If there was a case among one of the pre-9:30 p.m. returnees who had not requested treatment, a 'special report' would be submitted through the Director of Medical Services to the Minister for Defence. This would be with a view to considering changing the cut-off time from 9:30 p.m. to 8 p.m.– Higgins' originally suggested time. Furthermore, treatment would not apply to officers, NCOs, married ranks, or to 'special privileged' lists which could be arranged by the Adjutant General and Director of Medical Services. Similarly, the Adjutant General directed that demonstrations 'instructing the soldier in the use of Prophylaxis' would be given by officers of the Army Medical Corps beginning on 26 January at Collins, Griffith, Portobello and McKee Barracks.[8]

'MENS PRAVA IN CORPORE SANO'
('A PERVERTED MIND IN A HEALTHY BODY')

It seemed that there was progress being made on the matter of venereal disease and that medical science and pragmatism were making headway over religious dogma. There was further empowerment of this approach that same month when the Adjutant General received written confirmation from the Minister's office on the verbal instruction of the previous September that infected soldiers could be returned to their units rather than discharged from the Army upon being declared effective and discharged from hospital.[9] However, Ryan was incensed by the proposal and drafted his own memorandum immediately after the meeting, as the following sections illustrate:

The gravity of the step which was advocated at our conference last evening is so terrible that I wish to have on record the HEAD CHAPLAIN'S views on the subject.

Before adopting such treatment, the moral effect on the troops must be considered. Supposing that 10% of any unit is morally low and that a further 15% is weak, I fear that a subjective sense of immunity will drag this part into the line of promiscuous sinners, with the result that you have ¼ of the unit vitiated. There is no sin that has a more degrading effect on man. It smashes the fundamental respect of manhood for the honour of woman, even for his own mother. It tends to surreptitious habits. It is the negation of honour, comradeship and self-respect. Restraint imposed by the Almighty God in this respect is one of the greatest tests of our allegiance to Him. For the soldier whose prime virtue is self-control, and discipline, it renders one and the other practically impossible. In all questions of morality, fear is a motive as well as love. The sense of immunity, even from physical consequences, in this case is almost an invitation for the weak to flout his Creator.

I think principally of the 75% of clean, religious, God-fearing boys. To compel them to submit to such treatment shames their deep reverence for Christian modesty. Many of them are married men, and many of them have honourable love for the girls they intend to make their wives. They are all frail. A new temptation is put in their path. With suspicion on their integrity, in addition to companionship with the unit, 25% of which are morally undermined, we're heading for moral degradation. The proposed step may give us a physically fit Army, but we need not look to the Chaplain's Branch for commensurate improvement in morale. <u>Mens prava in Corpore sano</u> [Trans: A perverted mind in a healthy body].

Before the Country we shall mark the Army with a brand which does not represent its real position as Catholic and Irish.[10]

On 21 January, while Ryan was undergoing a short stay in hospital, the Dublin chaplains met at GHQ to discuss the matter. They recommended the postponement of 'direct methods' of treatment for a further six months, in favour of the methods of 'education and recreation', arguing that they had only been recently introduced but were already resulting in a 'marked improvement'. They buttressed Ryan's previous suggestion that 75 per cent of the soldiers were 'clean living, self-respecting boys' who need not be subjected to the indignities of prophylactic treatment. Of the other 25 per cent, they reported, 'the vast majority are the victims of bad women, who live by this traffic', urging that action should be taken in the first instance against 'the civilian element in this matter'.[11]

While their report was duly transmitted via the chain of command to the Minister for Defence the following week, their action irked the Adjutant General. He wrote to Ryan describing their 'method of protest' as 'highly irregular'. As far as he was concerned, Ryan, as Head Chaplain, took his opportunity to respond to the conference which had been convened earlier that month by the Minister and at which a certain course of action had been adopted:

> Now, we find that four subordinate Chaplains assemble and suggest that the Minister's decision be countermanded at this stage. I quite realize and appreciate the zeal and sense of responsibility which has always been evident among our Army Chaplains, but I certainly cannot let this incident pass without letting you have my views.[12]

While Ryan stood over their motivation as well-intentioned, he accepted that they had overstepped the mark and conveyed his regrets to the Minister for the irregularity.[13]

THE INTERDEPARTMENTAL COMMITTEE ON VENEREAL DISEASE CONVENES

On 16 February 1925, Colonel Higgins received a phone call from the Department of Justice, notifying him that the first sitting of the Interdepartmental Committee on Venereal Disease was scheduled for 4 p.m. the following day. Having received no communication on the matter from the Army, he attended. However, only the Department of Justice and Department of Local Government representatives (Mr John Duff and Dr McDonald respectively) were in attendance. There was no secretary, and no terms of reference or any directions whatsoever. They decided it best to adjourn until they received further instructions.[14]

This inauspicious start was perhaps suggestive of the reluctance of the other departments involved to take ownership of the issue.

The Adjutant General described it to the Minster as 'very discouraging ... when the Department of Defence is at last grappling with this problem in a sensible thorough-going fashion, to find the other Departments apparently still viewing it in the old lackadaisical fashion'. If Justice and Local Government and Public Health were going to allow Defence to 'fight this plague unaided' then the Army's efforts were 'already doomed to failure from the national aspect'.[15] The Secretary to the Minister for Defence addressed the matter with his counterparts in Justice and Local Government and Public Health. While addressing the fact that all three departments had to act together to elicit the full benefits, he still echoed the preconception that venereal disease was primarily an Army problem, stating the Minister's opinion that the benefits of the committee's recommendations would 'accrue to the Defence Forces in particular'.[16] The Minister for Justice deferred the matters of administration and terms of reference to the Minister for Local Government and Public Health, as the committee's initiating department.[17]

On 2 March, the Minster for Local Government and Public Health published the terms of reference for the Interdepartmental Committee on Venereal Disease: 'To make enquiries as to the steps, if any, which are desirable to secure that the extent of Venereal Disease may be diminished.' McDonnell was appointed as chairman and a barrister, Mr D.E. Meagher of the Department of Local Government and Public Health, as secretary. The committee set to work and would publish the first draft of its report in March 1926, though it would ultimately be suppressed by the government.

OUTCOMES OF THE INQUIRY

As the committee's terms of reference covered instances of venereal disease within the whole of the state, many of its findings are not relevant to this social history of the first decade of the Irish Army. That said, it still had significant outcomes for the military. Most importantly, it disproved the thesis that venereal disease was primarily an Army problem. This bias had been rooted in a logical fallacy – being subject to medical discipline, the Army was the one body that was able to provide detailed and accurate statistics as well as pro-actively addressing the issue. The lack of broader national statistics had been misrepresented (perhaps deliberately by some with malign intent) as representing a lack of infection within the wider population.

The report also found that the Army's definition of a 'prostitute' (previously mentioned as referring to the 'amateur' and 'professional' classes of prostitutes) was unhelpfully vague, broad and ill-defined. A woman was classed by the Army authorities as a prostitute, the committee noted, 'if the smallest reward, even a bottle of stout, was given to her by the soldier'.[18] This, they said, demonstrated that the view of prostitution as the principal cause of venereal disease was incorrect. It is not surprising though, given the more broad and moralistic definition, that some of the committee's twenty-four witnesses were adamant that prostitution was the whole problem, including the National Army's *éminence grise* and religious counsel to Mulcahy, Fr Richard Devane.

THE SUCCESS OF THE 'DIRECT METHOD' PROPHYLACTIC TREATMENT SCHEME

By the time of the report, venereal disease in the Army was much improved compared to what it had been a few years previously. While the inquiry was in progress, Higgins' prophylactic scheme was proving relatively successful but generally too narrow in its application. On 20 February 1925, Higgins reported 4,703 treatments given, 429 defaulters, 150 men admitting exposure and just one case of venereal disease after prophylaxis on the day of exposure, and in this case the patient had only received partial treatment as he had been drunk.

While the figures were encouraging, Higgins reported that the number of hospital admissions were as high as ever. The scale – 4,703 men treated over twenty-one days, an average of 224 per day in an Army of 15,000 – was too small to affect any real rate of change. A shortfall of medical staff resulted in treatment being provided in only three Dublin barracks (Collins, Portobello and Griffith) and only beginning at 9:30 p.m. Higgins advocated the need to extend it to all Dublin barracks. While the majority of the country's barracks and posts would still be excluded from the Dublin-centric scheme, he believed that the results would prove its efficacy. Islandbridge and McKee were included in the scheme by the beginning of March with expected positive results, though three infections in soldiers returning to barracks before 9:30 p.m. resulted in Higgins pushing again for an earlier treatment start time of 8:45 p.m.[19]

While the term 'prophylactic treatment' may be both a vague and a euphemistic term, Higgins, the pragmatic and straight-talking doctor, explained in his report in detail what exactly the simple

process – deemed by the chaplains as one scandalising and trauma-
tising to the '75% of clean, religious, God-fearing boys' – entailed:

> We begin by treating each case with a prepared ointment, this was
> followed by an injection. We found that the injection was irritat-
> ing and officers of the Medical Service who tried it on themselves
> recommended a less complete process. I then altered the proce-
> dure, merely anointing each case, this being specific against Syphilis
> and not carrying out the full treatment unless the soldier admits
> exposure and asks for full treatment. This means that a soldier may
> contract Gonorrhea if he does not inform the Medical Officer in
> confidence that he exposed himself to infection. On the whole, I
> consider that the Scheme is working satisfactorily.[20]

NOTORIOUS AND BRAZEN WOMEN
IN THE WEST

By September of 1925, the misconception that venereal disease was a
Dublin-centric problem was no longer credible. Due to the increase
in venereal disease within parts of the Army's Western Command
the Adjutant General, in consultation with Higgins, decreed that
the prophylactic treatment scheme would be extended to the
affected posts and informed the Minster for Defence accordingly.[21]

Unsurprisingly, the compulsory prophylactic treatment scheme
met with the opposition of Fr Feely, the chaplain to No. 2 Brigade
of the Western Command. Feely was of the opinion that this was
a temporary spike in view of the 'brigade's comparatively clean
record hitherto'. His suggestion as to where the blame lay was the
familiar one, as was his almost histrionic appraisal of the desultory
and morally harmful nature of a rather perfunctory treatment:

If, as I am convinced, our troops have been the victims of a passing circumstance which is no longer manifest, viz. the brazen attention of two notorious women, one in Athlone and one in Ballinasloe, (the only places, by the way, which became abnormal), surely it is not rational to compel 99% of them to submit unnecessarily to an indecent remedy calculated to degrade and demoralise them, and to destroy at once every vestige of inherent modesty, cause needless physical suffering, and induce a nauseating social atmosphere.[22]

Feely suggested that 'the desperate evil' of venereal disease be given 'reasonable time to establish itself' before the equally evil concept of the prophylactic scheme be considered. Compared to Dublin the figures in the Western Command were small: Athlone had eight cases from April to August; Longford had nine and Ballinasloe had three from August to September; and Boyle and Galway had one case each in April and June respectively. Nonetheless, Higgins vehemently objected to Feely's arguably warped and moralising logic of allowing venereal disease to become established before taking action, informing the Adjutant General of the same.[23]

FIGHTING AGAINST THE TIDE

Despite the misconception of the Catholic Church in Ireland during the 1920s as being *all* powerful (as opposed to just powerful), the chaplains were fighting against the tide in this case and professional medical advice won out. In November of 1925, a General Routine Order (GRO 11/1925) was drafted by the new Adjutant General, Major General Michael Brennan, extending prophylactic treatment to the entire Defence Forces.

The GRO came into force on 10 December 'with a view to reducing the incidence of Venereal Disease to a minimum in the Forces'.[24] The order required that: all NCOs and all married private soldiers who may have exposed themselves to venereal infection would report immediately to the prophylactic centre of the respective units; all unmarried private soldiers returning to barracks after 7 p.m. (winter time) or 9 p.m. (summer time), whether in danger of infection or not, would report to their prophylactic centre and should admit if they had been exposed. NCOs and privates were liable to face charges under the Defence Forces (Temporary Provisions) Acts for failure to comply. However, just as Beggars Bush Barracks was exempt under the earlier Dublin prophylactic scheme 'for obvious reasons', the prophylactic treatment of officers did not fall under the remit of this GRO. This absence is very telling in relation to the social and moral conceptions, both internally and externally, of the 'officer class' during these formative years.

THE CHAPLAINCY – EXPANDING ITS MINISTRY IN A CONTRACTING FORCE

During this period, the Chaplaincy had to consolidate its roles and remits just like the rest of the force. In July of 1925 the Head Chaplain wrote to the Archbishop of Dublin on what he considered the undesirable situation of members of An Garda Síochána and civilians (including the wives and families of soldiers) attending Mass at Arbour Hill Military Church. The latter was partly due to his concern about the implied responsibility for baptisms, marriages and sick calls falling to the chaplains and partly as the attendance of the wives and children of privates and

NCOs (officers' families were fine apparently) 'may hamper the freedom which the chaplains should have when addressing the Troops'. He sought direction from the Archbishop to the local parish churches forbidding them from attending, as the Adjutant General had refused and the military authorities had no objection to it.[25]

That same month, the Head Chaplain secured funding to employ part-time or contract clergymen to minister to certain posts including the Army School of Music based at Beggars Bush. In this case, it was particularly highlighted that 'the number of young boys in training' required a chaplain to give 'at least three lectures per week and generally contribute to the moral and educational welfare' of the boys.[26]

There was also more prosaic administration to be attended to, reflective of the wider conditions of the drastically reduced post-Civil War Army taking shape and finding its feet, as well as internal politics. GOC Eastern Brigade had an interview with the Archbishop of Dublin in August 1925 during which it was decided that St Bricin's Hospital would not have a dedicated chaplain attached but that a senior chaplain would be appointed for GHQ members based at Parkgate, McKee Barracks and Islandbridge, and that this chaplain would also cover St Bricin's Hospital. This appointment, for which a Fr Jack O'Callaghan was identified, would reside in McKee Barracks and assume responsibility for Arbour Hill. O'Callaghan, who had been until then the chaplain at Baldonnel Aerodrome, would be replaced by a junior chaplain.[27] While the Head Chaplain had expressed concern at the excessive duties this implied for the Arbour Hill chaplaincy,[28] the move was expedited by a certain amount of friction that had developed between O'Callaghan and the Officer Commanding the Air Corps, which resulted in the military authorities requesting his transfer.[29]

CHAPTER 13

SATISFACTORY MORALE

In 1926 there were rumblings of dissatisfaction towards the Head Chaplain from many of the Dublin-based chaplains as well as senior officers. This was not new – O'Duffy had been critical of Fr Ryan in his reports to the Executive Council during 1924. In replying to inquiries from the Bishop of Ardagh and Clonmacnoise, Joseph Hoare, into the matter during 1926, Fr Feeley, the Athlone Command Chaplain, described Ryan's interaction with chaplains outside of Dublin as being generally 'confined to receiving occasional communications of a routine nature' and that his 'influence outside Dublin' was 'scarcely palpable'.[1] This, however, he attributed to the scope and nature of his office rather than his qualifications. While Feeley was aware of 'positive dissatisfaction amongst the chaplains and senior officers in Dublin generally' its cause he could not determine, his feeling being that they were due to 'local jealousies and squabbles' between Ryan and some of the chaplains. He had heard officers express the opinion that Ryan lacked the 'organising or personality necessary for the success of his office' – an attitude he believed was fashioned by the influence of these officers' own chaplains. Others were more direct in expressing the 'grave dissatisfaction' felt towards Ryan, however, describing him as 'not only useless but a misfortunate' man who was unpopular among both chaplains and officers.[2]

The Head Chaplain certainly had a lot on his plate in Dublin, as evidenced in the following extract from his letter to the Archbishop of Dublin from October 1926. As well as illustrating the internal politics of city chaplains, it alludes to the disruption to the spiritual life of the Army that could be produced by an inconsistent chaplaincy service:

> I beg to submit that an interchange of Chaplains in the city area is desirable, also that a more equal distribution of the duties of the Chaplains working in Arbour Hill Church would render their efforts for the Spiritual interests of the Troops more effective.
>
> From the beginning the question of seniority was in evidence in connection with the Chaplains attached to Collins Barracks. Your Grace will recall that Father Gleeson was appointed to Collins Barracks as Command Chaplain, and Father Pigott as Chaplain in charge of the same station. Fr. Gleeson's zeal was unquestionable, but co-operation between him and Fr. Pigott was wanting. Before many months helpful relations between the Command Military authorities and Fr. Gleeson ceased. The Military looked to their Chaplain in all matters concerning the Command, and so rendered Fr. Gleeson's office more or less futile.
>
> On Fr. Kennedy's appointment the situation did not improve as regards co-operation. True there was no direct conflict, but in many details the original difficulty remains. The Military still turn to their Chaplain of the Barracks and regard him as in charge of Arbour Hill. Fr. Kennedy experiences difficulty in finding a channel for his suggestions to the Military, and more difficulty in having them put into execution. The result is that the best interests of the men are not served.
>
> My suggestion is that Fr. Casey be transferred to Collins Barracks and be responsible, in addition, for the Troops at Islandbridge and

the Detention Prison. As Senior he should take charge of Arbour Hill Church. Fr. Kennedy be made responsible for McKee Barracks and St Bricin's Hospital, assisting Fr. Casey in the common Services at Arbour Hill Church. Fr. Pigott be made responsible for Portobello Barracks and Griffith Barracks, with supervision over the area and outposts.

Fr. Casey being in the senior position (ecclesiastically and officially) should clear the existing state of things from the Military point of view. I have no doubt that perfect co-operation would exist between him and Fr. Kennedy. I am also of the opinion that Fr. Pigott would do good work in Portobello untrammelled by the ties which these few years of misunderstanding has generated. The station is well organised – its Sodality is one of the most constant in the Army. On the other hand, the position in Arbour Hill needs a thorough overhauling. Fr. Kennedy was handicapped from the start on account of his inexperience and position. Fr. Casey will tackle the work with energy and tact.

I shall be grateful for Your Grace's consideration of these suggestions. If they meet with your approval, I request that they be put into effect as soon as convenient. Just now steps are being taken to organise activities for the welfare and comforts of the men. It is well that the Chaplain concerned may have a controlling influence from the start. Something more than routine Services is needed to stimulate the religious life of the troops stationed in the Northern area of the city.[3]

In this letter, Ryan's own words corroborate many of the complaints and criticisms levelled against him by both O'Duffy and some of the other chaplains. While he could not be blamed for personal animosities between individual chaplains, this situation arose under his leadership. He intimates to the Archbishop that 'Fr Kennedy experiences difficulty in finding a channel for his suggestions to the Military' – surely this channel should have been the Head Chaplain.

FINDING EQUILIBRIUM

Adjustments to the Army during 1929, most significantly the abolition of the brigade stationed at Collins Barracks, necessitated a commensurate reduction in the quantity and location of spiritual care provision, with the Minster for Defence writing to the Archbishop of Dublin to ensure the proposed scheme had his approval. As Minister, Desmond Fitzgerald had been reluctant to encroach upon the magisterium of the Church, noting that he had 'always endeavored to act in accordance with the general agreement come to some years ago between a sub-committee' under the Archbishop and representatives of the Hierarchy.[4] By this stage the Chaplaincy Service was as fundamental an element of the Defence Forces as any other. Subsequent movements of troops due to various exigencies in 1930 were accounted for and administered between the Head Chaplain and the Archbishop in the same functional manner as between any other staff officer and general of GHQ.

Following the death of Bishop Foley in 1926 and the taking ill of Archbishop Byrne, the bishops' sub-committee on chaplains began to fail in its proper functioning. In 1931, the Minster for Defence raised for clarification the exact nature of the original agreement between the Army and the Church in relation to the operation of the Chaplaincy Service, with a particular focus on cost-cutting. Arising from this, new regulations covering the Chaplaincy published in 1932 simply restated the arrangements made in 1923 but notably reduced the Head Chaplain's salary. This drive to reduce associated costs saw the abolition of the post of Head Chaplain the following year and marked the end of Ryan's time with the Army. Fr Casey assumed his responsibilities but it was several more years before he was formally appointed.[5]

The general themes of correspondence from 1927 onward became predominantly concerned more with the practical affairs of remuneration, house keepers and the various responsibilities of chaplains for religious services than imminent moral perils to the troops. Ryan still fought the case for Christian marriage though, condemning the Defence Forces' regulations governing the admission of soldiers onto the married strength (the structure of the Army allowed for a set number of the strength of a unit to be married, known as the 'married strength') and objecting to it on moral grounds. Soldiers could not be included on the married strength (and receive the accompanying benefits in terms of pay and accommodation) unless they had given five years' continuous service and were at least twenty-six years old. Neither was allowance made for a family of more than four. In general, however, the Chaplaincy Service and the Defence Forces were now navigating much calmer spiritual waters. In 1930, for example, the Head Chaplain reported that:

> The general morale of the Army continues satisfactory. There is very little excessive drinking. The medical returns indicate a vast improvement as regards venereal disease. The number per month is now only three or four as compared with five times that number a few years ago. There is a marked decrease in the number of those seeking prophylactic treatment.[6]

The medical reports concurred with the clerical assessments. After a bit of toing-and-froing the method of prophylactic treatment in barracks was eventually fine-tuned. By early 1928 Colonel Shields, the commanding officer of the Athlone district, was able to report to the Adjutant General that, having tried a few methods that turned out to be 'cumbrous and generally unsatisfactory' he had finally devised one so satisfactory that he recommended it be considered as 'worthy of general adoption'. All that was needed to carry it out properly, was 'a supply of printed cardboard passes'.[7]

While it was decided best to allow freedom of action to district and unit commanders to implement a system most suitable to their own particular circumstances, it was codified in a new General Routine Order, No. 12 of 1928, superseding GRO No. 11 of 1925. Less prescriptive but clearer that its predecessor, the GRO directed any NCO or private soldier who had exposed himself to the risk of venereal disease was to report forthwith for treatment to the prophylactic centre established for his unit 'or such other place as is available for treatment of NCOs and men of the Unit when the Centre is not open'. In this regard, the Medical Corps had succeeded in undertaking the prevention and treatment of venereal disease in the same way as any other ailment. Contracting venereal disease was now treated as evidence of the soldier's failure to comply with an order and incurred disciplinary action accordingly.

This is not to say that moral panic surrounding venereal disease among soldiers was completely eliminated. In 1929, the Director of Medical Services wrote to the officer in charge of the Army laboratory, in order to clarify for the Adjutant General reports based on punishments issued under GRO No. 12 of 1928, which indicated that there was a preponderance of venereal disease among NCOs as opposed to the private soldiers. The evidence to hand was inconclusive, mitigated by questions of whether the accused admitted or denied exposure, or was able to provide evidence of receiving prophylactic treatment etc. He suggested, however, that it was 'quite likely that the men are much more resourceful or less honest in these matters than NCOs and so may escape punishment oftener'.[8]

185

CHAPTER 14

THE MOST CATHOLIC STATE

The year 1929 was seminal for the expansion of Irish relations with the Catholic Church. Pontifical High Mass, attended by a crowd of 300,000 people, was celebrated in the Phoenix Park on Sunday 24 June, closing the centenary celebrations of Catholic Emancipation. With these events acting as a practice run, it was also the year that Ireland entered into diplomatic relations with the Holy See, setting in motion events that would culminate in Ireland hosting the 1932 Eucharistic Congress,[1] an international showcase for Catholicism at which the Army would play a prominent role.

The 31st Eucharistic Congress, which took place in Dublin between 22 and 26 June 1932, was as much a triumphalist expression of nationhood as it was one of Roman Catholic devotion. It represented an occasion for simultaneously establishing international recognition and confirming national identity. It was not, as some contend, a manifestation of a domineering Catholic hierarchy over an oppressed population – in fact its success was at least as much due to a dedicated laity and rank-and-file clerics.[2]

Just a decade after the pastoral letter condemned to excommunication those who took up arms against the Free State and deprived them of the spiritual aid of priests, for the newly elected Fianna Fáil government –and its leader Éamon de Valera in particular – it offered a form of redemption and a chance to demonstrate their unquestionable Catholic devotion. At the same time, it was 'characterised by continuity in Church-State relations' since both 'Church and State leaders, irrespective of political party, shared a desire to develop the country according to a philosophy of Catholic nationalism'.[3]

Having been formed in 1926 by Éamon de Valera following a split from Sinn Féin, this new party opted to take their seats in Dáil Éireann rather than continuing to pursue abstention. In January 1932, President W.T. Cosgrave had dissolved the 6th Dáil partly in order to ensure political stability in advance of the Eucharistic Congress. The results of this election saw Fianna Fáil becoming the largest party in the chamber and forming a government with the support of the Labour Party.

The imminent prospect of former Civil War adversaries heading for ministerial office understandably caused nervousness among many senior Army officers in particular. There were rumours, among others, that they were to be replaced with anti-Treaty republicans. Immediately prior to the handover of power the Minster for Defence, Desmond Fitzgerald, issued an order to the Army to burn certain Civil War records including those relating to executions, fearing reprisals should these details fall into the wrong hands. Certain elements within the state's civil and military services even contemplated a coup, with Eoin O'Duffy canvassing support within the Army for a military dictatorship with himself in charge. The Chief of Staff, Major General Michael Brennan, swiftly quashed any such seditious ideas, and the Defence Forces remained steadfast and loyal during the transition of power.[4] The loyalty of the Defence Forces had not been tested like this since the Army Mutiny of 1924. Following the mutiny, disloyal and anti-democratic elements has been purged, with professionalisation and the copper-fastening of democratic ideals ensuing. With the peaceful transition of power in 1932, the nomenclature of the Defence Forces as 'the servant of the nation'[5] was affirmed anew.

As for Fianna Fáil, they now inherited a Defence Forces which was at an all-time low in terms of both men and equipment – reaching a nadir of under 5,000 in 1931 and never exceeding 6,000 for most of that decade. While they had previously been critical of Cumann na nGaedheal's defence policy, Fianna Fáil followed their lead and kept the military on life support up until the sudden panic of 1938 when it became very clear that war was imminent in Europe.[6] That said, the Defence Forces, as the lawfully-raised, mandated and armed military body of the state, held important symbolic and ideological value for the new government as the visual embodiment of independence. This is evidenced in de Valera's comments to James Henry Thomas, UK Secretary of State for Dominion Affairs, which also present a tempered and sympathetic disposition to those soldiers who took the pro-Treaty side, ironically echoing Collins' 'stepping-stone' attitude to the Treaty:

> This agreement divided the people of Ireland into two hostile camps, those who deemed it a duty to resist, facing the consequences, and those who deemed it prudent in the national interest temporarily to submit, the latter being placed in the no less cruel position of having apparently to hold Ireland for England with 'an economy of English lives' ... To England this agreement gave peace and added prestige. In Ireland it raised brother's hand against brother, gave us ten years of blood and tears and besmirched the name of Ireland wherever a foul propaganda has been able to misrepresent us.[7]

This was not the only echo of de Valera's predecessors. The Defence Forces' prominent participation in an event as nation-defining as the Eucharistic Congress undoubtedly embodied the culmination of the aspirations and ideals of the 'spirit of manly loyalty to God' and of being 'pioneers in a new State' which had been envisioned in 1922 by Mulcahy and Devane.

DIPLOMATIC RELATIONS WITH THE VATICAN

In 1929, the Irish diplomat Charles Bewley was made the Irish Free State's ambassador to the Vatican, the Vatican having been formally recognised as a sovereign state under the Lateran Treaty signed the same year. It had always been to the forefront of the intentions of the Cumann na nGaedheal government 'to effect an exchange of ligations with the Vatican'.[8] Joseph Walshe, the Secretary of the Department of External Affairs, explained this as the natural expression of the Irish people's affection for the Holy See. However, there was an aspect about it too of Ireland simultaneously looking beyond its borders and to its past: 'the Government had also felt that the Irish race scattered all over the world wanted some manifest sign that the new Ireland had forgotten none of her old affections ... and to give to the Irish people everywhere a new bond of union with the Church by the bond of official relations with the Holy See'.[9]

Bewley had been an interesting choice of ambassador; coming from a famous Dublin Quaker family, he had embraced both republicanism and Roman Catholicism. He was, among other things, a well-known anti-Semite, and had been known as such to his contemporaries since 1921. He would be dismissed from diplomatic service in 1939 and ended up working for Nazi propagandist-in-chief Joseph Goebbels.

Bewley visited the Pontifical Irish College in Rome in 1929 accompanied by Walshe. Reporting on the visit to the Minister for

External Affairs, Patrick McGilligan (successor to the murdered Kevin O'Higgins), he described a positively discourteous reception from Monsignor Michael Curran, the vice-rector of the college. Curran had made a point of conspicuously ignoring their diplomatic positions, treating them instead like 'two tourists'.[10] Despite this visit from two high-ranking official representatives of Saorstát Éireann, Monsignor John Hagan, the rector of the college, was absent during the visit. Bewley described his reception as 'part of a general campaign for the discrediting of the Irish Free State', unsurprising, he said, given 'the notorious fact that Mons. Hagan is in the closest touch with the leaders of the Fianna Fáil party'. Both Hagan and Curran had opposed the Anglo-Irish Treaty but favoured constitutional as opposed to armed opposition. Curran's views hardened following the executions of republican prisoners during the Civil War. Both Curran and Hagan had used the Irish College to assist anti-Treaty representatives and Curran 'maintained a frosty attitude during subsequent visits by representatives of the Cumann na nGaedheal government'.[11] This attitude extended to all students of the Irish College, with Bewley commenting that 'it is hard to imagine anything more dangerous for the future of the country than the continued training of the future priesthood in a spirit of active disloyalty to the Government'. In the course of official entertainments given by Walshe, it was not unusual for the Irish ligation to be snubbed by the Irish College with all the other colleges and religious orders in Rome being represented among the attendees.[12] While the Free State enjoyed the support of the Catholic Church during the Civil War, this had not been the case with the Irish College in Rome. While clerical opposition had generally been directed towards violent methods, the Catholic Church had aligned with majority nationalist sentiment throughout the struggle for independence.

Part of Bewley's mission, as he acknowledged it himself, was to 'make clear that the Holy See and the international diplomacy of Rome have no doubts about the status of Saorstát Éireann, and will make it much more difficult for any individual to take up the position of not being willing to recognize it'.[13] To this end, it was a major achievement for the government to secure Dublin as the venue for the 1932 Eucharistic Congress. The year 1932 was significant as it marked the 1,500th anniversary of St Patrick's arrival in Ireland and promised a unique opportunity to evidence the new state's ancient Christian credentials as well as demonstrate its capability to conduct such a grand international event and exhibit its identity on the world stage.

While the Archbishop of Armagh, Joseph MacRory, was made a cardinal in December of 1929, the Cumann na nGaedheal government were eager for the Vatican to appoint the Archbishop of Dublin (Byrne) as a cardinal in conjunction with the Eucharistic Congress. This is unsurprising – as Daithí Ó Corráin has described it, 'the partition of Ireland reinforced the association of political allegiance and religious affiliation on both sides of the border after 1920'.[14] The symbolism of a Dublin cardinal would have been a triumph for the Irish Free State.

Bewley fought hard for this but was unsuccessful. During his time in Rome he had had to correct the Vatican's Secretary of State, Cardinal Pietro Gasparri, of his misapprehension that the 'Red Hat' had traditionally gone to the Archbishop of Armagh. Walshe advised Bewley to pursue the cardinalate in grandiose terms that nonetheless illustrated the totality of the Free State's self-conception of its uncompromisingly Roman Catholic character:

It would be regarded with profound gratitude by all the Catholics in all the English speaking countries of the world as a reward for Ireland's contribution to Catholicism through her children everywhere and … it would greatly enhance our prestige as a Catholic State as well as confirm the Catholic character of the State. The Holy See through your good offices is now probably fully alive to the fact that Ireland is the most Catholic State in the world without exception.[15]

In terms of Irish identity, it is interesting that when it came to Roman Catholicism official Ireland was more than happy to emphasise its *English*-speaking credentials in vying for recognition as a leader among English-speaking Catholic countries. At the same time, old antagonisms with England were played out by proxy in Rome. Bewley was critical of Cardinal Francesco Marchetti-Selvaggiani's potential candidacy for appointment as Papal Legate for the Eucharistic Congress due to his reputation as 'definitely anti-Irish' and someone who had 'for many years spent some part of his vacation in England … and rather cultivates English circles in Rome'.[16] The rumour that it could be the English Cardinal Francis Bourne was one that Walshe wanted to 'kill as soon as possible'.[17] Walshe was forthright in his opinions of the English clerics in Rome as being granted too much influence and as usurpers to a position that he considered as rightfully belonging to Ireland:

With the English representatives in general here it is all take and no give. England is first rather too ostensibly all the time … Their influence in Roman circles is quite comparable (though far greater) to that of the English Embassy in Washington. The Irish clergy do not count … [they] have persuaded the Vatican by their action and real leadership that they are the true representatives of the English speaking Catholics all over the world.[18]

In very exercised terms, Walshe attributed this 'in very large measure to the passivity and mediocrity of the Irish College and to the complete indifference of the Irish Bishops to the position of Ireland in Rome'. As far as the Vatican was concerned, he opined, 'the Ireland of Saints and Scholars might just as well have accepted the reformation and waxed fat and prosperous'.[19]

While the English bishops betokened Ireland's wider relationship with its former colonial masters, having its envoys at the Vatican gave Ireland another avenue to reach out to cement friendships across the water. During his 1931 St Patrick's Day message to the USA, W.T. Cosgrave looked forward to marking the fifteenth centenary of St Patrick's mission to Ireland, and commenting that it would be 'a special pleasure to welcome our kinsfolk and the many friends of Ireland from the United States of America who will come to participate'[20] in the Eucharistic Congress.

ECHOES OF THE CIVIL WAR: THE PUBLIC SAFETY ACT

In October of 1930, the Head Chaplain circulated a proposed rate of subscriptions to be collected from the Army to be contributed to the Eucharistic Congress. Ryan estimated that £500 could be raised based on a sliding scale of contributions based on rank, ranging from 1/- for privates, 2/- to 2/6 from NCOs and 5/- to 20/- from officers.[21] That same year, the IRA had protested against hosting the Eucharistic Congress in an Ireland that was not yet fully free. Consequently, an armed rising was a very real worry for both the Irish Free State and the Vatican as potentially detrimental to both the Congress and Ireland's reputation in Rome. The IRA was again becoming a concern, particularly following their murder of Garda Superintendent Seán Curtin and John Ryan. There were echoes of the 1922 pastoral letter the following year. In an audience with Cardinal Pacelli on 4 September 1931, Bewley told him that 'the [Irish] Government was doing everything possible to overcome the danger, but that in a Catholic country like Ireland, where there was, at the same time, a tradition of hostility to the law, a condemnation by the Irish Episcopate would have far more effect, as Irish Catholic boys were induced to join what they believed to be merely a patriotic organization, and were led into crime'.[22]

That November the Pope himself (Pius XI) raised with Bewley his concerns regarding communist and anti-Catholic propaganda, and the threat of armed insurrection, expressing his surprise that such things could find willing listeners in a country as committedly Catholic as Ireland.[23] Attempts to formulate a national defence policy in the mid-1920s had, in fact, assessed the Army as being generally orientated towards dealing with internal security, in particular the threat of an outbreak by the IRA and serious riots or disturbances by ex-Army men or communists.[24] Bewley reassured the Pope that the Irish Free State would not allow the IRA to disrupt the Eucharistic Congress, describing for him in particular the measures introduced in the Constitutional Amendment Act (1931), known popularly as the Public Safety Act.

In order to tackle subversive activity with the force required, this allowed for the establishment of the Constitution (Special Powers) Tribunal. This was comprised of five Defence Forces' officers of at least the rank of commandant who could impose sentences up to and including the death penalty. It also gave special policing powers to both An Garda Síochána and the Defence Forces, defined and proscribed 'unlawful organisations' and went as far as prohibiting the distribution or possession of documents from any organisation deemed 'unlawful'.[25] Bewley even translated certain key sections into Italian for the cardinals.[26] Following their meeting, Bewley reflected that:

> The Pope struck me as being very well informed about affairs in Ireland. I endeavoured, without giving too alarming a picture of affairs, to urge the necessity of any such measures as had been taken, and to prepare him for the possibility of more severe action becoming inevitable, while expressing the hope that it might be avoided.[27]

Against this background the significance is abundantly clear, notwithstanding its established ceremonial function, of asserting the Defence Forces' position in connection with, and during, the Eucharistic Congress, as the lawfully raised military of a democratic, independent state.

THE CARRIGAN REPORT

While plans were in motion to demonstrate Ireland's implacable Roman Catholic credentials to the world, a festering underbelly of the state-building project of the previous decade was being exposed. In June 1930, the government appointed the Committee on the Criminal Law Amendment Acts and Juvenile Prostitution. Chaired my Mr William Carrigan KC it was tasked with considering whether the Criminal Law Amendment Acts (1880–1885) needed modification and if new legislation was needed to address juvenile prostitution. The committee had seventeen sittings at which twenty-nine witnesses presented evidence. Among these witnesses, and perhaps the most prominent, were two highly influential figures on the moral and disciplinary development of the

Defence Forces in its formative years – Fr Richard Devane and General Eoin O'Duffy.

Unique among his fellow clerics in appearing before Carrigan, Devane identified several underlying problems determining immorality in the Free State, 'articulating critical problems that would remain prominent in sociological debates for decades to come'. Such problems included the dual standard of morality applied to women and men in issues of sexual morality and the 'impersonal attitude' whereby 'any other's child or sister is envisaged [as the victim of abuse or engaged in prostitution] rather than one's own'.[28]

General O'Duffy's testimony, as one would expect from the Garda Commissioner, centred on prosecutions for sexual offences and the need for modern nations to legislate against immorality, in particular crimes like incest, paedophilia and rape. 'O'Duffy, more than any other witness, influenced the shape of the committee's final report as well as the eventual legislation'.[29]

The findings of the Carrigan Report were delivered in August 1931 and recommended a combination of enlightened social reform and punitive measures. It provided irrefutable evidence of widespread sexual crime in Ireland. It painted a picture of an Irish legal system that operated to the detriment of children 'leading to their sometimes being treated as accomplices in a crime rather than victims'.[30] It revealed a country in which a significant and increasing number of sexual crimes, particularly against girls under sixteen, were taking place but where there was a lack of prosecutions due to anxiety among parents not to subject their children to the courts out of a combination of care and shame, and of course due to the difficulties in corroborating evidence which is very often a characteristic of sexual crimes.

The government followed the advice from the Department of Justice not to publish the report and failed to implement its recommendations. While Carrigan had, for example, advocated for the extension of the offence of 'solicitation' to apply to men as well as women, raising the age of consent to eighteen and revising judicial practice that required the corroboration of a minor's testimony, 'the view of the Department was that it was unbalanced to be too severe on men, while overlooking the shortcomings of women in these matters, and the, at times, highly coloured imaginations of children'.[31] Prior to addressing the committee, O'Duffy had provided a detailed report on sexual crimes in Ireland for the previous six years. This, like the Carrigan Report, was not published.

In light of all of this, General Hugo MacNeill's vociferous objection to the portrayal of the Defence Forces as a singular source of immorality and, specifically, venereal disease is elucidated and vindicated in a more broadly applicable way than was done by the report of the Interdepartmental Committee on Venereal Disease. That the values and principles of the Defence Forces were (and are) a reflection of wider Irish society became increasingly clear. Captain Brophil and his patrols to reconnoitre the threat of 'immoral women' to Army men; Mulcahy's disapproval of recruiting men with 'illegitimate children' or 'unmarried wives'; the chaplains' concerns with the corrupting effects of 'notorious' and 'brazen' women on 'innocent Army boys' favouring punishment for the former and increased creature comforts for the latter: as the Irish Free State dredged its own deep and murky waters, it became clear that all of these things were a reflection of wider Irish societal attitudes and pervasive behaviours.

The findings of the Carrigan Report were addressed by Fianna Fáil in the ensuing limp and watered-down Criminal Law Amendment Act of 1935. This, for example, saw the sale of contraceptives banned, an increase in the age of consent from sixteen to seventeen (not eighteen as Carrigan had recommended) and sex with a girl aged fifteen to seventeen categorised as a misdemean-our rather than a felony. So as Ireland prepared for the Eucharistic Congress, ready to enter the international arena as a major player within the English-speaking Catholic world, it remained, as those in power knew, one in which vice and immorality were simplisti-cally conflated and where a Catholic 'obsession with the visibility of sex deflected attention from the plight of individuals occluded by sexual immorality, specifically the unmarried mother, illegiti-mate child and victims of rape, incest and pedophilia'.[32]

THE ARMY – 'THE ONLY COMPETENT PARTY TO RUN A CAMP'

Following the announcement that the 31st Eucharistic Congress was coming to Dublin, a committee was established and head-quartered at 8 Lower Abbey St, Dublin. Mr Frank O'Reilly, a prominent lay Catholic and secretary of the Catholic Truth Society, was appointed as its director of organisation by Archbishop Byrne. Faced with an enormous logistical task in anticipation of up to 70,000 visitors, O'Reilly's natural port of call was the Army and the Department of Defence.

What proceeded was the first instance of what would become a familiar motif in the government's utilisation of the Defence Forces over the course of the following century and a country that has never known exactly what do to with its military forces. From an army established in haste in the heat of a civil war and initially rife with indiscipline only eight years previously, the Defence Forces were now being called upon to be at the forefront of both the Irish Catholic Church's and the Irish Free State's largest and most ambi-tious project since independence. While this represented pride in, and recognition of, the Defence Forces' professionalism and ability, it was also not a military task and symptomatic of an enduring attitude towards the Irish Defence Forces as a jack-of-all-trades most useful in plugging gaps for the civil authority and civil power. As described by Eoin McNamara, one that suffers from a 'political acceptance of military underfunding' symptomatic of 'a wide civil-military gap' in Ireland which resulted in the military becoming 'a very distant institution in Irish society'.[33]

Undertaking such a substantial task as the Eucharistic Congress also highlighted the enduring paradox of Ireland's concurrent nationalist separatism and national reliance on Great Britain as illustrated in the following note from Colonel E.V. O'Carroll (Quartermaster General) to the Secretary of the Department of Defence:

> Mr. O'Reilly, who is dealing with the Eucharistic Congress (1932) arrangements, spoke to me on the phone some days ago regarding the question of tentage and camps. He is very concerned about the matter of accommodation and feels that a very considerable number will have to be put under canvas. Accordingly, he suggested that I should lay the following proposals before the Minister:
>
> That the Minister explore the possibility of the British Army authorities supplying tentage for approximately 8,000 people (2,000 bell tents).
>
> He explained that owing to the Malta crisis, the Bishops felt that it would not be an opportune time for the British Cardinal to approach the British Government on such a matter and that representations coming from the Minister would have a much better hearing. He would be anxious to discuss this and other matters with the minister at some future date but desired that he should have time to digest the proposal beforehand.

Another question which he is very anxious to discuss is the possibility of the Army taking on complete control of such camps when established. He feels that to entrust such a work to a committee would result in the work being done very badly and that as experience of running camps is so very critical, and as strict discipline must be enforced, the only competent party to run a camp is the Army. He also wished to emphasize that the 1932 congress arrangements should be regarded as a National duty and that all the facilities and services of the state should be utilized to the fullest. Of course he is well aware that expenses incurred by such state services will have to be met by the committee organizing the arrangements for the Congress.

I would like you to bring the matter before the Minister if he wishes to meet Mr. O'Reilly perhaps you would arrange.[34]

In support of this mass movement of people into and around Ireland, the Army planned to call up three battalions (approximately 2,500 men) in support. Even making allowance for what the Army could supply, the logistical requirements from the British Army were staggering. The Minster for Defence, Desmond Fitzgerald, sent a request through Walshe for the loan of the necessary equipment.[35] O'Reilly calculated that they would need 39,500 beds or bed boards, 46,300 mattresses, 109,600 blankets, 36,000 sheets, 51,500 coverlets, 94,100 pillows, 74,100 pillowcases, 18,000 tents and 1,000 marquees.[36] While any spare space would be utilised to get pilgrims under a roof (spare rooms in houses, hotels, schools, convents etc.) there was still a need for extensive camp accommodation. However, old national antagonisms arose again in September of that year when the Archbishop of Dublin (Byrne) instructed O'Reilly that he was 'not inclined to apply to the British War Authorities for any material' and so

O'Reilly wrote to the Minister for Defence withdrawing his previous letter.[37]

The Army Corps of Engineers played a central role in the establishment of campgrounds. They began inspecting agreed and proposed sites during the summer of 1930. Entrance and exit routes, transportation facilities, accommodation, water supply, cooking, dining, washing and latrine facilities all had to be thoroughly surveyed. Even when the president of the GAA informed O'Reilly that they would take charge of the camp site and hostel at Croke Park, O'Reilly put it first for consideration to the Army Engineer Corps and offered complete control of the sites to the Army should the Quartermaster General prefer.[38]

POMP AND CEREMONY

The Army took pride of place in the pomp and ceremony of the Eucharistic Congress, and nowhere was this more conspicuous than in the establishment of the Ceremonial Mounted Escort in 1932. More commonly known as the 'Blue Hussars', they escorted the Papal Legate, resplendent in sapphire blue tunic and breeches with gold frogging and lace of the 'hussar' pattern, with black sealskin busby hat adorned with orange-yellow plumes. A total of £2,165 was spent on producing seventy of these uniforms.

Such a function would traditionally be associated with cavalry soldiers. However, the Army had not had a mounted cavalry since the unit that mutinied and was disbanded in the autumn of 1922. The three officers, four NCOs and fifty-three men were supplied by the Artillery Corps, as one of the corps that still heavily relied on horse transport. Stocks of saddlery were supplied by the Supply and Transport Corps, under which the Army Equitation School fell.[39]

When the Papal Legate, Cardinal Lorenzo Lauri, arrived by mail steamer into Dún Laoghaire on 20 June 1932, he was greeted by six Air Corps Avro Cadets flying in cruciform formation. As his boat reached the Kish Bank the Papal Flag was hoisted and a salute of nineteen minute-guns was fired. After this, the papal flag was lowered and the national flag raised. A guard of honour and the Army Band greeted him at Carlisle Pier. These formalities were repeated on his departure.

At Dún Laoghaire he was met by de Valera, and both were escorted by the Blue Hussars to the Pro-Cathedral in Dublin. Following the service at the Pro-Cathedral the Hussars escorted him to the Archbishop's Palace in Drumcondra. The next day the Hussars escorted Lauri from the Archbishop's Palace to Dublin Castle for a state banquet in his honour, where he was greeted by another guard of honour and music from the Army Band.[40]

En route to the Pro-Cathedral following Lauri's arrival, the procession had stopped at the Greater Dublin boundary where the Papal Legate was received by the Lord Mayor, the hugely popular Alfie Byrne, who then joined the procession in the Lord Mayor's gold coach. Just the week before, Byrne had reported that he had neither the horses nor the men to take charge of the coach and other civic ceremonial functions during the procession. These were also supplied by the Army, with the men donning the traditional costumes for which the Lord Mayor claimed he could not find any suitable men elsewhere.[41] The Equitation School provided a coachman, four footmen and two outriders 'selected from the tallest and smartest men in the school'. The Artillery Corps provided six grey horses, while the School of Music provided four trumpeters 'to blow the necessary calls from the City Gate Towers'.[42]

Before providing these Army men and horses, however, the Minister for Defence, Frank Aiken, wanted assurance from Byrne that they could not be obtained by other means – noting that 'applications for free performances by members of the Army band have always been turned down on the ground that there is a considerable number of unemployed musicians in the City'.[43] It also seems that Byrne had tried to take advantage of the Army through this last minute request for men and horses, translating military professionalism and competency into the previously described role as a 'jack-of-all-trades' for national contingencies. Aiken enquired of the Chief of Staff how this matter of providing horses and men to the Lord Mayor has arisen in the first place. It seemed that it had been presented by Byrne as a fait accompli and the Quartermaster General (Colonel J.J. 'Ginger' O'Connell) had mistakenly, but understandably, assumed that it was the case that Byrne had surely gone through government channels. O'Connell noted that:

> It was only at about 1600 hrs on Thursday, yesterday, that I learned that the whole affair was quite irregular, and that the Lord Mayor had rushed us. Because, evidently, certain preparations i.e. overhaul of the State Coach, arrangements for fitting out men, etc. must have been in train for some time before anything came to light as far as I was concerned.[44]

At the Pontifical High Mass to close the Congress, the highlight of the week, the Army was once again positioned in pride of place. This open-air Mass held in the Phoenix Park was a tremendous spectacle – a million people attended, Count John McCormack performed the offertory motet *Panis Angelicus* and there was a live broadcast from the Pope at the Vatican. In 1923, Mulcahy had dreamed of officers having the opportunity to dedicate 'their swords during a day or so of vigil like the soldiers of more romantic times in other Catholic countries'. Now, at the Consecration of the

Eucharist, a guard of thirty-six Army officers 'rendered swords' to the Host in a striking reverential gesture of salute while trumpeters played the 'royal salute'. As G.K. Chesterton described it:

> All along the front there ran, like a sudden lightening, the light upon the lifted swords; for all the soldiers standing before the altar saluted with a blazing salute of steel, carrying the hilt to the head in the old swordsman's salutation, and then striking outwards, in the ancient gesture of the Romans. Her face was like a King's Command when all the swords are drawn.[45]

The man hand-picked to command the guard of honour was Colonel James (Séamus) McGauran. On 8 June, McGauran, who was at that time based at the Command and Staff School in the Curragh, received word that he had been selected for the task. McGauran was summoned to a meeting with the Chief of Staff who briefed him personally. This episode in itself illustrates the monumental significance of the Eucharistic Congress to the Irish state. For context, the guard of honour for the state visit to Ireland of Queen Elizabeth II in 2011, perhaps the most historically significant in recent times, was commanded by a captain (Thomas Holmes) and it was certainly not deemed necessary that he be personally briefed in preparation by the Chief of Staff.

Following the Mass, the members of the guard of honour attended a dinner hosted by the new Fianna Fáil government. Captain Seán Clancy recalled the unease they felt dining in the company of men against whom they had fought in the Civil War. The tension was broken when de Valera invited McGauran to take a seat beside him during the meal. In an oral history interview, Clancy reminisced that:

We sat down to a well-earned lunch and Dev announced, now he said 'I want the officer in charge of the guard of honour sit on my right for this meal and the Ceann Comhairle of Dáil Éireann on my left' and then what happened? Frank Fahey was the Ceann Comhairle I remember at the time and he sat on Dev's left and our officer sat on his right. And we had a fine meal and we talked and chatted with each other and had a very good relationship and we were all on different sides of the Civil War you see. So that brings us back to what you said earlier about bad feelings and hard feelings now. There was no hard feeling there anyhow that day.[46]

Almost ten years previously to the day, Dubliners had woken to the sound of the National Army shelling their erstwhile comrades of the anti-Treaty IRA in the Four Courts, heralding the death, suffering and destruction of the Civil War. Now, an Army officer and the anti-Treaty leader through whom his professional loyalty to the state was pledged, dined side-by-side, marking the end of a week of the most extraordinary Roman Catholic devotional festivities. Perhaps this image, like some reimagining or reinvention of Seán Keating's *An Allegory*, most adequately invokes the disciplinary and religious trajectory of that most unique arm of the Irish state, the Defence Forces, during its first decade of existence.

CONCLUSION

'ÓGLAIGH NA HÉIREANN HAS BEEN THE PEOPLE, IS THE PEOPLE, AND WILL BE THE PEOPLE'

As Cardinal Lauri sailed away from Dún Laoghaire, his ship left in its wake an Irish state that was entering its peak decades of Roman Catholic influence and power. Coinciding with this, the anti-Treatyites of Fianna Fáil coming to power by popular election heralded the end of the sometimes dirty, more often perfunctory, unglamorous or tedious work of consolidating the revolution (or counter-revolution, depending on your position) and establishing the mechanisms of a functioning, independent state that had fallen to Cumann na nGaedheal. Pulling off a national event as immense as a Eucharistic Congress, mobilising the necessary infrastructure, resources and administration, had shown the world that Ireland was a functioning, modern state. But following a respite from the years of fighting from 1919–23, it was a state again ready for national idealism; one that needed to discard the dead weight of Cumann na nGaedheal, a party associated with establishing and defending a Treaty that was, for many, only a stepping-stone, and one associated with various (arguably necessary but nonetheless unpleasant) draconian public safety measures. This national idealism however, translated into a state where the establishment, in particular through its religious, political, legislative, judicial and medical institutions, would exert control over virtually all aspects of life until the latter part of the twentieth century.

This model had, of course, had its mould cast during the first decade post-independence. As the preceding chapters have illustrated, this wider triumvirate of Church, government and medical powerbases were reflected in miniature within the Defence Forces' Chaplaincy Service, GHQ / Department of Defence, and Medical Service. As Ireland entered the 1930s, while the body politic could shake off Cumann na nGaedheal, it was stuck with its army, and attitudes towards it reflected this. The Army became a showpiece – the Equitation School and School of Music came into the ascendant, providing a positive public image while, in reality, as a fighting force it was neutered, starved of resources and left to wither on the vine.

The necessity of fighting the Civil War and establishing a democracy based on the rule-of-law, as rough and ready as it may have been at times, was muted within the collective consciousness. Despite over 810 of its members dying in the process, the National Army lost the battle for commemoration to the IRA in the decades that followed. This is something that only began to be addressed during the centenary of the Civil War; although the state stopped short of a government-led commemoration specifically for the National Army dead, there was, however, a Defence Forces-led ceremony in July 2023, rededicating the National Army monument in Glasnevin cemetery attended by members of government.

Arguably, the redesignation of the National Army as the Defence Forces in October 1924 allowed the creation of a dissonance between the former and the latter, allowing the former to become the sin-eater for the Irish Free State, carrying the burden of the bloody and brutal cost of securing democracy. The latter, then, inherited the original sin. The Defence Forces has existed in a liminal space in social and political consciousness, applauded for displays of the more performative trappings of military service – be it rendering guards of honour for presidents, archbishops or royalty, or being waved off while heading overseas on peace-keeping service with the United Nations – but becoming a source of public or political discomfort when the real-life implications or requirements of the employment of military force are raised. Within its own borders especially, it has been a force deployed to do everything from aiding the civil power to combatting militant subversion, to erecting tented villages for the Special Olympics and refugees, to clearing snow from the roads, to collecting rubbish during a refuse-collectors' strike, but it has never been endowed with the military capacity to defend the state from armed aggression in any meaningful way.

During the Emergency – the term given to the Second World War period in Ireland, derived from the Emergency Powers Act and referring, for ostensibly neutral Ireland, to the penultimate planning phase before a state of war and not a twee euphemism as sometimes incorrectly asserted – the Defence Forces increased in numbers again and with it, the attending disciplinary issues arose. Venereal disease rates increased as large numbers of new permanent and reserve members flooded in. De Valera's banning of the prophylaxis treatment fought so hard for by Colonel Higgins did not help.[1] Despite the initial surge in enthusiasm when invasion seemed a distinct possibility, as the war progressed and the

Germans turned their attention east towards Russia, as had been the case after the Civil War, boredom and disenchantment – the two worst enemies of discipline among soldiers anywhere in the world – set in. This time, thousands deserted, many joining the Allied forces to take up arms against the evil of nazism, or simply in search of adventure.

In 1958, with the permission of Archbishop John Charles McQuaid,[2] the Defence Forces attended the first International Military Pilgrimage to Lourdes, with members attending every year since. Seven years previously, on the Feast of Our Lady, Queen of the Most Holy Rosary, in October 1951, the Archbishop of Dublin had invoked Her as the 'Patroness and Protector of the Defence Forces'. Reflecting on this in terms that echoed Mulcahy, Devane and O'Duffy, one member of the first pilgrimage organising committee described it as 'fitting that our young army still forming its military traditions and linking them with those of Ireland's past, should thus publicly attest its devotion to the Mother of God, which has always been such an admirable trait of the Irish people'.[3]

Such was the pattern throughout the century, no less so than when Ireland began participating in overseas military service with the United Nations. As the Defence Forces became the physical representation of increasingly outward-looking and multilateral Irish foreign policy, so their values and what they represented came to be a focus for wider Irish values. This was demonstrated in the formal and ceremonial exhibition of both national grief and respect following the Niemba Ambush, when, on 8 November 1960, nine Irish soldiers were killed by Baluba tribesmen in the Congo. It also arguably contributed to the moral injury inflicted on the men of 'A' Company, 35th Infantry Battalion, who were involved in the Siege of Jadotville.

For a week in September 1961 these men bravely defended their position from a numerically superior and better-armed mercenary force until their commander, Commandant Pat Quinlan, agreed to surrender in order to save their lives. Rather than being treated as heroes, the men were egregiously cast as cowards for their surrender in an example of both military and national immaturity and insecurity.

The most significant shift in collective Irish values began in the 1990s. Beginning with the decriminalisation of homosexual activity in 1993, followed in 1997 by the legalisation of divorce, the stage was set for a twenty-first century which would see Ireland become one of the most socially liberal countries in Europe. In 2015 Ireland became the first country in the world to introduce same-sex marriage by popular vote and in 2019 the constitutional ban on abortion was finally removed by referendum.

This sea change naturally resonated within the Defence Forces. Following the amendment of the Criminal Law (Sexual Offences) Act 1993, which decriminalised homosexual activity, and the subsequent statement by the Minister for Defence that homosexuals would not be prohibited from joining the Defence Forces, the Head Chaplain (later bishop), Monsignor Raymond Field, advised the Defence Forces Code of Conduct Study Group that the Chaplaincy was concerned with the 'likely serious and harmful consequences'[4] that would follow without 'decisive initiative' and the establishment of an adequate code of conduct to govern the behaviour of all members of the organisation. As it had been in the time of his earliest predecessor, Dominik Ryan, religious and disciplinary advice bled into one another.

One of Field's recommendations was that the Defence Forces 'formulate and state for the guidance of its members its own policy on moral values' and that programmes be 'devised to assist the moral formation and development of the individual ... and initiated particularly in the Cadet School, the Apprentice Schools and with Recruit Classes'. While confirming that any member of the Defence Forces who approached the Chaplaincy for advice, assistance or counselling would be treated with 'kindness, charity, understanding and the strictest confidence', Field's other recommendations demonstrated the particular moralising tone and biases of the pastoral care on offer. In respect to 'homosexuals that were known to be such' his recommendations were laden with assumptions and stereotypes, and only related to gay *men*: they should not be required to work 'in places or positions which would be an unfair source of temptation, including male-dominated camps; on overseas service 'where life tends to be somewhat unreal and situations at times, highly charged emotionally'; or 'in positions of authority over young people' or in any situation where 'their professed way of life could be an influence on the more vulnerable such as Cadets, Apprentices or Recruits'.

It was not just matters of homosexuality that concerned Field. He advised that the 'widespread availability and pervasive use of pornography in the Defence Forces' be curtailed, stating that 'it is not uncommon for pornographic videos to be shown nightly' in places like barrack duty rooms and that it was very much 'a feature of life overseas'. As well as its inherent tendency to 'deprave and corrupt', in some circumstances pornography infringed upon the rights of those service personnel who did not want to watch it but were precluded from leaving the room, or victimised for objecting.

Alcohol abuse also remained an issue of concern to the Chaplaincy, as did gambling, borrowing and lending money, and, to a limited extent, drug taking. With respect to alcohol, something which remained problematic in the Defence Forces until the 2000s, Field identified certain practices which lent themselves to alcohol abuse, including: canteens boosting sales to increase income, particularly overseas; officers and NCOs detailing subordinates to keep messes and bars open after hours; the failure of senior ranks to intervene in cases of alcohol abuse for fear of possible future career and overseas service repercussions for the individuals concerned; and the toleration of alcohol abuse to facilitate the individual reaching their pensionable age. Field made enlightened suggestions regarding the need for a programme of education on the effects of alcohol and, continuing in the tradition of both services working closely together, commended the excellence of the Medical Corps in this regard already.

By this stage, however, within the Defence Forces many of these issues and remits were moving into a more ecumenical realm which in some ways subsumed – or at least complimented – the pastoral role of the Chaplaincy. It was in 1992 that the Defence Forces established the Personnel Support Service (PSS). This service continues to provide support, counselling, information and assistance on a range of matters from marital, family and relationship issues, stress, alcohol and substance abuse, to tax issues, financial problems and housing assistance, working closely with the Chaplaincy Service. Reflecting and adapting to the greater diversity of people under its care, the modern Chaplaincy Service remains a very relevant one, increasingly focused on its pastoral mission more so than its spiritual one. The chaplains, though fewer in number, remain important and popular figures around barracks at home and overseas; friends and confidants to all ranks, uniformed and part of the force but without the attendant formality of professional relationships within the chain of command.

Recent times have seen issues concerning Defence Forces discipline and values come to the fore in very public forums, reflecting the increasingly open and transparent nature of Irish society. Tom Cloonan's PhD research in the year 2000 on 'The Status and Roles Assigned to Female Personnel in the Permanent Defence Forces' highlighted issues of bullying, assault and sexual harassment. The subsequently established Independent Monitoring Group was allowed to peter out by the Department of Defence. Two decades later, following the report of the Independent Review Group (IRG), instigated following the campaigning of the Women of Honour group, it was reported that these problems were still ongoing and had not been properly addressed. The first Ombudsman to the Defence Forces, Paulyn Marrinan Quinn, who submitted her final report to the Department in 2011, commented angrily in the *Irish Times* following the IRG report:

> Before I left, I wrote a letter and sent a memo to the department minister, and I said that there were a number of things that needed to be tweaked. I was advocating at that stage, strongly, that we would bring in our own monitoring provision. Where my greatest anger now is, that opportunity for the independent monitoring group, the ball was dropped or was the ball buried?[5]

In urging appropriate action be taken, starting with the reinstatement of the Independent Monitoring Group, former army officer and TD, Dr Cathal Berry, pointed out that Ireland's defence apparatus does not consist solely of the Defence Forces but includes the Minister and Department of Defence. Berry called for the establishment of a statutory inquiry in light of the IRG report, stating:

> The IRG was a scoping exercise rather than a fact-finding inquiry. Aside from the accusations of sexual misconduct there are also

concerning allegations of bullying and abuse of power. In order to protect the victims of such abhorrent behaviour and to pursue justice, the allegations it uncovered need to be established in fact. Otherwise, we risk making sweeping generalisations and engaging in negative stereotyping of entire cohorts of people based on the reported actions of a few. This is increasingly likely when those criticised are denied the right of reply. Because no chronology is attributed to the allegations in the IRG report it is unclear whether the reported incidents are historical or more recent in nature and whether the allegations reflect the organisation in 2023 and current standards of conduct. As these facts are clarified, consideration might be given to granting the Chief of Staff powers to suspend personnel pending investigation, without prejudice to the outcome, should sufficient preliminary evidence warrant this. Such powers are already given to the Garda Commissioner but do not exist in the Defence Forces.[6]

In relation to the announcement of the establishment of an external oversight body for the Defence Forces, which Berry welcomed, he re-emphasised 'the concerns expressed by other interested parties regarding the inclusion of the secretary general of the Department of Defence', something that he said 'completely undermines the integrity and the credibility of the oversight body and ensures that it will be neither independent nor external'. In addressing this issue solely towards the Defence Forces without the inclusion of the other two elements of the state's defence apparatus, there were echoes of the government attitude to the Defence Forces prior to the Interdepartmental Committee on Venereal Disease. President Michael D. Higgins, the Supreme Commander of the Defence Forces, in response to the IRG report, said that he was 'left with the greatest anxiety that this institutional failure is far from confined

to the Defence Forces, and in many cases there are lessons to be
drawn, and transformations to be made, that are now urgent, not
only within the Defence Forces, but across our society and many
of our institutions'.[7] The metaphor from this book's introduction,
of the canary in the mineshaft, comes to mind again. Higgins'
statement was not one written in a tone of resignation, however,
but of aspiration to address 'deeply unacceptable, indeed criminal,
behaviour'. He described as a 'precious resource' 'the pride which
Irish people rightly feel in the over 60 years of UN peacekeeping
by members of the Defence Forces' and his 'hope the many young
people currently considering a career in the Defence Forces will
join an organisation that they can feel confident is going to be
reformed.'

***

At the graveside of Michael Collins, Richard Mulcahy said that
'Óglaigh na hÉireann has been the people, is the people, and
will be the people.' Both the successes and the shortcomings
of the Defence Forces are *generally* reflective of wider society
and *specifically* symptomatic of the unique features and exigencies of military life everywhere (its culture, psychology, ethics,
values etc.) – simultaneously the weathervane and the canary in
the mine. That said, just as the inheritance of two millennia of
Christian thought contains both thesis and antithesis to the great
debates of modern society, as elucidated by Tom Holland and
referenced in the introduction, the values by which the shortcomings will be addressed are just as inherent to the Defence
Forces' ethos and philosophy. Perhaps during its first decade it
did not become the bastion of Gaelic, Godly, pioneering spiritual
warriors of a Christian state envisioned by Mulcahy or Devane.

Projecting such naively idealistic and nationalistic aspirations on any government institution or human endeavour is destined to disappoint. But the seeds of these values, whether based in discipline, religion, morality, regulation or culture, were planted by the characters who featured in this book and cultivated by their successors. These evolved, as the Irish state did, over the course of a century and have been influenced by every citizen who has put on the uniform. Perhaps not necessarily 'pioneers in a new state', but always 'the servant of the nation'.

ENDNOTES

Introduction

1   Dublin Diocesan Archives (DDA), Papers of Archbishop Edward Byrne, AB8/b/LIII, Adjutant General to Archbishop Byrne, 12 October 1923.

2   The exception being Lieutenant (Dr) Brigid Lyons Thornton, who was commissioned into the National Army's Medical Service, serving from 1922–24. She would be the only woman to serve in the Defence Forces until the first female cadets joined the short-lived Women's Service Corps in 1980, followed by the first female recruits being enlisted in 1981.

3   Damien Brennan, *Irish Insanity, 1800–2000* (UK: Routledge, 2014).

4   Joe Humphreys, 'Professional and local interests had stake in keeping asylums, says major study', *The Irish Times*, 25 October 2013, accessed 19 June 2023, www.irishtimes.com/news/health/professional-and-local-interests-had-stake-in-keeping-aslyums-says-major-study-1.1572258

5   John Gibney, *A Short History of Ireland, 1500–2000* (London: Yale≈University Press, 2018), pp. 209–11.

6   Francis Fukuyama, *The End of History and the Last Man* (New York: Free Press, 1992), pp. 212–13.

7   Ernest Gellner, *Nations and Nationalism* (New York: Cornell University Press, 1983), p. 1.

8   Irish Military Archives (IMA), Commander-in-Chief: Chaplains. Suggestions re Spiritual Welfare of National Forces. Retreats, Sodalities, etc., DOD/A/7092, 'Liam Lynch to Richard Mulcahy', 30 May 1922.

9   Colin Barr, 'Paul Cullen', *Dictionary of Irish Biography*, accessed 8 June 2023, www.dib.ie/biography/cullen-paul-a2281

10 Diarmaid Ferriter, 'Irish Catholicism is rooted in class prejudice', *The Irish Times*, 25 August 2018, accessed 8 June 2023, www.irishtimes.com/opinion/diarmaid-ferriter-irish-catholicism-is-rooted-in-class-prejudice-1.3606614

11 Niall O'Dowd, *A New Ireland: How Europe's Most Conservative Country Became its Most Liberal* (New York: Skyhorse, 2020).

12 Tom Holland, *Dominion: The Making of the Western Mind* (UK: Abacus, 2020).

13 Larry Siedentop, *Inventing the Individual: The Origins of Western Liberalism* (UK: Penguin Random House, 2015).

14 Diarmaid Ferriter, 'Opinion and analysis: A people ravaged by civil war had their faith in common', *The Irish Times*, 25 November 2022, p. 16.

15 Caitriona Beaumont, 'Women, Citizenship and Catholicism in the Irish Free State, 1922–1948', *Women's History Review*, Volume 6, No. 4 (1997), p. 565.

16 *The Irish Times*, 23 February 1924, p. 6.

17 Thomas Mohr, 'Religious Minorities under the Constitution of the Irish Free State, 1922–1937', *American Journal of Legal History*, Volume 61, No. 2 (June 2021), pp. 253–4.

18 *Constitution of Ireland*, www.irishstatutebook.ie/eli/cons/en/html

19 Mohr (2021), p. 257.

20 The sixty senators that first sat in 1922 were made up of thirty-six Catholics, twenty Protestants, three Quakers, and one Jew.

21 Mohr (2021), pp. 247–8.

22 Ibid., p. 250.

Chapter 1

1 While it had been occasionally used previously to refer to the IRA during the War of Independence, the earliest use of the term 'national army' in relation to the armed forces of the Provisional Government appears to be attributable to Alec McCabe, TD for Sligo. The *Evening Herald* of 4 January 1922 and the *Freeman's Journal* of 5 January 1922 record him using the phrase, appearing in lower case, during the debate on the Treaty.

2 IMA, 'Memorandum on the Progress of the Forces, 1923–1927', HS/A/0876.

3 IMA, 'Publicity, Discipline, Morale', DOD/A/6906.

4 Archivist Lisa Dolan and volunteer Tony Kinsella researched and compiled the most comprehensive listing to date of National Army deaths, drawing on several of the Military Archives' sources, published in 2023.

5 IMA, Statement of Cahir Davitt to the Army Inquiry Committee, 24 April 1924, AMTY/3/60.

6 'Our Chaplains', *An tÓglach,* Volume 1, No. 7 (new series), 19 May 1923, p. 18.

7 Dáil Éireann debates, 1 March 1923, Volume 2 No. 35.

8 Jason Knirck, *Afterimage of the Revolution* (Wisconsin: University of Wisconsin Press, 2014), pp. 5–6.

9 Gerry Adams in interview with Niall O'Dowd, *Irish Central*, 2 April 2018, accessed 6 July 2023, www.irishcentral.com/opinion/gerry-adams-1916-easter-rising

10 Michael Laffan, *The Resurrection of Ireland: The Sinn Féin Party 1916–1923* (Cambridge: Cambridge University Press, 1999), p. 49.

11 Ibid., p. 53.

12 Dáil Éireann debates, 26 June 1923, Volume 3, No. 34.

13 Knirck (2014), p. 41.

14 Ibid., pp. 105–40.

15 Diarmaid Ferriter, *Between Two Hells: The Irish Civil War* (UK: Profile, 2021), p. 169.

16 Richard Mulcahy, *To the Men of the Army*, 23 August 1922.

Chapter 2

1 Pádraig Ó Caoimh, *Richard Mulcahy: From the Politics of War to the Politics of Peace, 1913–1924* (Dublin: Irish Academic Press, 2019), p. 2.

2 Ibid., p. 10.

3 Martin Walsh, *Richard Devane SJ: Social Commentator and Advocate 1867–1951* (Dublin: Messenger Publications, 2019), p. 53.

4 Ibid., p. 54.

5 Ibid., p. 56.

6 Ibid., p. 83.

7 Ibid., p. 62.

8 Ibid., pp. 64–5.

9 IMA, DOD/A/7092.

10 Ronan Fanning, 'Richard Mulcahy', *Dictionary of Irish Biography* (Dublin: Royal Irish Academy, 2009).

11 IMA, DOD/A/7092, 'Mulcahy memorandum', 25 May 1922.

12 IMA, DOD/A/7092, 'Lynch to Mulcahy', 30 May 1922.

13 John P. Duggan, *A History of the Irish Army* (Dublin: Gill and Macmillan, 1991), p. 77.

14 IMA, DOD/A/7092, 'O'Sullivan to Mulcahy', 1 June 1922.

15 IMA, DOD/A/7092, 'O'Duffy to Mulcahy', 30 May 1922.

16 The Delaney Archive at Carlow College, KL/PF/MC/022, 'Adjutant General to Bishop of Kildare and Leighlin', 2 May 1922.

17 IMA, DOD/A/7092, 'Mulcahy to Donnelly', 16 June 1922.

18 The model schools were a non-denominational educational system established in 1831. One of the primary purposes was to provide trained teachers to work in the new national schools, by enabling and encouraging pupils to stay at national school as monitors and train under an experienced teacher.

19 Maurice Hartigan, 'The 'reverend gentlemen' of the early years of the Irish Army Chaplaincy Service', *The Irish Sword* (Winter 2019), Volume. XXXII, No. 128, p. 185.

20 DDA, Archbishop Byrne Papers, AB8/b/LIII, 'W Miller, Braganza House, to "Pat"', 26–28 October 1926.

21 Ó Caoimh (2019), p. 126.

22 IMA, DOD/A/7092, 'President's Office to Mulcahy', 17 October 1922.

23 IMA, DOD/A/7092, 'A Prayer' [1922].

24 IMA, DOD/A/7092, 'Sisters of Mercy, Ballyragget, to Mulcahy', 18 November 1922.

25 IMA, DOD/A/7092, 'Mollie Hand to Mulcahy', 30 November 1922.

26 IMA, DOD/A/7092, 'Annie M. Hearne to Mulcahy', 27 January 1923.

27 Ó Caoimh (2019), p. 109.

28 IMA, DOD/A/7092, 'Hannon to Mulcahy', 27 January 1923.

29 The Royal Hibernian Military School was built in 1771 to educate orphaned children of members of the British armed forces in Ireland. In 1922 it moved to Shorncliffe, in Folkestone, Kent, and the building was taken over by the National Army.

30 IMA, DOD/A/7092, 'Fahy to Hannon', 7 February 1923.

31 IMA, DOD/A/7092, 'Mulcahy to Hannon', 14 February 1923.

32 IMA, DOD/A/7092, 'Byrne to Mulcahy', 12 February 1923.

33 IMA, DOD/A/7092, 'Fahy to Mulcahy', 19 February 1923.

34 IMA, DOD/A/7092, 'Mulcahy to
   MacMahon', 25 February 1923.
35 'Weekend Retreat for Officers (from
   one who was there)', *An tÓglach*,
   Volume 1, No.1 (new series),
   24 February 1923, p. 12.
36 Gavin Foster, *The Irish Civil War and
   Society: Politics, Class and Conflict* (UK:
   Palgrave, 2015), p. 117.
37 Ibid., p. 125.
38 Ibid., p. 55–6.
39 IMA, DOD/A/7092, 'Mulcahy to
   O'Sullivan', 10 May 1923.

Chapter 3

1 I wish to acknowledge the work of
  Maurice Hartigan on the history of
  the Chaplaincy, which has appeared
  in several editions of the *Irish Sword*.
  I only came across Hartigan's research
  after I had written the first draft of this
  book, it having been recommended to
  me following peer review. It was very
  apparent that we had accessed and
  referenced many of the same records
  from both the Military Archives and
  the Dublin Diocesan Archives and
  so the content of our narratives was
  broadly similar. So least I be accused
  of plagiarism, let the record show that
  Hartigan trod this path first.
2 Hartigan (2019), p. 179.
3 IMA, DOD/A/6909, Defence Order
  No.9, 'Chief of General Staff to
  Commander-in-Chief', 29 July 1922.
4 IMA, DOD/A/6909, 'Note from
  Bishop of Cloyne', [June] 1922.
5 At this time the Army Council consisted of the Commander-in-Chief,
  Chief of Staff, Adjutant General,
  Director of Operations and Director
  of Intelligence. The Quartermaster

General joined the Council in January
1923, with the appointment of Seán Ó
Murthuile.
6 IMA, DOD/A/7091, Commander-in-
  Chief: Chaplains (other than Catholic)
  Appointments and Allocation.
7 DDA, AB8/b/LIII, Army GHQ
  Correspondence re Chaplains, 1922–
  1924, 'Memorandum [undated]'.
8 Hartigan (2019), p. 180.
9 DDA, AB8/b/LIII, 'Archbishop
  Byrne to Adjutant General',
  13 February 1923.
10 'Our Chaplains', *An tÓglach*,
   Volume 1, No. 7 (new series),
   19 May 1923, p. 18.
11 DDA, AB8/b/LIII, 'Fr. Gleeson to
   Monsignor Hickey', 9 March 1923.
12 DDA, AB8/b/LIII, Episcopal Sub-
   Committee on Army Chaplains
   1931–1932, 'Archbishop Byrne to
   Archbishop Logue', 17 April 1923.
13 Scheme adopted by the Standing
   Committee of the Bishops, appendix
   to Byrne to Logue, 17 April 1923.
14 DDA, AB8/b/LIII, 'Adjutant General
   to Archbishop Byrne', 12 October
   1923.
15 *An tÓglach*, 24 February 1923, p. 13.
16 IMA, DOD/A/6878, Chapels –
   Dublin Barracks, 'Quartermaster
   General to Commander-in-Chief',
   31 July 1922.
17 IMA, DOD/A/6878, 'Minute Sheet,
   Commander-in-Chief', 15 March 1923.
18 *An tÓglach*, 24 March 1923, pp. 3–6.
19 *An tÓglach*, 7 April 1923, p. 17.
20 Ibid.
21 *An tÓglach*, 11 August 1923, p. 7.
22 Ibid., p. 8.
23 *An tÓglach*, 1 September 1923,
   pp. 12–13.

24   IMA, DOD/A/6909, 'Memo on the Chaplaincy Department 1922–1931' [1931].

Chapter 4

1   Ferriter (2021), p. 9.
2   Hartigan (2019), p. 181.
3   IMA, DOD/A/8402, Chaplains, Catholic, Irregular Activities, 'O'Hegarty to Mulcahy', 15 December 1922.
4   Ibid.
5   DDA, 'Kevin O'Higgins to Archbishop Byrne', 20 December 1922, South Dublin County Library Source, https://hdl.handle.net/10599/12603
6   Cardinal Michael Logue, *Pastoral letter of his eminence Cardinal Logue, the archbishops and bishops of Ireland. To the priests and people of Ireland* (Dublin: Brown and Nolan, 1922), p. 4.
7   Ibid., p. 7.
8   IMA, DOD/A/8402, 'Kevin O'Mahony to Mulcahy', December 1922.
9   IMA, DOD/A/8402, 'O'Higgins to Byrne', 20 December 1922.
10   IMA, DOD/A/8402, 'Cosgrave to Gavin', 21 December 1922.
11   IMA, DOD/A/8402, 'Gavin to Cosgrave', 27 December 1922.
12   Susannah Riordan, 'Cultural Policy and Religion in Independent Ireland', *History Hub's Educational Resources Podcast*, April 2021, retrieved from Spotify.
13   IMA, DOD/A/8402, 'Captain Hegarty to Mulcahy,', January 1923.
14   DDA, AB8/b/LIII, 'Fr. Gleeson to Fr. Dunne', 5 June 1923.

15   IMA, DOD/A/8402, 'Costello to Mulcahy', 6 March 1923.
16   IMA, DOD/A/8402, 'Mulcahy to Byrne', 13 March 1923.
17   IE/MA/DOD/A/8402, 'Hodnett to Mulcahy', February 1923.
18   IE/MA/DOD/A/8402, 'Mulcahy to Foley', 22 March 1923
19   IE/MA/DOD/A/8402, 'Foley to Mulcahy', 26 March 1923
20   'An Unholy Trinity', *Documentary on One Podcast*, 2017, RTÉ Player.

Chapter 5

1   Duggan (1991), pp. 84–5.
2   'Military Courts – General Regulations as to Trial of Civilians', 2 October 1922, irishstatutebook.ie.
3   IMA, AMTY/3/27, Army Inquiry Committee Papers, 'Statement of Seán Mac Mahon', 6 May 1924.
4   Defence Order No.1, 19 October 1922.
5   IMA, DOD/A/08325, Civic Power, Special Infantry Corps, Organisations and Distribution, 'O'Higgins to Mulcahy', 15 March 1923.
6   IMA, CMA/002, Army Finance Office Circulars, 'JAG to Adjutant General', 19 February 1923.
7   IMA, CMA/002, 'Army Finance Department Circular No. 6', 31 October 1922.
8   IMA, CMA/002, 'Army Finance Department Circular No. 14', 12 December 1922.
9   IMA, CMA/006, Availability of Officers for Courts Martial, 'GOC Curragh Camp to Chief Legal Officer', 24 September 1922.
10   IMA, CMA/006, 'Director of Organisation to Chief Legal Officer', 2 December 1922.

11 IMA, CMA/024, The Mutiny of the Mounted Services, 'JAG to CSLO, Custume Barracks', 15 December 1922.

12 IMA, CMA/002, 'JAG to Adjutant General', 19 February 1923.

13 General Routine Order No.14, 18 January 1923.

14 IMA, CMA/036, Record of Military Courts and Courts Martial, 1922–1924.

15 IMA, AMTY/3/27, 'Statement of Seán Mac Mahon to Army Inquiry Committee', 6 May 1924.

16 IMA, 24649 Dominick McGreal.

17 IMA, DOD/A/7213, Suspensions: McGreal – Cavalry Officers – Curragh, 'Director of Operations to GSO Staff Duties', 1 November 1922.

18 IMA, CMA/024, 'Statement of SSM Joseph Kinsella, Martin Slattery (Equitation Instructor), Troop Sergeant James Reid and SQMS William Bracken, to Commandant Cusack', 7 October 1922.

19 IMA, DOD/A/7213, 'Report of Staff Captain Coghlan', 9 October 1922.

20 IMA, CMA/024, 'Statement of Colonel Michael Dunphy', October 1922.

21 IMA, CMA/024, 'Seamus O'Broin to GOC Curragh Camp', 10 October 1922.

22 IMA, CMA/024, 'Statement of SSM Joseph Kinsella, Martin Slattery (Equitation Instructor), Troop Sergeant James Reid and SQMS William Bracken, to Commandant Cusack', 7 October 1922.

23 IMA, CMA/024, 'Statement of Corporal Edward Purcell', 10 October 1922.

24 Battalion Sergeant Major W. Lamphier, Quarter Master Sergeant W. Bracken, Sergeant Major J. Kinsella, Sergeant J. Maher, Sergeant P. Murphy, Sergeant J. Reid, Sergeant M. Slattery, Company Sergeant Major D. Shannon and Corporal J. O'Donnell.

25 IMA, DOD/A/7213, 'JAG to Commander-in-Chief', 5 October 1922.

26 IMA, CMA/028, Captain Thomas Buckley – Mounted Services.

27 IMA, CMA/024, 'JAG to Commander-in-Chief', 31 October 1922.

28 Seosamh Ó Longaigh, Emergency Law in Independent Ireland 1922–1948 (Dublin: Four Courts, 2006), p. 26.

29 Seán Enright, The Irish Civil War: Law, Execution and Atrocity, (Dublin: Merrion Press, 2019), pp. 1–7.

30 Gemma Clark, 'Violence against women in the Irish Civil War, 1922–3: Gender-based harm in global perspective', Irish Historical Studies, Cambridge University Press, Volume 44, No. 165 (August 2020), pp. 75–90.

31 Ciara Breathnach and Eunan O'Halpin, 'Sexual assault and fatal violence against women during the Irish War of Independence, 1919–1921: Kate Maher's murder in context', Medical Humanities, 48, (2022) pp. 94–103.

32 '16 ways you can stand against rape culture', UN Women (website), 18 November 2019, accessed 19 May 2023, www.unwomen.org/en/news/stories/2019/11/compilation-ways-you-can-stand-against-rape-culture

33 Laffan (1999), p. 295.

34 Linda Connolly, 'Sexual violence and the Irish Revolution: An inconvenient truth?', *History Ireland*, November/December 2019, Volume 27, No. 6.

35 While this may be an unconventional endnote, the statement of Canon Henry is referred to but not contained in the Department of Defence file on Margaret Doherty's case at the Military Archives (DOD/A/11837). Based on records preserved, catalogued and made available by the Military Archives, the story of Margaret Doherty has been highlighted by Professor Linda Connolly, who has worked closely with the Doherty family who are still sensitive to the terrible experiences of their ancestor. The statement of Canon Henry would be a very valuable piece of Margaret's story, should any reader happen to come across it in the course of their own research.

36 IMA, DOD/A/11837, Charge against Lieuts Waters, Benson + Mulholland, Ballina. Alleged assault on Miss M. Doherty, 'Adjutant General to Minster for Defence', 15 July 1923.

37 IMA, DOD/A/11837, 'Commander-in-Chief to Adjutant General', 10 July 1923.

38 IMA, DOD/A/11837, 'Deputy Judge Advocate General to Military Secretary', 30 July 1923.

39 IMA, DOD/A/11837, 'Secretary, Department of Defence, to Judge Advocate General', 24 August 1923.

40 IMA, Military Service (1916–1923) Pensions Collection (MSPC), DP2100, Margaret Doherty.

41 IMA, Bureau of Military History (BMH), 'Witness Statement 1751: Cahir Davitt'.

42 IMA, CMA/151, Kenmare Case, 'Judge Advocate General to Adjutant General', 3 July 1923.

43 Ibid.

44 IMA, BMH, 'Witness Statement 1751: Cahir Davitt'.

45 Ibid.

46 Ibid.

47 Ibid.

48 IMA, BMH, 'Witness Statement 939: Ernest Blythe'.

49 Ibid.

50 IMA, CMA/151, 'Judge Advocate General to Adjutant General', 1 August 1923.

51 Diarmaid Ferriter, *Occasions of Sin: Sex and Society in Modern Ireland* (London: Profile, 2009), p. 141.

52 IMA, DOD/A/8079, Commander-in-Chief, Operations, Claremorris Command, 'McGrath to Mulcahy', 26 September 1923.

53 IMA, DOD/A/8079, 'Staff Officer Operations to Secretary Minister for Defence', 19 October 1923.

54 IMA, DOD/A/8079, 'Fr. T. O'Hara to Joe McGrath', 24 November 1923.

55 IMA, DOD/A/8079, 'Condition of Galway, [1923]'.

56 IMA, DOD/A/8079, 'Inspection of Intelligence in Claremorris Command, Special Report, Enemy Electioneering Activities', 15 August 1923.

57 IMA, DOD/A/8079, 'Report for fortnight ending 11 August 1923'.

58 Ibid.

Chapter 6

1 IMA, DOD/A/3525, Venereal Diseases, 'Murphy to Brophil', 23 September 1923.

2 IMA, DOD/A/3525, 'Farrell to Brophil', 24 September 1923.

3 IMA, DOD/A/3525, 'Feeney to Brophil', 24 September 1923.

4 IMA, DOD/A/3525, 'Lacey to Brophil', 24 September 1923.

5 IMA, DOD/A/3525, 'Gough to Brophil', 24 September 1923.

6 IMA, DOD/A/3525, 'Foley to Brophil', 24 September 1923.

7 Mary McAuliffe, 'Treaty details signal the end of unity in Cumann na mBan', *The Irish Times*, 25 May 2021.

8 Ferriter (2021), p. 10.

9 James Smith, 'Politics of Sexual Knowledge: The Carrigan Report (Paper presentation)', Boston College, 25 March 2014, accessed 6 June 2023, https://www.youtube.com/watch?v=LAkODkD1Wk8&t=491s

10 Ferriter (2009), p. 128.

11 IMA, DOD/A/7152, Medical Corps – History, Organisation, Training, Pay.

12 IMA, DOD/A/3525, 'Brophil to O'Sullivan', 24 September 1923.

13 IMA, DOD/A/3525, 'O'Sullivan to Mulcahy', 24 September 1923.

14 IMA, DOD/A/3525, 'Brophil to O'Sullivan', 25 September 1923.

15 IMA, DOD/A/3525, 'Brophil to O'Sullivan', 26 September 1923.

16 IMA, DOD/A/3525, 'Gough to Brophil', 25 September 1923.

17 IMA, CMA/016, 'Memorandum on Venereal Disease Affecting Officers and Other Ranks, Major General Maurice Hayes', [February] 1924.

18 IMA, DOD/A/3525, 'Brophil to O'Sullivan', 29 September 1923.

19 Ibid.

20 DDA, AB8/b/LIII, 'Major Carroll to Head Chaplain', 23 October 1924.

21 IMA, DOD/A/6608, Dependents of Unmarried Soldiers, 'O'Sullivan to Mulcahy', 5 September 1922.

22 IMA, DOD/A/6608, 'Circular from C.B. O'Connor to General Staff', 8 September 1922.

23 Ferriter (2009), p. 36.

24 IMA, DOD/A/6608, 'O'Hegarty to Mulcahy', 9 September 1922.

25 IMA, DOD/A/6608, 'Memorandum from Mulcahy', 22 September 1922.

26 IMA, MSPC, Private Patrick Perry, W2D133PatrickPerry; DOD/A/6608, 'C.B. O'Connor to Thomas Gorman'.

27 IMA, MSPC, Private Patrick Perry, W2D133PatrickPerry.

28 IMA, DOD/A/13977, Chaplains Report, Illegitimate Children, 'Moloney to Lavery', 17 March 1923.

29 A/13977, 'Fr. Casey to Head Chaplain', 10 November 1924.

Chapter 7

1 Susannah Riordan, 'Venereal Disease in the Irish Free State: The Politics of Public Health', *Irish Historical Studies*, XXXV, No. 39 (May 2007), pp. 346–7.

2 IMA, DOD/A/9796, Medical Services Weekly Medical Reports, 'Annual Medical Report 1923', 15 February 1924.

3 IMA, CMA/16, Major General Maurice Hayes, [February] 1924.

4 IMA, DOD/A/3525, 'Fr. Feely to Secretary, Minister for Defence', 17 September 1923.

5   IMA, DOD/A/7207, Poteen, 'Minister for Agriculture to Minister for Defence', 9 January 1923.

6   IMA, DOD/A/7207, 'Minster for Agriculture to President of Dáil Éireann', 9 January 1923.

7   IMA, DOD/A/7207, 'Minister for Home Affairs to Minster for Defence', 22 March 1923.

8   *General Regulations as to the Trial of Civilians by Military Courts (L.C. 501)* (Dublin: Eason and Son, 2 October 1922). These drew their authority from the Army Emergency Powers Resolution of An Dáil, 28 September 1922.

9   IMA, DOD/A/7207, 'Proclamation by the Army Council', May 1923.

10   IMA, DOD/A/7207, 'OC 3 Southern Command circular', 22 December 1922.

11   IMA, DOD/A/9985, Adjutant General: Hospital: Haulbowline.

12   IMA, DOD/A/3525, 'O'Connor to O'Sullivan', 19 September 1923.

13   IMA, DOD/A/3525, 'Director of Medical Service to O'Sullivan', 20 September 1923.

14   IMA, DOD/A/3525, 'O'Sullivan to C.B. O'Connor', 26 September 1923.

15   IMA, HS/A/0876, 'Memorandum on the Progress of the Forces, 1923–1927'.

Chapter 8

1   IMA, Chiefs of Staff reports to Executive Council (CREC), 'General Eoin O'Duffy's Monthly Report to Executive Council of Dáil Éireann', CREC/06, 7 April 1924.

2   Patrick Long, 'Eoin O'Duffy', *Dictionary of Irish Biography* (Dublin: Royal Irish Academy, 2009).

3   Dáil Debates, Volume 4, No. 16, 24 July 1923.

4   IMA, CMA/002, Army Finance Office Circulars, 'Army Finance Circular No. 30', 2 April 1924.

5   IMA, CMA/002, 'JAG to Adjutant General', 25 October 1923.

6   *An tÓglach*, 12 January 1924, p. 2.

7   IMA, DOD/A/7092, 'Head Chaplain to Minister for Defence', 29 January 1924.

8   DDA, AB8/b/LIII, 'Report from the Catholic Head Chaplain', 7 January 1924.

9   T.F. Higgins was the brother of Kevin O'Higgins, the Minister for Justice assassinated in 1927. While Higgins was born to Thomas and Anne Higgins, and the *Dictionary of Irish Biography* notes that he changed his name to *O'Higgins* in 1921, in the referenced official documents his name appears as *Higgins*. This is why it appears as such in this book.

10   IMA, DOD/A/13570, 'Medical Services Annual Report 1924', 17 January 1925.

11   IMA, DOD/A/3525, 'Adjutant General memo', 20 February 1924.

12   IMA, DOD/A/3831, Church Statements, 'Dublin Command Chaplain to Head Chaplain', 11 January 1924.

13   IMA, DOD/A/3831, 'Fr. Galvin, Gormanston Camp, to Dublin Command Chaplain', 15 February 1924.

14   IMA, DOD/A/3831, 'Fr. Fahy, Baldonnel Aerodrome, to Dublin Command Chaplain', 20 February 1924.

15   IMA, DOD/A/3831, 'Fr Pigott, Collins Barracks, to Dublin Command Chaplain', 15 February 1924.

16   *An tÓglách*, 23 February 1924, p. 13.

17   *An tÓglách*, 12 January 1924, p. 2.

18   *An tÓglach*, 26 April 1924, p. 11.

19   *An tÓglach*, 24 May 1924, p. 13.

20   *An tÓglach*, 19 July 1924, p. 5.

Chapter 9

1   IMA, Papers of the Army Inquiry Committee 1924 (AMTY), 'Major General Liam Tobin and Colonel C.F. Dalton to President W.T. Cosgrave', 6 March 1924.

2   Defence Order No. 58, 9 October 1924.

3   IMA, DOD/A/3651, Chapels, Seating etc. Complaints RE., 'Head Chaplain to Minister for Defence', 7 October 1924.

4   Dáil Debates, 11 March 1924.

5   Defence Order No. 47, 14 March 1924.

6   IMA, CREC/06, 'O'Duffy's Report to Executive Council', 7 April 1924.

7   IMA, CREC/06, 'O'Duffy's Report to Executive Council', 14 April 1924.

8   IMA, DOD/A/10552, Disinfectors, 'Adjutant General Weekly Report for week ending 9th February 1924'.

9   IMA, CREC/06, 'O'Duffy's Report to Executive Council', 7 May 1924.

10   Ibid.

11   IMA, CREC/06, 'O'Duffy's Report to Executive Council', 29 May 1924.

12   IMA, CREC/06, 'O'Duffy's Report to Executive Council', 12 June 1924.

13   A minimum sentence of twenty-eight days was required for a soldier to be remanded to a detention barracks.

14   IMA, CREC/06, 'O'Duffy's Report to Executive Council', 12 June 1924.

15   IMA, CREC/06, 'O'Duffy's Report to Executive Council', 5 July 1924.

16   Ibid.

17   Ibid.

18   IE/MA/HS/A/0876, Memorandum on the Development of the Force in the Period 1923–1927.

19   IMA, CREC/06, 'O'Duffy's Report to Executive Council', 8 September 1924.

20   IMA, CREC/06, 'O'Duffy's Report to Executive Council', 30 September 1924.

21   Ferriter (2021), p. 162.

Chapter 10

1   DDA, AB8/b/LIII, 'Major J. Donal Carroll to Head Chaplain', 23 October 1924.

2   Built *c.* 1860, the Isolation Hospital was associated with the former Royal Military Hospital on the opposite (west) side of Infirmary Road. This type of facility was commonly used to control the spread of infectious diseases in the nineteenth century, necessitated by soldiers serving throughout the British Empire.

3   IMA, DOD/A/10513, Private Hynes MTC Collins Barracks, 'Allegation against Private Murray, MCT', 1924.

4   IMA, DOD/A/3525, 'Secretary, Department of Local Government and Public Health, to President's Office', 27 November 1924.

5   IMA, DOD/A/3525, 'Memorandum on Venereal Disease by Director of Medical Services', 9 December 1924.

6   IMA, DOD/A/3525, 'Adjutant General to Minister for Defence', 4 November 1924.

7   IMA, DOD/A/3525, 'Secretary, Department of Local Government and

Public Health, to President's Office', 27 November 1924.

8   IMA, DOD/A/3525, Dr R.P. McDonnell's 'Synopsis of attached report for circulation amongst members of the Executive Council', [November] 1924.

9   IMA, DOD/A/3525, 'C.B. O'Connor to E.P. McCarron', 9 December 1924.

10 IMA, DOD/A/3525, 'Adjutant General to Minister for Defence', 12 December 1924.

11 IMA, DOD/A/3525, 'Memorandum on Venereal Disease by Director of Medical Services', 9 December 1924.

12 IMA, DOD/A/3525, 'Memorandum', 18 December 1924.

13 IMA, DOD/A/3525, 'O'Connor to McCarron', 23 December 1924.

14 An tÓglách, 23 December 1922, p. 1.

15 IMA, DOD/A/13570, Medical Services Annual Report 1924, 17 January 1925.

16 IMA, DOD/A/7156, Sanitation Officer, 'Sanitation Report, Memorandum on Sanitation', 1924.

17 IMA, DOD/A/13395, Adjutant General: Soldiers' Welfare, 16 December 1924.

18 IMA, DOD/A/6909, 'Memo on the Chaplaincy Department 1922–1931' [1931].

Chapter 11

1   David McCullagh, 'David McCullagh on the centenary of the Defence Forces', RTE.ie, 17 April 2023, accessed 18 April 2023, www.rte.ie/culture/2023/0417/1376822-david-mccullagh-on-a-century-of-the-irish-defence-forces

2   IMA, 'Report of the Army Organisation Board', July 1926.

3   National Archives of Ireland (NAI), DT/S4541, 'Defence Policy Memorandum', 13 November 1925.

4   An tÓglách, 11 August 1923, p. 7.

5   Daniel Ayiotis, 'Irish Military Neutrality: A Historical Perspective for Modern Consideration', The EU, Irish Defence Forces and Contemporary Security (Carroll, O'Neill, Williams (eds)) (Switzerland: Palgrave Macmillan, 2023), p. 394.

6   IMA, CREC/10, 'Monthly Report', 15 January 1925.

7   IMA, CREC/10.

8   IMA, CREC/10, 'Monthly Report', 14 February 1925.

9   IMA, CREC/10, 'Monthly Report', 8 September 1926.

10 IE/MA/HS/A/0876, Memorandum on the Development of the Force in the Period 1923–1927.

11 IMA, DOD/A/15978, Objectionable Material, 'Fr. Donnelly to GOC Curragh Camp' and 'Fr Donnelly to Head Chaplain', 10 September 1925.

12 IMA, DOD/A/15978, 'Minute Sheet, Head Chaplain to Adjutant General', 22 September 1924.

13 IMA, DOD/A/15978, 'Adjutant General to GOC Curragh Camp', 9 January 1925.

14 IMA, DOD/A/15978, 'Charles Eason to Colonel M. Dunphy', 12 January 1925.

15 IMA, DOD/A/15978, 'Colonel M. Dunphy to Messrs Eason and Son Ltd.', 12 February 1925.

16 IMA, DOD/A/7184, Traffic Accidents, 'Army Finance Meeting', 10 July 1924.

17 IMA, DOD/A/7184, 'Adjutant General's Memo No.45: Courts of Inquiry: Investigation of Accidents

Involving Army Transport Vehicles',
6 March 1925.

18 IMA, DOD/A/7184, 'Director of
Transport Accident Report', 6 April
1925.

Chapter 12

1 IMA, D OD/A/3651, 'Army Finance
Officer to OC Army Corps of
Engineers', 12 January 1925.

2 IMA, CREC/10, 'Monthly Report',
14 April 1925.

3 DDA, AB8/b/LIII, 'Approved Military
Syllabus'.

4 DDA, AB8/b/LIII, 'Approved Military
Lecture to Serve as a Basis for Talks to
Men in Camp'.

5 IMA, DOD/A/3525, 'Adjutant General
to Secretary, Department of Defence',
3 January 1925.

6 IMA, DOD/A/3525, 'Conference
Held as Minister's Room, Portobello
Barracks (memo)', 8 January 1925.

7 IMA, DOD/A/3525, 'Mac Neill to
O'Connor', 2 March 1925.

8 IMA, DOD/A/3525, 'Adjutant General
to GOC Eastern Command',
19 January 1925.

9 IMA, DOD/A/3525, 'O'Connor to
Mac Neill', 14 January 1925.

10 IMA, DOD/A/3525, 'Memo from
Head Chaplain', 9 January 1925.

11 IMA, DOD/A/3525, 'Fr. O'Callaghan,
Byrne, Casey and Pigoid [sic] to
Adjutant General', 28 January 1925.

12 IMA, DOD/A/3525, 'Adjutant General
to Head Chaplain', 28 January 1925.

13 IMA, DOD/A/3525, 'Head Chaplain
to Adjutant General', 29 January 1925.

14 IMA, DOD/A/3525, 'Colonel
Higgins to Adjutant General',
18 February 1925.

15 IMA, DOD/A/3525, 'Adjutant General
to Minister for Defence', 23 February
1925.

16 IMA, DOD/A/3525, 'Secretary,
Department of Defence to Secretary,
Department of Justice / Secretary
Department of Local Government and
Public Health', 27 February 1925.

17 IMA, DOD/A/3525, Secretary,
Department of Justice to Secretary,
Department of Defence', 2 March
1925.

18 IMA, DOD/A/3525, 'Report of the
Inter-departmental Committee of
Inquiry Regarding Venereal Disease',
12 February 1926.

19 IMA, DOD/A/3525, 'Adjutant General
to Secretary, Minister for Defence',
2 March 1925.

20 IMA, DOD/A/3525, 'Colonel Higgins
to Adjutant General', 20 February
1925.

21 IMA, DOD/A/3525, 'Adjutant
General to Minister for Defence',
8 September 1925.

22 IMA, DOD/A/3525, 'Fr. Feely to Head
Chaplain', 23 September 1925.

23 IMA, DOD/A/3525, 'Colonel Higgins
to Adjutant General', 6 October 1925.

24 GRO 11/1925, Prophylactic Treatment,
V.D., 10 December 1925.

25 DDA, AB8/b/LIII, 'Head Chaplain to
Archbishop of Dublin', 22 July 1925.

26 DDA, AB8/b/LIII, 'Head Chaplain to
Archbishop of Dublin', 11 July 1925.

27 DDA, AB8/b/LIII, 'Acting Military
Secretary to Head Chaplain',
11 August 1925.

28 DDA, AB8/b/LIII, 'Head Chaplain to
Archbishop of Dublin', 15 September
1925.

29   DDA, AB8/b/LIII, 'Head Chaplain to Archbishop of Dublin', 6 October 1925.

Chapter 13

1   DDA, AB8/b/LIII, 'Fr. Feeley to Bishop Joseph Hoare', 10 April 1926.
2   DDA, AB8/b/LIII, 'Bishop James Downey to Archbishop of Dublin', 2 April 1926.
3   DDA, AB8/b/LIII, 'Head Chaplain to Archbishop of Dublin', 25 November 1926.
4   DDA, AB8/b/LIII, 'Minister for Defence to Archbishop of Dubin', 23 January 1923.
5   Hartigan (2019), p. 198.
6   DDA, AB8/b/LIII, 'Head Chaplain to Archbishop of Dublin', 14 June 1930.
7   IMA, DOD/A/3525, 'Commanding Officer Athlone Military District to Adjutant General', 10 February 1928.
8   IMA, DOD/A/3525, 'Officer in Charge Army Laboratory to Director of Medical Services', 12 December 1929.

Chapter 14

1   In Roman Catholicism, a Eucharistic Congress is a gathering of clergy, religious, and laity to bear witness to the Real Presence of Jesus in the Eucharist.
2   Gerry Kane, 'The Eucharistic Congress 1932', *The Furrow*, Volume 58, No. 6 (2007), pp. 343–6, http://www.jstor.org/stable/27665556
3   Daithí Ó Corráin, 'The Catholic Church, the State and Society in Independent Ireland, 1922–2022', in *Working Notes*, 21 January 2022, accessed 16

May 2023, www.jcfj.ie/article/the-catholic-church-the-state-and-society-in-independent-ireland-1922-2022
4   Eoin Kinsella, *The Irish Defence Forces 1922–2022: Servant of the Nation* (Dublin: Four Courts, 2023), pp. 96–9.
5   *An tÓglách*, 16 December 1921.
6   Kinsella (2023), pp. 105–27.
7   NAI, DT S2264, 'Dispatch from Eamon de Valera to J.H. Thomas', 5 April 1932.
8   NAI, DT S5857B, 'Letter from Joseph P. Walshe to Sean Murphy', 20 April 1929.
9   Ibid.
10   NAI, DFA Secretary's Files, S28A, 'Memorandum from Charles Bewley to Joseph P. Walshe' [1929].
11   Patrick Maume, 'Michael J. Curran', *Dictionary of Irish Biography*.
12   NAI, DFA Secretary's Files, S28A, 'Letter from Joseph P. Walshe to Seán Murphy', 8 May 1929.
13   NAI, DFA EA 231/4, 'Confidential Report from Charles Bewley to Joseph P. Walshe', 26 July 1930.
14   Ó Corráin (2022).
15   NAI, DFA 19/1B, 'Joseph P. Walshe to Charles Bewley', 30 July 1931.
16   NAI, DFA 19/1B, 'Confidential Report from Charles Bewley to Joseph P. Walshe', 1 June 1931.
17   NAI, DFA 19/1B, 'Joseph P. Walshe to Charles Bewley', 6 November 1931.
18   NAI, DFA Secretary's Files S28A, 'Joseph P. Walshe to Seán Murphy', 8 May 1929.
19   Ibid.
20   NAI DFA 7/20, 'St. Patrick's Day Message by William T. Cosgrave to the

United States of America', 17 March 1931.

21 DDA, AB8/b/LIII, 'Eucharistic Congress 1932, Head Chaplain to Department of Defence', 25 October 1925.

22 NAI DFA/19/1B, 'Confidential Report from Charles Bewley to John P. Walshe', 5 September 1931.

23 NAI DFA/19/1B, 'Confidential Report from Charles Bewley to John P. Walshe', 10 November 1931.

24 IMA, 'Report of the Army Organisation Board', July 1926.

25 Constitution (Amendment No. 17) Act, 1931, www.irishstatutebook.ie/ eli/1931/act/37/

26 NAI DFA 19/1B, 'Confidential Report from Charles Bewley to Joseph P. Walshe', 2 November 1931.

27 NAI DFA/19/1B, 'Confidential Report from Charles Bewley to Joseph P. Walshe', 10 November 1931.

28 Smith (2014).

29 Ibid.

30 Finola Kennedy quoted in 'An Irishman's Diary', *The Irish Times*, 10 January 2001.

31 Ibid.

32 Smith (2014).

33 Eoin McNamara, 'Ireland's Defence Deficit', *Royal United Services Institute* (website), 21 December 2022, accessed 7 July 20232, www.rusi.org/ explore-our-research/publications/ commentary/irelands-defence-deficit

34 IMA, DOD/2/24162, Eucharistic Congress 1932, application for loan of camp equipment, bedding etc. from British Government, 'Handwritten note from Colonel E.V. O'Carroll,

Quartermaster General, to Secretary, Department of Defence', 11 June 1930.

35 IMA, DOD/2/24162, 'Minister for Defence to Joseph P. Walshe', 10 July 1930.

36 IMA, DOD/2/24162, 'Frank O'Reilly to Minister for Defence', 25 July 1930.

37 IMA, DOD/2/24162, 'Frank O'Reilly to Minister for Defence', 22 September 1930.

38 IMA, DOD/2/24163, Eucharistic Congress 1932, Visitors' camp sites, surveys of, by Army Corps of Engineers, 'Frank O'Reilly to Quartermaster General', 25 July 1930.

39 IMA, DOD/2/29969, Harnesses and Saddlery – Equipment of Ceremonial Mounted Unit, Eucharistic Congress 1932.

40 IMA, DOD/2/30337, Ceremonial Reception of His Eminence The Papal Legate on 20 and 21 June 1932, 'Secretary Department of External Affairs to Secretary Department of Defence', 24 May 1932.

41 IMA, DOD/2/30337, 'Minister for Defence and Colonel E.V. O'Carroll', 16–17 June 1932.

42 IMA, DOD/2/30337, 'Quartermaster General to Department of Defence', 15 June 1932.

43 IMA, DOD/2/30337, 'Minister for Defence to Quartermaster General', 16 May 1932.

44 IMA, DOD/2/30337, 'Quartermaster General to Minister for Defence', 17 May 1932.

45 G.K. Chesterton, *Christendom in Dublin: Personal Impressions of the 31st Eucharistic Congress in Dublin 1932* (New York: Shed and Ward, 1932), p. 68.

46 IMA, PRCN 65, Oral History
    Interview of Lieutenant Colonel Seán
    Clancy with Dr Charles Flynn,
    24 June 2002.

Conclusion

1   Ferriter (2009), p. 136.
2   John Charles McQuaid (1895–1973)
    served as Catholic Archbishop of
    Dublin and Primate of Ireland from
    1940 until 1973. Éamon de Valera
    (1882–1975) formed Fianna Fáil in
    1926, becoming President of the
    Executive Council of Dáil Éireann
    when they won power from Cumann
    na nGaedheal in 1932. In 1937, with
    the introduction of a new constitution,
    his position automatically transitioned
    to the newly created equivalent office
    of Taoiseach. He held this appoint-
    ment until 1948, again from 1951–4,
    and again from 1957–9. In 1959 he was
    inaugurated as President of Ireland,
    the Head of the Irish State. He held
    this appointment until 1973.
3   *60th International Military Pilgrimage
    to Lourdes Souvenir Booklet* (Defence
    Forces Printing Press, 2018).
4   IMA, 'Guidance letter of Head
    Chaplain to Defence Forces Code of
    Conduct Study Group', 1993.
5   'Former Defence Forces Ombudsman
    "so angry" at revelations of abuse
    within the ranks', *The Irish Times*,
    8 April 2023, accessed 14 June 2023,
    www.independent.ie/irish-news/
    former-defence-forces-ombudsman-
    so-angry-at-revelations-of-abuse-with-
    in-the-ranks/42424673.html
6   'Any review of misconduct in Defence
    Forces must include department and
    Minister', *The Irish Times,* 13 April
    2023, accessed 14 June 2023, www.
    irishtimes.com/opinion/2023/04/13/

any-review-of-misconduct-in-defence-
forces-must-include-department-and-
minister/

7   'Statement by President Higgins
     on the report of the Independent
     Review Group into the Defence
     Forces', 31 March 2023, accessed
     14 June 2023, www.president.ie/
     en/media-library/news-releases/
     statement-by-president-higgins-on-
     the-report-of-the-independent-review-
     group-into-the-defence-forces

INDEX

Ward, Margaret 85
Watters, Lt J.J. 70
welfare of soldiers, the 149–50
women and equality in the Irish Free State 85
women in the Defence Forces 213
Women of Honour Group, the 213

Yeats, W.B. xvii